Muslim Students, Education and Neoliberalism

Máirtín Mac an Ghaill • Chris Haywood
Editors

Muslim Students, Education and Neoliberalism

Schooling a 'Suspect Community'

Editors
Máirtín Mac an Ghaill
Graduate School
Newman University
Birmingham, United Kingdom

Chris Haywood
Media and Cultural Studies
Newcastle University
Newcastle Upon Tyne
United Kingdom

ISBN 978-1-137-56920-2   ISBN 978-1-137-56921-9 (eBook)
DOI 10.1057/978-1-137-56921-9

Library of Congress Control Number: 2017931311

Cover illustration: © Olivier Asselin / Alamy Stock Photo

Printed on acid-free paper

This Palgrave Macmillan imprint is published by Springer Nature
The registered company is Macmillan Publishers Ltd.
The registered company address is: The Campus, 4 Crinan Street, London, N1 9XW, United Kingdom

ACKNOWLEDGEMENTS

We would like to take this opportunity to thank all the contributors. We would also like to thank the editorial team at Palgrave Macmillan.

CONTENTS

LIST OF TABLES

CHAPTER 1

Introduction

Máirtín Mac an Ghaill and Chris Haywood

What Is the Book About?

A Greek Tragedy came to Birmingham schools in March 2014. This involved an alleged Islamist plot to take over schools in predominantly Muslim areas, which was claimed in a leaked letter that was sent to the Birmingham City Council, which was then circulated in the media. In turn, this was followed by two major formal investigations, 21 OFSTED inspection reports and a report by the Education Funding Agency, into what became known as the Trojan Horse affair (Miah 2014). What occurred in these schools, the response of the then Secretary of State for Education, Michael Gove, the wide range of reports and the policy changes have and continue to be highly contested across education and the wider society. Here, we are not directly concerned with the substantive issues involved as there is an existing literature available that provides sophisticated accounts (Miah 2015; Arthur 2015). Rather, we wish to

M. Mac an Ghaill (✉)
Graduate School, Newman University, Birmingham, UK
e-mail: m.macanghaill@newman.ac.uk

C. Haywood
Media and Cultural Studies, Newcastle University, Newcastle upon Tyne, UK
e-mail: chris.haywood@newcastle.ac.uk

© The Author(s) 2017   1
M. Mac an Ghaill, C. Haywood (eds.), *Muslim Students, Education and Neoliberalism*, DOI 10.1057/978-1-137-56921-9_1

argue that the reductive political and media framing of this event is illustrative of a broader cultural limiting representation of the emergence of the Muslim figure, nationally and globally.

Most immediately, this collection emerges from our research in the city of Birmingham. In carrying out empirical work in the local area, a key theme that emerged from educational theorists, teachers, policy-makers and local politicians was that of intense confusion about what was going on in relation to the Trojan Horse affair. While many of them *publically* challenged the racialisation of Muslim students, in terms of their being associated with terrorism and radicalism, *privately* there was ambivalence about the role of (organised) religion in (secular) education. For some, their ambivalence was implicitly linked with a perception of the Muslim community marked by increasing social separateness, cultural fixity and boundedness, and more specifically, the association of Islam with an ana-chronistic tradition and Muslims projected as figures of 'anti-modernity' in cosmopolitan urban spaces (Said 1993). In other words, a major rationale for this edited collection is to address educators' confusion and ambiva-lence about the generationally specific reconfiguration of education and its impact on the education of Muslim students.

In response, we set out to make a new and exciting conceptual inter-vention in existing studies in this field of inquiry. *Muslim Students, Education and Neoliberalism* has a number of interrelated aims. The book provides up-to-date accounts of research and writing on schooling Muslim students across different educational sites. It offers a nuanced appreciation of highly contested debates by focusing upon specific themes that critically engage with the complexity of the field. The last decade has witnessed a fundamental shift, both nationally and internationally, in dominant political and media discourses that have positioned the Muslim community and, more specifically, young Muslim men and women as a major social problem for the state (Bhattacharya 2008; McGhee 2012; UK Government 2009). For example, within a British context, the media-led projected refusal of Muslims to integrate into society has manifested itself in pervasive images of a traditional religious community living a self-segregating, anti-modern existence that is alien to a British way of life (Poole 2002). Within broader state, media and popular narratives, Muslims are projected as having broken the multi-cultural social contract that emerged during the 1970s around a notion of ethnic integration that was assumed to be played out in schools (Nagle 2009). In response, this edited collection brings together leading scholars in education, who make a number of interconnecting interventions at the level of educational theory, representation, policy, practice and politics in exploring contemporary schooling and higher education (set out below). In so doing, we seek to understand both how state educational discourses position diverse internationally located Muslim communities and how late-modern generations of Muslim students are responding to this positioning.

The 'Muslim Question' is currently projected as a major international political, social and security issue across government, media and civil society discourses. Central to this projection of the state-led public anxiety is the schooling of Muslim students. Faas (2010, p. 6) in his text, *Negotiating Political Identities: Multi-ethnic Schools and Youth in Europe*, explains a shifting landscape around ethnic, religious and cultural belonging within a European perspective of a pervasive hostile visibility, as an effect of the development of an 'anti-immigration, anti-Muslim platform'. Historically, for migrant groups and ethnic minority communities, schooling strategically has been perceived as a primary institution for social mobility, and for the wider society the institution in which the multicultural society would be created and lived out (Abbas 2004). Within a British contemporary context, Shain (2011, p. 16) maintains that 'education is central to current discourses of radicalisation and extremism' which are projected onto young Muslim men and women, hence its continuing strategic significance, in a period marked by the central government's claim of the emergence of the 'enemy within' and the end of multiculturalism as a means of attaining inclusion in civil society (Fekete 2004; Ansari 2004; Choudhurry 2007).

Our starting point is that currently we appear to be at a critical moment, an intellectual, political and cultural interregnum in which 'the old (educational) politics and identities have been in decline, but the new have still to emerge' (Rutherford 1990, p. 23), within a rapidly shifting geopolitical, local (national) and institutional (educational) environment. More specifically, there is a fragmentation of the theorisation of contemporary schooling and racialisation and a sense that the 'old theories' are not able to capture the 'new times' of a younger generation of minority (and majority) ethnic students (Mirza 2009; Gilroy 2004). At the same time, reading through the literature on the education of Muslim students, there is an exclusive focus on their shifting identities, for example from ethnicity to religion, that are frequently under-conceptualised. This is accompanied by a relative silence on the theorisation of the impact on the students' schooling experiences of historical shifts in state policy frameworks, which has seen the global emergence of neoliberalism and performative schooling in which exclusion has been reconceptualised as an individualised responsibility.

MAKING INTERVENTIONS

As indicated above, in response, this book draws upon the work of leading scholars in education, who make a number of interconnecting theoretical, conceptual and empirical contributions to the field. One of the ways that this collection engages with the field is through its international breadth and in so doing highlights the different experiences of being Muslim in education. With an underlying commitment to equality in areas such as gender, 'race'/ethnicity, age, sexuality and disability and as part of an ongoing dialogue with the contributors, we have explored the cultural specificity and international relevance of religious and ethnic categories across a wide range of contexts. The aim of ensuring an international field is in order to connect to a global agenda where the concept of a suspect community might be critically explored and scrutinised in the pursuit of establishing its empirical viability and conceptual purchase in global, national and local contexts. The contributors are highly aware of how theories and concepts embedded in the West are often unproblematically applied to other non-Western contexts. As a result, the contributors in this collection draw upon several key themes, discussed below, that inform theoretical, conceptual and empirical interventions.

Alongside this, the collection recognises that, at a time when social and cultural theory has disconnected from 'old' institutional spaces, such as schools, it is important to make available a range of theoretical frameworks that enable us critically to explore highly contested debates about the education of Muslim students. The Introductory section sets out four major educational perspectives: political-economic, late-modernity, Islamic discourses on education and critical realism and Islamic realism perspectives. In addition, the introductory section includes a comparative European-based perspective that synthesises theoretical and policy approaches. These theoretical perspectives set out an overview of the central issues that have defined this area of inquiry during the last 50 years. A specific objective of the book is to bring together early and more recent theoretical and empirical work to provide a critical reflection on the relative adequacy of different frameworks of educating Muslim students. An advantage of this kind of structure is that it allows us to consider not only the relative adequacy of different theoretical accounts through a series of contrasts, but also encourages a view of these theories as alternative explanations, which make different assumptions about educating Muslim students. In turn, this suggests different political and policy interventions at both local and global levels.

In order to provide a range of theoretical approaches, the collection makes Muslim students, education and neoliberalism a central focus of the book. Neoliberalism operates at a number of levels, but two key areas for consideration focus on how nation-states cultivate values such as competition, entrepreneurialism and individual responsibility through educational policies and how, at more local levels, individuals are responding to the deployment of such values (Torres 2009; Rizvi and Engel 2009). Giroux (2012) argues that neoliberal processes provide a context in which: 'The value of knowledge is now linked to a crude instrumentalism, and the only mode of education that seems to matter is one that enthusiastically endorses learning marketable skills, embracing a survival of the fittest ethic, and defining the good life solely through accumulation and disposing of the latest consumer goods'. The implication of this is that neoliberalism creates the discourses through which academic achievement and failure become understood and, in so doing, shapes social and cultural interpretations of students' behaviours. As Stromquist and Monkman (2000) suggest, knowledge within a neoliberal context becomes a commodity, and as a result pedagogy is imbricated within marketplace relations.

One of the ways of understanding neoliberalism, education and Muslim identities has been to ground it in local contexts. In the UK, it is possible to provide a mapping that documents a move from *local* multi-cultural comprehensive (neighbourhood) schools to *global* neoliberal performing academies. An archaeology of the field of policy might identify a shift from assimilation (1960s), through integration (1970s) to multi-culturalism/ anti-racism (1980s). This is not to suggest a simple mapping of each policy ideology onto each decade. Rather, these ideologies were in tension with an emerging emphasis that played out differentially across different regions. During the last two decades, we can identify a return to assimilation through the implementation of a neoliberal policy regulatory regime across public institutions, including education (Kundnani 2009). The disturbances in Northern towns in 2001 signalled a shift away from materialist accounts of institutional racism in schools to an emphasis on community cohesion that intensified following the 9/11 attacks and the

London bombings in July 2005 (Miah 2015). Most recently, the shifting emphasis from neoliberal discourses that attempted to promote community cohesion to neoliberal regimes that view diversity as problematic to citizenship is evident in forms of legislation such as the Prevention of Violent Extremism (McGhee 2012). Sian et al. (2012) highlight how a toolkit designed for schools to prevent extremism specifically targets young Muslim (men). This toolkit places teachers at the centre of surveillance and monitoring through an Islamophobic discourse that elides racial extremism with religion (see Miah, Chapter 9, for a detailed account of the Counter-Terrorism and Securities Act 2015 and its impact on education policy in the UK). It is within this context that Muslim young men and women as a 'suspect community' are subjected to an exclusionary discourse that is constituted through the deployment of neoliberal pedagogy, racial profiling and religious fundamentalism. Our recent empirical work in Birmingham areas involved in the Trojan Horse affair illustrates an up-to-date case history of a highly confused situation involving the visibility of the militarisation and securitisation of state schooling (across government, media and educational discourses) being accompanied by the invisibility about the pedagogical lives of Muslim male and female students (Mac an Ghaill and Haywood 2014, 2015).

Connected to a commitment to the focus on neoliberalism is an emphasis on providing innovative methodological insights, emphasising the autonomy of methodology from theoretical and substantive issues (Popoviciu and Mac an Ghaill 2004; Mac an Ghaill and Haywood 2005). The Muslim students represented in this edited collection inhabit specific lifestyles within a spatial context of diverse social trajectories among changing Muslim diasporas across several diverse societies (ONS 2006, 2012; DfES 2007). Therefore, it is the exploration of Muslim students' meaningful experiences that is a key objective of the research design throughout the empirical-based chapters in Sections 2 and 3 in this edited collection (Alvesson and Skoldberg 2000). The collection provides an inclusive methodological space that includes a range of methods, including ethnography, content analysis, quantitative research and discourse analysis as part of a wider critical methodological reflection on the impact of globally inflected change upon the local formation of Muslim young women's and men's subjectivity, identity formation and agency within educational contexts (Appadurai 1991; Ansari 2004). In collecting empirical data, the chapters enable the research participants to inhabit alternative representational spaces that provide insightful narratives about the complexity of taking up subject positions across schooling sites. For example, Bagguley and Hussain (2014) in earlier work with South Asian women wonderfully capture the specificities of the experiences of current higher education students, referring to them as cultural navigators (Ballard 1994), translators, adaptors and reflexive communicators. Reading through the educational literature, post-modernist and post-structuralist accounts of subjectivity and identity formation among minority ethnic students have opened up a range of possibilities or 'ways of looking' at Muslim students' school lives. However, it may be argued that this current explosion of *new* knowledge is accompanied by *old* methodological techniques. In response, the authors in this collection develop innovative epistemological and methodological understandings (see Pini and Pease 2013). Providing a space where a shared critical reflexivity of their educational experiences can be expressed is particularly of significance when young Muslim women and men experience censorship about publically engaging in discussions about Islam and being Muslim. Carrying out empirical research in this field of inquiry presents major theoretical and methodological issues to ensure we do not reinscribe Muslim students as a social problem for the state and more specifically an institutional problem for educational institutions.

Finally, this book captures emerging Muslim student subjectivities and identities, at a time when young men and women are experiencing a new cultural condition of which we know little. There is a need to shift beyond the logics of *potential jihadist* and *Islamophobic victim* to capture the disparate voices of a late-modern generation of Muslim students. As achievement and academic success become reframed through notions of individualised responsibility, the chapters examine students' experience of educational exclusionary practices, including reifying religion as an ethnic category and addressing the (intersecting) gendering and class dynamics of Muslim students across the sectors of education. For example, exploring how education policy changes have both helped shape and been a response to shifting dominant public representations of young Muslim men from an ascribed image as *law abiding citizens* to the current image of *dangerous brown men* (Bhattacharrya 2008), who are a threat to the British nation (Shain 2011). At the same time, there is an examination of new forms of inclusion and exclusion in relation to female and male Muslim students' experience of marginalisation through class differentiation after a decade of austerity that continues to have differential effects on different social groups (Mac an Ghaill and Haywood 2012).

OVERVIEW OF THE BOOK

The book opens with a chapter by Farzana Shain providing a political-economic analysis. She suggests that Muslim boys in England, especially those from Pakistani and Bangladeshi backgrounds, have come to occupy the status of a folk devil or what Cohen (2002) refers to as 'visible reminders of what we should not be'. Once regarded as passive, hard-working and law abiding, they have been, in recent years, recast in the public imagination as volatile, aggressive, hotheads who are either 'at risk' of being brainwashed into terrorism or involvement in gangs, drugs or other such criminal activities. This chapter draws on Gramscian concepts of hegemony and articulation to make sense of the current location of Muslim boys as a threat to the social order. In doing so, it engages with theoretical issues beyond education, to explore the socio-historical significance of state-led campaigns, such as the War on Terror in the manufacture of consent for the state's political legitimacy at a time of intense global economic crisis. A central concern of the chapter is to establish and analyse how Muslim boys and young men have come to be the targets of punitive state measures over the last two decades.

This is followed in Chapter 3 by Bagguley and Hussain, who reflect upon what it means to be a 'late-modern' Muslim student in contemporary Britain. They maintain that for Muslims at university there is both the late-modern liquid character of Islamic identities and the on-going securitisation of Islam and Muslims. It is argued that young Muslims both have ever-greater opportunities to reflect on their Islamic identities and are forced to choose how and where to locate themselves by the ever-unfolding hegemonic securitisation of Islam. These themes are explored through how universities are increasingly required to take on securitising roles in relation to their students through the new counter-terrorist legislation and programme known as Prevent. The theme of securitisation is developed further by Saeeda Shah in Chapter 4, who begins by suggesting that education of children in multi-cultural, multi-faith schools in the UK and elsewhere is a complex pedagogic challenge. This challenge is intensified in the case of Muslim students in the backdrop of growing assumptions regarding association of Muslims and Islam with religious extremism and violence. The resulting political, educational and social practices and discourses have impacted on the education of Muslims, increasing their concerns about relevant state policies and provisions. Drawing on pertinent literature and research, this chapter discusses how this context of mistrust and turbulence has been shaping Muslims' expectations from education and their educational choices, and with what implications for wider society.

In Chapter 5 Matthew Wilkinson outlines critical realism and Islamic realism perspectives. He opens with his argument that classical sociology has tended to reduce faith and the human dimension of the spirit to other experiential factors and this reductionism is problematic for researchers of young Muslims, for whom faith is an elemental and causally determinate factor in their identities, daily praxis and educational outcomes. This chapter shows how 'laminated' and 'articulated' ontologies of the Muslim learner derived from the philosophy of critical realism can provide multi-dimensional, nuanced frameworks for factoring-in the faith and faith-based identities of Muslim young people into research without swamping research with considerations of faith. This model and the importance of factoring-in faith fairly are illustrated with results from an empirical study of the effects of History education on a cohort of 307 Muslim young people in education in England.

In Chapter 6 Daniel Faas provides a comparative European-based perspective, bringing together theoretical and policy approaches, based on the educational experiences of Turkish Muslim students in Germany and Britain. Drawing on mainly qualitative data, the chapter argues that when the concept of Europe is allied to multi-culturalism, there is the possibility of including minority ethnic groups, like the Turkish Muslims and giving them the opportunity of relating to the European project and identity in a positive way. If, however, Europe is framed as a white Christian concept, then Turkish Muslim students will struggle to relate positively to Europe as a political identity. Faas theorises the education of Muslim students in European societies and, in so doing, he contributes to on-going debates about the challenges of constructing and promoting inclusive, multi-cultural, multi-religious models of Europe and the nation-state.

The second section addresses schooling the 'crisis', exploring the interconnections between neoliberalism, claims of the post-racial state and militarisation/securitisation. It opens with Chapter 7, in which Sunaina Maria reports on ethnographic research in Silicon Valley about post-9/11 Muslim American youth activism and coalitions linking Arab, South Asian and Afghan American college students, exploring how campus activism related to Palestine is the object of intense repression, but also the site of cross-racial, pan-Islamic and transnational solidarities. The experience of Palestine solidarity activism and the exceptional silencing of the Palestinian narrative in the USA, including in educational contexts, produces what the author calls 'Palestinianisation' for Arab as well as non-Arab Americans. Furthermore, the inadmissibility of Palestinian rights as human rights forces youth to confront the limitations of liberal human and civil rights and explore alternative political paradigms.

In Chapter 8 Ahmed examines the issue of schooling Muslim students in the USA and Europe, and how and why the counterparts of these new 'challenges', 'suspects', 'problems', a few decades ago, were seen as some of the top achievers whose numbers ranked among the highest percentages of university candidates, competing in the fields of medicine, engineering and the sciences, their communities, some of the most law abiding, productive and successful in society. The chapter draws attention to the idea that today's governments and academic institutions may seem confused and are at a loss as to how to deal with this new 'enemy within', yet they fail to recognise that these may be the by-products of the past decade of political rhetoric that has alienated these students, if not directly through the school systems and the 'neoliberal pedagogy', but through the political rhetoric that has deemed their communities as threats and enemies to societies-venomous rhetoric which has trickled into the classroom.

In Chapter 9 Shamim Miah addresses the radical transformation of education policy framing of Muslim communities in Britain, following the London bombings 10 years ago this year. The events signified a radical shift away from the politics of racial inequality/multi-culturalism to racialised politics of securitisation. By focusing on recent legislation and policy announcements, this chapter highlights minority communities in general and Muslim communities in particular are racialised and also criminalised as can be seen through the politics associated with the Counter-Terrorism and Securities Act 2015 and its impact on education policy. This chapter further explores the relationship between Muslims, securitisation and racial governmentality.

The third section of the book addresses emerging Muslim student perspectives and identities as a late-modern generation. It begins with Chapter 10, in which Bakali provides a timely examination of the presence of Islamophobia in Quebec secondary schools in the post-9/11 context. Employing a critical ethnographic approach stemming from institutional ethnography, this chapter explores systemic and institutional racism experienced by young Muslim men in their secondary schools and possible causes for this treatment. Through engaging with participants in individual interviews and focus group discussions, Bakali describes how participants regularly encountered bias from classmates and teachers relating their perceived faith. The findings in this chapter suggest that anti-Muslim racism experienced by participants was inextricably linked to the effects of the War on Terror in the North American context. Moreover, these experiences were also impacted by Quebec state practices, policies and political and media discourses.

In Chapter 11 Enneli and Enneli provide an account of the interaction between Islam and neoliberalism in Turkey on a basis of female university students who openly express their religious identities by wearing a headscarf. The chapter underlines how Islamic expressions and representations have recently become much more apparent and used for providing privileges in the unequal economic structure. Based on a qualitative research in two universities, one private and one public, Enneli and Enneli draw attention to the students' dissimilar modes of marking headscarf and religiosity and conclude with a relationship between them and the labour market opportunities, thought to be available in the future.

In Chapter 12 Mingyue Gu and Xiaoyan Guo explore identity construction and multi-lingual practices of a group of tertiary-level Uyghur students in China within their intra-national migration. Interviews and observations were conducted in three rounds of fieldwork. Findings indicate that participants experienced multiple marginalisations constituted by linguistic practices underpinned by the infiltration of neoliberal values and practices into the spheres of education and of social reality. Participants struggled over the (re)ethnicisation process and contested their disadvantageous social positions by capitalising on a repertoire of linguistic and cultural resources. Moreover, they tried to negotiate an educated Uyghur elite identity by marking boundaries between themselves and Uyghur counterparts in less prestigious institutions. In spite of this, the minority elites faced potential challenges when translating symbolic resources into economic capital in the neoliberal economy.

In Chapter 13 Mac an Ghaill and Haywood pick up a theme resonant throughout the book, exploring young Muslim people's experiences of education to examine what inclusion/exclusion means to them in late-modern conditions. In their case study, they use qualitative research undertaken with 48 Pakistani and Bangladeshi young men living in areas of the West Midlands, England. The young men highlighted three key areas: the emergence of a schooling regime operating through neoliberal principles, the recognition of class difference between themselves and teachers and their awareness of how racialisation operated through codes of masculinity. In conclusion, it is argued that research on issues of inclusion/exclusion should be cautious when interpreting new forms of class identity through conventional categories of ethnicity.

In the final Chapter 14, Tania Saeed addresses a major question of educating Muslim students and their continuing implication in the British state's counter-terrorism agenda, thus underscoring the subtitle of this edited collection. She argues that with government policies 'monitoring', ergo 'assisting' young Muslims in schools by preventing their possible radicalisation, the entire Muslim community, from children to adults have become 'suspect'. However, misunderstanding and ignorance about the Muslim identity already existed before 7/7. The chapter presents biographical accounts of Muslim women who reflect on their schooling experiences before and after 7/7, suggesting how racism and ignorance about the troubled 'Paki' was already prevalent in schools, which has now taken the guise of the dangerous 'would-be' terrorist. While participant experiences vary based on school demographics, their narratives are nonetheless instrumental in highlighting the limitations of a security policy that incite greater anxiety about the Muslim student.

Writing from our own national contexts and local neighbourhoods and aware of the interconnections with global geopolitical shifts, it is clear to us that these chapters are a small contribution to the complex questions of late-modern education that addresses the widest range of overlapping ideas about inequality, difference, subjectivity, representation and generational reflexivity that is being worked through in embodied classed and gendered lives. We hope the chapters resonate with the work of future researchers in the field.

REFERENCES

Abbas, T. (2004). *The education of British South Asians*. London: Palgrave Macmillan.

Alvesson, M., & Skoldberg, K. (2000). *Reflexive methodology: New vistas for qualitative research*. London: Sage.

Ansari, H. (2004). *'The Infidel Within': Muslims in Britain since 1800*. London: C. Hurst and Co.

Appadurai, A. (1991). Global ethnoscapes: Notes and queries for a transnational anthropology. In R. G. Fox (Ed.), *Recapturing anthropology: Working in the present*. Santa Fe, CA: School of American Research.

Arthur, J. (2015). Extremism and neo-liberal education policy: A contextual critique of the Trojan Horse affair in Birmingham schools. *British Journal of Educational Studies*, 63(3), 311–328.

Bagguley, P., & Hussain, Y. (2014). Negotiating mobility: South Asian women and higher education. *Sociology*, IFirst, 1–17.

Ballard, R. (1994). Introduction: The emergence of Desh Pardesh. In R. Ballard (Ed.), *Desh Pardesh: The South Asian presence in Britain*. London: Hurst and Company.

Bhattacharya, G. (2008). *Dangerous brown men: Exploiting sex, violence and feminism in the war on terror*. London: Zed.

Choudhurry, T. (2007). *The role of Muslim identity politics in radicalisation (a study in progress)*. London: Department of Communities and Local Government.

Cohen, S. (2002). *Folk devils and moral panics: The creation of the mods and rockers*. London: Routledge.

Department for Education and Skills. (2007). *Diversity and citizenship curriculum review*. London: Department for Children, Schools and Families.

Faas, D. (2010). *Negotiating political identities: Multi-ethnic schools and youth in Europe*. Farnham: Ashgate.

Fekete, L. (2004). Anti-Muslim racism and the European security state. *Race and Class*, 43, 95–103.

Gilroy, P. (2004). *After empire: Melancholia or convivial culture*. London: Routledge.

Giroux, H. (2012). The post-9/11 militarization of higher education and the popular culture of depravity: Threats to the future of American democracy. *International Journal of Sociology of Education*, 1(1), 27–53.

Kundnani, A. (2009). *The end of tolerance. Racism in 21st century Britain*. London: Pluto.

Mac an Ghaill, M., & Haywood, C. (2012). Schooling, masculinity and class analysis: Towards an aesthetics of subjectivity. *British Journal of Sociology of Education*, 32(5), 729–744.

Mac an Ghaill, M., & Haywood, C. (2014). Pakistani and Bangladeshi young men: Re-racialization, class and masculinity within the neo-liberal school. *British Journal of Sociology of Education*, 35(5), 753–776.

Mac an Ghaill, M., & Haywood, C. (2015). British-born Pakistani and Bangladeshi young men: Exploring unstable concepts of Muslim, Islamophobia and racialization. *Critical Sociology*, 4(1), 97–114.

Mac an Ghaill, M., & Haywood, C. (2005). *Young Bangladeshi people's experience of transition to adulthood*. York: Joseph Rowntree Foundation.

McGhee, D. (2012). Responding to the post 9/11 challenges facing 'post-secular societies': Critical reflections on Habermas's dialogic solutions'. *Ethnicities*. doi:10.1177/1468796812450860.

Miah, S. (2014, July). Trojan Horse, Ofsted and the 'Prevent'ing of Education. *Discover Society, 1.*

Miah, S. (2015). *Muslims, schooling and the question of self-segregation.* Basingstoke: Palgrave Macmillan.

Mirza, H. S. (2009). *Race, gender and educational desire: Why black women succeed and fail.* London: Routledge.

Nagle, J. (2009). *Multiculturalism's double bind: Creating inclusivity, cosmopolitanism and difference.* Farnham: Ashgate.

Office for National Statistics. (2006). *Religion-labour market.* London: Office for National Statistics.

Office for National Statistics. (2012). 2011 Census: Religion (Detailed), local authorities in England and Wales, Table QS210EW. http://www.ons.gov.uk.

Pini, B., & Pease, B. (2013). *Men, masculinities and methodologies.* London: Palgrave Macmillan.

Poole, E. (2002). *Reporting Islam: Media representation of British Muslims.* London: I. B. Taurus.

Popoviciu, L., & Mac an Ghaill, M.. (2004). Racisms, ethnicities and British nation-making. In F. Devine & M. C. Walters (Eds.), *Social identities in comparative perspective.* London: Blackwell.

Rizvi, F., & Engel, L. C. (2009). Neo-liberal globalization, educational policy, and the struggle for social justice. In W. Ayers, T. Quinn, & D. Stovall (Eds.), The handbook of social justice in education (pp. 529–541). Lanham, MD: Rowman & Littlefield Publishers.

Rutherford, J. (1990). A place called home: Identity and the cultural politics of difference. In J. Rutherford (Ed.), *Identity: Community, culture and difference.* London: Lawrence and Wishart.

Said, E. W. (1993). *Culture and imperialism.* London: Vintage.

Shain, F. (2011). *The new folk devils: Muslim boys and education in England.* Stoke on Trent: Trentham Books.

Sian, K. I. L., & Sayyid, S. (2012). *Debates on difference and integration in education: Muslims in the UK.* Centre for Ethnicity and Racism Studies, University of Leeds. http://www.ces.uc.pt/projectos/tolerace/media/WP4/WorkingPapers%204_UK.pdf.

Stromquist, N. P., & Monkman, K. (2000). Defining globalization and assessing its implications on knowledge and education. In N. P. Stromquist & K. Monkman (Eds.), *Globalization and education: Integration and contestation across cultures.* Lanham, MD: Rowman and Littlefield.

Torres, C. A. (2009). *Education and neoliberal globalization.* New York: Routledge.

U.K. Government. (2009). *The United Kingdom's strategy for countering international terrorism.* Home Office, London: The Stationary Office.

Máirtín Mac an Ghaill is Professor and Director of Graduate School at Newman University. He is the author of The Making of Men: Masculinities, Sexuality and Schooling. He has published books and articles with Chris Haywood, including Men and Masculinities; Education and Masculinities: Social, Cultural and Global Transformations.

Chris Haywood is a Senior Lecturer at Newcastle University whose main interests focus on men and masculinities. He is currently exploring the emergence of new sexual cultures with a particular focus on anonymous sex with strangers. This is part of a broader study on men's dating practices with a particular focus on mobile dating, online dating and speed dating. Overall, he is interested in pushing the conceptual limits of masculinity models to consider ways of gendering that are not reducible to masculinity or femininity.

CHAPTER 2

Dangerous Radicals or Symbols of Crisis and Change: Re-theorising the Status of Muslim Boys as a Threat to the Social Order

Farzana Shain

INTRODUCTION

Since the mid-1980s, Muslims in England, especially boys and young men of Pakistani and Bangladeshi origin, have come to be regarded as 'folk devils' or what Cohen (2002: 2) refers to as 'visible reminders of what we should not be'. Once compared positively with their African-Caribbean counterparts as passive and law abiding, they have been recast in the public imagination as a threat to the social order. British Muslims are among the most deprived communities in the UK with 46 % (1.22 million) of the Muslim population residing in the 10 % most deprived local authority districts in England. Pakistani and Bangladeshi boys and men are also among the groups that have the lowest educational attainment and highest rates of unemployment (ONS 2014). However, discourses of self-segregation (Cantle 2001; Denham 2002) and global (in)security posed by the War on Terror have positioned them simultaneously as the victims of cultural and religious practices and as a threat to the social order.

F. Shain (✉)
Keele University, Keele, UK
e-mail: f.shain@keele.ac.uk

© The Author(s) 2017
M. Mac an Ghaill, C. Haywood (eds.), *Muslim Students, Education and Neoliberalism*, DOI 10.1057/978-1-137-56921-9_2

Public and political anxieties about radicalisation and 'extremism' – in circulation from the late 1980s – intensified to a point of frenzy after the London transport bombings in July 2005 were attributed to 'home-grown' suicide-bombers. Since then, Muslim communities have come under exceptional scrutiny and surveillance; at the same time, their loyalty to the British state has been significantly questioned. Concerns about 'Muslim extremism' have also intersected with national and European-level discourses of integration. Across several European countries, political and social commentators have made arguments linking the 'Muslimness' of their disadvantaged ethnic groups to predominant economic and political problems faced within and by European nation-states since the 1970s (see, e.g. Sarazzin 2010).

Young working-class men have often been the focus of adult anxieties and fears, particularly in periods of economic crisis and social change in England (Pearson 1983; Hebdige 1979). Mods, Rockers, skinheads, muggers, hoodies, chavs and Asian gangs are among the list of anti-heroes cited by Delamont (2000). Pearson (1983) also traces a long history, going back to the seventeenth century, of moral campaigners and political figures, comparing young people today with an apparently more disciplined, idealised youth in the past. Extending this theme, Cohen (2002) applied the concept of folk devil to a group of Mods and Rockers who, in the 1960s and 1970s, became scapegoated as the symbols of society's ills. Through a spiralling sequence of media reports, public letters and public reactions, they came to be represented as a 'threat to the nation'. Cohen drew on the notion of moral panic to explain this spiralling sequence:

> A condition, episode, person or groups of persons emerges to become defined as a threat to societal values and interests; its nature is presented in a stylized and stereotypical fashion by the mass media; the moral barricades are manned by editors, bishops, politicians and other right-thinking people; socially accredited experts pronounce their diagnoses and solutions; ways of coping are evolved (or more often) resorted to; the condition then disappears, submerges or deteriorates and becomes more visible. (Cohen 2002: 9)

Cohen's notion of moral panic has been critiqued, evaluated and reassessed by researchers, including Cohen himself, in the light of new concepts and theories (see Garland 2008 for a review). Jefferson (2008) argues that Cohen's original definition answered the *what* and *who* questions but not the *why*: that is, why moral panics take root around particular folk devils in particular societies at particular moments in history. This is the central concern in this chapter. Drawing on Gramscian concepts, I argue that Muslim boys, in particular, have come to be demonised in England, at a time of significant economic, political and cultural global change. Their emergence as folk devils is located not only in the crisis politics that have gripped the UK since the 1970s, but also in the related and interlinked global shifts marked by the end of Cold War politics and the emergence of Islam as a new, global enemy. The chapter is structured as follows: the first section briefly discusses the theoretical assumptions and concepts that frame my analysis; the second section considers the question of how and why Muslims have come to symbolise a threat to 'the West' since the end of the Cold War. In the third section, I review the English policy and political context that has given rise to the construction of young Muslims as the 'unacceptable other' of 'Western values' of 'freedom' and 'democracy' (Shain 2013).

THEORETICAL ASSUMPTIONS AND FRAMING

A key theoretical assumption underpinning this chapter is that the economic, political and social forces that have given rise to the contemporary status of Muslim young people as a social threat are global and systemic and that the post-Cold War realities and dynamics of US global hegemony form a central backdrop to the current status of Muslims boys as folk devils in England.

The Gramscian concept of hegemony emphasises the way a particular 'world view' comes to secure the domination of a ruling elite or 'ruling bloc' within a state or systems of states. A dominant group, itself, often a coalition of competing interests, may lead by force but this leadership is likely to be short-lived. To achieve long-term success, a ruling bloc needs to secure and maintain the consent of the majority of the subordinate class, though this hegemony is never complete. For Gramsci, the state which comprises political society (the police and judiciary) and civil society (family, media and education) is the central arena where this consent is manufactured; it is 'hegemony protected by the armour of coercion' (Gramsci 1971: 262–3). That is, even in periods of relative consensus, coercion always remains in reserve. It is in the realm of civil society, however, that 'the successful mobilisation and reproduction of the active consent of the dominated groups by the ruling class "takes place" through their exercise of intellectual, moral and political leadership' (Jessop 1982: 146).

Some theorists argue that we are now 'post-hegemony' in the sense that 'neoliberal regimes construct and rely upon new forms of rule for which ideology no longer plays a part' (Beasley-Murray 2003: 118), but I agree with Johnson (2007) that hegemony has never been a more relevant concept for understanding the post 9/11 world order and the construction of political Islam as a threat to the social order. The neo-conservative Project for a New American Century (PNAC 1997) predated 9/11 but its various elements and goals were subsequently brought together and legitimated via the War on Terror. These goals included but were not limited to: an emphasis of US global leadership as the goal of its foreign policy; a commitment to spreading/exporting US values of (market) freedom and liberal democracy; investment in the military as the foundation of US global power; and a pre-emptive strike doctrine. The War on Terror, the practical exercise of the PNAC project, enabled a redefinition of the global 'enemy' and the security environment in a post-Cold War environment. As Johnson (2007) argues, the post 9/11 speeches of George Bush and Tony Blair were critical in building consent for subsequent military actions through the linking, ideologically, of many familiar elements including:

> a hatred of the Other, an absolute and racialized division between good and evil, powerfully emotive constructions of nations, forms of gendered masculine address, the impersonation of national-popular heroes, a wholesale absolution for consumerist ways of life . . . and a more than implied civilizational superiority associated with religion. (Johnson 2007)

The speeches were not merely discursive but enabled a geopolitical strategy aimed at the global promotion of US-centred neoliberal globalisation to be presented as a fight 'for our democratic values and way of life' (White House 2002: 31); the core ideas and values promoted by Bush and Blair had material consequences both globally (bombings, military invasions, regime change) and domestically (forced repatriation, new forms of security and surveillance, the general curtailment of civil liberties). Many, including Democrats in the USA and Labour Party members in the UK, were 'won over' to support the wars in Afghanistan in 2001 and Iraq in 2003 and alternative voices were rhetorically and actively silenced, for example, as 'terrorist sympathisers'.

It is also now widely accepted that the military invasions in Afghanistan and Iraq and regime-change in Libya and Syria were centred on promoting US economic interests, including the seizure of oil supplies and the privatisation of public services in the interest of transnational corporations (Johnson 2007). This maintenance of US hegemony and positioning in a post-Cold War era forms an important backdrop for the contemporary construction of Muslims as problems to be contained and managed. However, to understand why specific ethnic groups have been the targets of punitive and coercive state policies within different regional/national contexts (e.g. Arabs and Asians in the USA, Lebanese young people in Australia, Turks in Germany and Holland, North Africans in France), we need to take account of the particular colonial histories that have shaped the development of these metropolitan contexts and young people's economic locations and social/cultural experiences within them. Gramsci's concepts of *Historical specificity* and *articulation* are relevant here. Historical specificity refers to the particular economic, political and ideological makeup of a society, at a particular moment in time. By articulation, Gramsci referred to the inter-relationship of economic, political and ideological structures in specific historical periods inferring that economic structures do not simply determine political policies and cultural processes but shape them, and in turn can be shaped by them. They become interlinked in specific periods to support particular hegemonic projects.

In the case of England, two major interlinked developments have been important in shaping the course of social policy in the last 50 years and are pertinent to making sense of why and how Muslims, predominantly Pakistanis and Bangladeshis, have come to be regarded as a 'problem'; the first is the significant economic decline that followed on from the end of the initial boom of the post-World War II period. This decline is associated with the economic restructuring that involved a shift in the economic base from a manufacturing to a service and financial sector. Beginning in the 1960s and developing as a result of increased competition from national economies such as Germany in the 1970s and China and India in the 1980s, this entailed significant costs in terms of unemployment and job insecurity that have had a lasting legacy in inner city areas in England.

The second development is the loss of Britain's colonies at the end of World War II, which was largely followed by the active recruitment of workers from the former colonies to fill labour shortages created in the immediate aftermath of the war. However, the loss of its colonies did not necessarily lead to a post-colonial state identity and culture for the British state in the initial decades. As Gilroy (2004) has argued, a post-colonial melancholia – the repeated failure to let go of its imperial past – has shaped British state relations and policy in relation to its ethnic minorities. Imperial and colonial notions of a 'superior British way of life' and the racialised inferiority or difference of minority groups have been rearticulated through modern constructions of minorities as 'backward', 'untrustworthy', ' hypersexualised' (CCCS 1982; Layton Henry 1992; Gilroy 2004) and more recently as ' terrorist suspects' and 'extremists'. Notions of a superior 'British way of life' are also embedded in social policies of integration and cohesion, and the 'British values' that are promoted through the education system. Through these soft forms of control, combined with the coercive and punitive measures justified by the British War on Terror, marginalised young people have come to symbolise the Other of Britishness. Muslims girls and women, especially those who wear their religion politically, through the *niqab, hijab* or *jilbab*, have become the most visible symbols of crisis and decline at a time of intense economic uncertainty. This argument is developed in the following sections.

FROM COLD WAR POLITICS TO THE RE-ARTICULATION OF ISLAMIC THREAT: US GLOBAL HEGEMONY

Current constructions of Islam as 'evil' and 'dangerous' are not new, of course, but have a long history going back to the period of the Crusades (eleventh to thirteenth centuries) when Islam was described as 'evil incarnate' and Turkish converts to Islam as a 'vile race' by Pope Urban II who led the first Crusade. Notions of Islam as monolithic, violent and uniquely sexist (Said 1978) have been reproduced in historically contingent ways since the Crusades. For example, they were rearticulated and reworked during the nineteenth and twentieth centuries to justify British and European colonialist projects and continue to underpin contemporary understandings of Muslims as 'suspect'.

However, there have also been periods when Muslims were differently constructed, for example, during the time of the Soviet invasion of Afghanistan (1979–1989) the Mujahidin, backed and trained by the USA (later regarded as terrorists), were referred to by US President Reagan in the 1980s as 'freedom fighters' (Ahmad 2011). This construction of Muslim political activists as 'our friends' occurred during the Cold War period (1945–1991) when the Soviet was the prime competitor of the USA.

The collapse of state socialist regimes in Eastern Europe and the Soviet Union in 1991 radically transformed the geopolitical and geoeconomic contexts of world politics ending the bipolar structure of world politics with the USA, now acknowledged as the only superpower – militarily, especially (Wallace 2002; Harvey 2003). Post-Cold War wars and campaigns have been centred on the manoeuvres of the USA, and its allies in Europe, over the division of resources and political/military control of Afro-Eurasia. These interventions have enabled the USA to gain a strong foothold in the lands between Western Europe to the west, Russian Federation to the north, China to the east and sub-Saharan Africa to the south, and turn this energy-rich strategic region increasingly into an American 'sphere of influence'.

The strengthening of US global control has relied as much on politics and ideology as on economic and military power. As Wallace (2002: 109) summarises, this 'hegemony rests upon a range of resources, of hard military power, economic weight, financial commitments, and the soft currency of hegemonic values, cultural influence and prestige'. US hegemony, since 1945, has been built on the ability to homogenise the political cultures of its allies around sets of ideological values and cultural perceptions constructed to serve US interests. This has largely been achieved via symbolic constructions, loosely connected to the Second World War experience and a Western-centric interpretation of the so-called 'clash of civilisations'.

During the Cold War period, the Soviet Union and Communist ideology were portrayed throughout the capitalist West, as the evil force that threatened 'Western freedoms' and 'free enterprise'. However, since 1979 – a key historical turning point in the West's relationship to Islam – a number of factors coalesced to replace the communist threat with political Islam. Those factors included the onset of the Iranian revolution, in 1979, and the Soviet invasion of Afghanistan after which Western-trained Islamic militants began to pose a sporadic threat to US global hegemony. With the demonisation of political Islam from the late 1980s onwards, Islam and fundamentalism became linked and 'Islamic fundamentalism' and 'Islamic terror' were progressed into dominant hate themes (Ahmad 2011). This value structure has been effectively embedded within Western political cultures since then, reshaping national security agendas through repeated international polarisations, the reporting and state handling of terrorist incidents and corresponding heavy-handed interventions since the end of the Cold War, from the military campaigns in the Gulf and Afghanistan to regime-change operations in Libya and Syria.

Under the Clinton administration and its hegemonic project of neoliberal globalisation, there was war in Serbia, but US interests were pushed primarily through a strategy of financialisation (Gowan 2009). It has been since the late 1990s, the latest period of US imperialism, that anti-Islamic terrorism has replaced anti-communism as the new millennium's all-purpose rationale for providing global US military/political and economic expansion. The post 9/11 military focused strategy of the US is seen by some (Harvey 2003; Arrighi 2005; Gowan 2009) to represent the politics of a declining super-power in economic terms - manufacturing declined since the early 1970s while the neo-financialisation project collapsed in the mid-2000s, leaving only military power. Others (Panitch and Gindin 2005; Kiely 2010) see the US as a still dominant power. There is, however, broad agreement across the views that the War on Terror, has been critical for managing and convincing domestic populations of the US led military advances of the 21st century.

Under the Obama leadership in the USA and since the Brown premiership in the UK, the language of War on Terror dissipated somewhat. There are few, if any, references to the War on Terror in the 2015 US National Security Strategy which declares that 'we have moved beyond the large ground wars in Iraq and Afghanistan that defined so much of American foreign policy over the past decade'. But the goal of US primacy remains that 'America must lead' and that '[s]ustaining our leadership depends on shaping an emerging global economic order that continues to reflect our interests and values' (White House 2015). All of these form an important backdrop against which the current 'Islamist threat' has come to fruition. How this changing global landscape has played out in the context of developments in England and Great Britain, the 'closest ally' of the USA in the 'New American Century', is explored below.

FROM THE NUMBERS GAME TO TERRORIST SUSPECTS: THE CHANGING STATUS OF YOUNG MUSLIMS IN ENGLAND

Since the 1950s, Muslim communities have consistently been characterised as policy problems in England. In the 1950s and 1960s, this was as 'black' migrant workers in economic competition for jobs and services. From the 1970s, themes of 'cultural deficit/clash/alienation' were applied to read the children of migrant workers and British-born minority youth as social problems. In the 1970s and 1980s, African-Caribbean young people were the main (but not the only) targets of the state's containment policies – both soft and coercive; however, since the mid-1980s as the discourse shifted from race to faith, Asian Muslims and asylum-seekers have become the most visible symbols of crisis and change in the UK. While the targets of containment policies have changed since the 1950s, there have been repeated calls, through state policies, on minorities to assimilate into a (superior) 'British way of life' (Grosvenor 1997) and these calls have been more pronounced in periods of economic uncertainty and geopolitical dislocations (Gilroy 2004).

The Numbers Game

Ethnic minorities made up 14 % of the population in 2011 but this figure looks set to rise to 20 % by 2051 (Tran 2010). In 2011, 2.7 million were identified as Muslims (ONS 2014), up from 1.8 million in 2001. Britain's long history of black immigration goes back 500 years (Fryer 1984) but it was in the post-Second World War period that large numbers of black workers were actively recruited by the British state to fill labour shortages following the economic boom of this period (Anwar 1986; Layton-Henry 1992). In the 1950s and 1960s, African-Caribbeans, Indians and Pakistanis (and later Bangladeshis) arrived to take up jobs – a small minority in professions as doctors and teachers but the majority in unskilled labouring work such as manufacturing and textiles. These were often the jobs the indigenous workers were not prepared to do, and involved immigrants working unsocial hours often for less pay (Solomos 1992). As the migrants were motivated by the need to find work, they tended to settle in urban areas where jobs and housing were readily available; these areas have subsequently suffered most from the decline in manufacturing since the 1970s with the long-term impacts, including widespread unemployment and accompanying disadvantage in educational and labour markets for the later generations.

As is now well documented, black commonwealth immigrants arriving in Britain to help re-build the economy after the Second World War, received a warm welcome but were soon treated with suspicion and hostility as competition for jobs and services grew. Throughout the 1950s and 1960s, public and private debates began to focus on the extent of black immigration and its supposed impact on housing, the welfare state, crime and social problems. This racialisation of immigration was not a simple reworking of old colonial racism but actively produced by the state (Solomos 1992) as the signs of economic and political decline began to emerge.

Whether identified as Keynesian (following the principles of economist John Maynard Keynes) or 'embedded liberalism' (e.g. Harvey 2007), the set of policies pursued by both Labour and Conservative governments from 1945 until the 1960s had been the result of high rates of economic growth which, accompanied by period of political and ideological consensus, lasted until the end of the 1960s when the growth slowed down and economic crises ensued.

Hall et al. (1978) argue that the end of the post-war liberal consensus created space for a new form of political leadership that required a more coercive state approach to manage the economic and political crisis caused by the decline of Britain's manufacturing base in the global economy. The conservative 'New Right' government led by Margaret Thatcher took up that space in 1979, setting out to find a radical solution to the economic decline and accompanying social and political problems. The policies of the Thatcher administration played a leading role in creating consent for what later came to be known as a 'neoliberal' and 'post-welfarist' agenda which set out to free capital from the constraints of state ownership and investment, and interference by unions. What followed was a radical restructuring of workers' rights and real wages in order to keep investments profitable for the capitalist economy. Similar policies were introduced in the USA and other leading capitalist economies in order to halt the declining rate of profit and to make investment profitable enough for capitalists. The Keynesian phase had emphasised state planning and in some instances state ownership of key sectors but these new neoliberal measures were underpinned by a global monetarism that was promoted by neoliberal economists such as Friedman. The neoliberal project set out to disembed capital from these constraints (Harvey 2007) and was put into practice by now right-wing political elite to enforce neoliberal restructuring on workers.

Race was a central political symbol in the New Right's manufacture of consent for its project of 'rolling back the state'. Moral panics about black 'criminals and muggers' helped to legitimate coercive state measures aimed at the population in general, but particularly targeted disadvantaged groups that were also the most severely affected by the rising unemployment. The increased surveillance of the population was achieved through measures such as 'stop and search', but these disproportionately targeted African-Caribbean men, and as a consequence, led to further unrest in towns and cities in the 1980s. By the mid-1980s, African-Caribbean youth were being characterised in policy and media discourse as a ticking time bomb (Solomos and Back 1994) and a threat, along with trade union power and (Irish Republican) terrorism, to the 'British way of life'.

From Black to Muslim Folk Devils

Thatcherite constructions divided Britain into a privileged nation of 'good', 'hardworking' citizens and a contained and subordinated nation which included ethnic minorities and much of the unskilled white working class outside the South East (Jessop 2003). Through repeated references to criminality and deviance, young black men came to be the prime visible symbols of crisis and change. However, from the 1980s, the British discourse on minorities began to shift from ethnicity towards religion. Young Muslim men are still sometimes regarded as passive and studious, but overwhelmingly constructed as dangerous. This re-racialisation of working-class youth as a 'problem' needs to be read in the context of the above-mentioned 'religious turn' which emerged in the space created by the end of Cold War politics and the demise of the former Soviet Eastern bloc in 1991. In England, the 'Rushdie affair' (the public protests in response to the publication of Salman Rushdie's 1988 novel, *The Satanic Verses*) was a major catalyst in the politicisation of Muslim identities. Groups previously identified as Pakistani, Mirpuri or Bangladeshi were now defined and some defined themselves as Muslims (Saghal and Yuval-Davis 1992).

The Rushdie affair served as a pivot for public and political debates about preserving a (white) British 'way of life', protecting Western values of freedom and liberalism against alien, uncivilised, uncultured and misogynistic Muslims. The debates drew on and revived colonial ideas of the 'backwardness' of Muslims which helped to refuel debates about the threat posed by unrestricted immigration. Followed by the Gulf War in 1991, the Bradford riots in 1995, this was an important turning point for British Muslims.

By the time the New Labour government was elected in 1997, concerns were being expressed about the growing inequalities resulting from the neoliberal reforms pursued by three successive Conservative governments. With an expressed commitment to tackling social exclusion and race inequality, the Blairite 'Third Way' between neoliberalism and social democracy looked set to deliver on the promise of 'equality for all'. However, as a number of analyses have shown, New Labour's policies did much to slow down the onset of the 2008 crisis but did not alter the broad patterns of structural inequality. New Labour governments also, especially from 2001, posed multi-culturalism and ethnic identification as a threat to 'the nation', and introduced some of the most draconian anti-immigration and anti-terror legislation that the country has ever seen. The ambitious project of redefining Britishness around notions of 'active citizenship', 'rights and responsibilities' and paid work (Worley 2005) positioned some groups, notably Muslims, asylum-seekers and generally those not in paid employment, as outside the nation and its interests.

New Labour Party's approach to dealing with 'race' and minorities in its second term (2001–2005) has been described variously as 'the new assimilationism' (Back et al. 2002: 452) and as naïve multi-culturalism (Gillborn 2008: 19). Flirtations with multi-cultural democracy were combined with melancholic appeals to imperial grandeur to produce a contradictory vision of 'the British nation'. Renewed calls on minorities to integrate into a 'British way of life', following the 'riots' in 2001, were given further fuel after the 9/11 terrorist attacks were officially connected to Islamist terrorism and the USA and Britain officially declared a War on Terror. The project of redefining British citizenship around notions of cohesion and integration and 'British values' was largely conceptualised and pursued through policies on immigration (Home Office 2002). However, the meaning of New Labour's Britishness was hard to pin down, shifting from 'fair play and tolerance' to 'hard work, effort and enterprise' (Brown 2006) and sometimes, the Other of genital mutilation or forced marriages.

Gillborn describes new Labour's final term (2005–2010) as an era of 'aggressive majoritarianism', when 'the rights and perspectives of a white majority were asserted' and, in the context of the War on Terror and its securitisation of everyday life, they now felt able to freely voice these prejudices in the name of 'integration' or 'security' (2008: 81). The 7/7 bombings, Britain's own War on Terror, were a critical factor in shaping the intense and unprecedented focus on young Muslims as the 'enemy within'. Islamic modes of dress, forced marriage and genital mutilation, already questioned, became the subjects of increasing and detailed debate, not only in Britain but across Europe. While Britain has not quite taken the steps that France has in banning the *niqab*, evidence of the horrific mistreatment of Iraqi prisoners in what has been called Britain's 'Abu Ghraib' (Cobain 2010) was revealing of the state's coercive power. This judicial abuse, torture and war crime, alongside 'home' measures, including forced repatriation and detention without trial, maintained the threat of state violence alongside a series of 'soft' or consensual measures to manage and contain 'problem' populations.

The 2008 economic and financial crisis was the platform for the election of the new Coalition government in May 2010. With the mantra of 'clearing up the mess inherited from the previous government', the Conservative/Liberal Democratic coalition pursued austerity measures with the assumption that the private sector will step in to provide jobs for the large numbers of unemployed as a result. But the real priority for the Coalition and subsequent Conservative government, elected in 2015, has been to satisfy the financial elite, bond markets and financial assessors. The British government's policies reflect a renewal and deepening of neoliberalisation in the context of the current financial crisis and persistent economic recession (Hall 2011). This intensification of neoliberal policy measures, based on punitive conditionality and economic rationality, has been portrayed by these governments as necessary to restore Britain's economic competitiveness. However, the large-scale public spending cuts have disproportionately affected poorer communities the most.

Race has not been mentioned overtly by the Coalition and Conservative governments, but the continuation of debates about forced marriages, 'extremism' and immigration, against the backcloth of US-led regime-change operations in the Middle East, have targeted racialised groups, namely Muslims and asylum-seekers. At the same time, the targeted cutting of public services, has and will, disproportionately affect all disadvantaged groups but especially poorer ethnic minorities because of their reliance on public services. Unemployment has risen for all groups since 2010 but more sharply for ethnic minorities. Prisons seem to be getting younger, blacker and more Muslim (Shaw 2015). There is a growing income gap between rich and poor in the UK. All these are indicators of deepening economic recession and decline. Surveillance and control measures have become widespread and the battle against 'extremism' has been the justification for embedding ever-tightening control measures that target the very communities that are at the sharp end of economic decline.

CONCLUSION

Muslim boys represent a social threat at a time of significant economic, political and cultural global change. Their emergence as folk devils is located in the global shifts marked by the end of Cold War politics and the emergence of Islamism as a new, global enemy. In Britain, the manufacturing base that attracted immigrant workers in the 1960s to settle in industrial towns and cities declined significantly, causing widespread unemployment and accompanying disadvantage in educational and labour markets for the later generations.

The War on Terror, the ideological justification for the US neo-conservative Project for a New American Century (Harvey 2003), has had profound implications for Muslims. In Britain, the Pakistani and Bangladeshi communities – already among the most disadvantaged of ethnic minority communities – have been subject to intense scrutiny and surveillance in debates about 'extremism' and the limits of multi-culturalism. These debates have been particularly heated since the inner city disturbances in 2001 and the London transport bombings in 2005. Muslim boys have emerged as symbols of crisis and change against this backdrop, and arguments about their supposed under-achievement in the educational and labour market have been used to underscore dominant discourses of dangerous and violent masculinity.

While global enemies have changed and the targets of containment and control policies have shifted over the course in the last 50 years in the UK, there has been, through British state policy pronouncements, a persistent desire to reconnect with Britain's imperial past. Against the background of rising unemployment and growing economic uncertainty, repeated appeals to Britishness come at a time when Britain's imperial power and status as a leading Western economy is being challenged by strong competition from countries such as China and India and other emerging economies (Gowan 2009; Gokay 2009). The forging of a renewed British identity can be read in this context as melancholic (Gilroy 2004) and as an ideological mechanism to deflect attention from a British economy in decline. Patriotic appeals to a mythic Britishness can be seen to support the illusion of a cohesive society at a time when disadvantage and class inequalities threaten to become stark as a result of savage cuts to public funding in the context of significant economic decline. Young Muslims are visible symbols of this crisis and decline.

REFERENCES

Ahmad, E. (2011). *Terrorism: Theirs & ours*. New York: Seven Stories Press.
Anwar, M. (1986). *Race and politics: Ethnic minorities and the British political system*. London: Tavistock Publications.

Arrighi, G. (2005). Hegemony unravelling. *New Left Review*, *32*, 23–80.
Back, L., Keith, M., Khan, A., Shukra, K., & Solomos, J. (2002). New Labour's white heart: Politics, multiculturalism and the return of assimilation. *The Political Quarterly*, *73*(4), 445–454.
Beasley-Murray, J. (2003). On posthegemony. *Bulletin of Latin American Research*, *22*(1), 117–125.
Brown, G. (2006) Britishness speech given to the Commonwealth Club, London. http://www.guardian.co.uk/politics/2007/feb/27/immigrationpolicy.race [Accessed July 2015].
Cantle, T. (2001). *Community cohesion*. London: Home Office.
CCCS (Centre for Contemporary cultural Studies). (1982). *The empire strikes back*. London: Hutchinson.
Cobain, I. (2010). Iraqi prisoners were abused at 'UK's Abu Ghraib', court hears. *Guardian*. November 6.
Cohen, S. (2002). *Folk devils and moral panics: The creation of the mods and rockers*. London: Routledge.
Delamont, S. (2000). The anomalous beasts: Hooligans and the history of sociology of education. *Sociology*, *34*(1), 95–111.
Denham, J. (2002). *Building cohesive communities: A report of the ministerial group on public order and community cohesion*. London: Home Office.
Fryer, P. (1984). *Staying power: The history of Black people in Britain*. London: Pluto.
Garland, D. (2008). On the concept of moral panic. *Crime Media Culture*, *4*, 9–30.
Gillborn, D. (2008). *Racism and education: Coincidence or conspiracy*. London: Routledge.
Gilroy, P. (2004). *After empire: Multiculture or postcolonial melancholia*. London: Routledge.
Gokay, B. (2009). Tectonic shifts and systemic faultlines: A global perspective to understand the 2008–9 world economic crisis. *Alternatives: Turkish Journal of International Relations*, *8*(1), 29–35.
Gowan, P. (2009). Crisis in the heartland, consequences of the new Wall Street system. *New Left Review*, *55*, 5–29.
Gramsci, A. (1971). *The prison notebooks*. London: Lawrence and Wishart.
Grosvenor, I. (1997). *Assimilating identities: Racism and educational policy in post 1945 Britain*. London: Lawrence and Wishart.
Hall, S. (2011). The neoliberal revolution. *Cultural Studies*, *25*(6), 705–728.
Hall, S., Critcher, C., Jefferson, T., Clark, J., & Roberts, B. (1978). *Policing the crisis: Mugging, the state and law and order*. London: Macmillan.
Harvey, D. (2003). *The new imperialism*. Oxford: Oxford University Press.
Harvey, D. (2007). *A brief history of neoliberalism*. Oxford: Oxford University Press.

Hebdige, D. (1979). *Subculture: The meaning of style.* New accents. London: Routledge.

Home Office. (2002). *Secure borders: Safe haven.* London: The Stationary Office.

Jefferson, T. (2008). Policing the crisis revisited: The state, masculinity, fear of crime and racism. *Crime, Media, Culture, 4*(1), 113–121.

Jessop, B. (1982). *The capitalist state: Marxist theories and methods.* Oxford: Martin Robertson.

Jessop, B. (2003). From Thatcherism to New Labour: neo-liberalism, workfarism and labour market regulation. In H. Overbeek (Ed.), *The political economy of European unemployment: European integration and the transnationalization of the employment question.* London: Routledge.

Johnson, R. (2007). Post-hegemony? I don't think so. *Theory, Culture & Society, 24*(3), 95–110.

Kiely, R. (2010). *Rethinking imperialism.* Basingstoke: Palgrave Macmillan.

Layton-Henry, Z. (1992). *The politics of immigration: Immigration, race and race relations in post-war Britain.* Oxford: Blackwell Publishers.

ONS. (2014) Office for National Statistics. 2011 Census: Key Statistics for England and Wales, March 2011.

Panitch, L., & Gindin, S. (2005). Global capitalism and American empire. *Socialist Register, 40*(40), 12–28.

Pearson, G. (1983). *Hooligan: A history of respectable fears.* Basingstoke: Macmillan.

Saghal, G., & Yuval-Davis, N. (1992). *Refusing holy orders.* London: Virago.

Said, E. (1978). *Orientalism.* 1979/1994 New York: Vintage.

Sarazzin, T. (2010). *Deutschland schafft sich ab: Wie wir unser Land aufs Spiel setzen, Deutsche Verlags-Anstalt.*

Shain, F. (2013). Race, nation and education. *Education Inquiry, 4*(1), 701–724.

Shaw, D. (2015, March 11). Why the surge in Muslim prisoners? *BBC News.*

Solomos, J. (1992). The politics of immigration since 1945. In P. Braham, A. Rattansi, & R. Skellington (Eds.), *Racism and anti racism.* London: Open University in association with Sage.

Solomos, J., & Back, L. (1994). Conceptualising racisms: Social theory, politics and research. *Sociology, 28*(1), 143–161.

Tran, M. (2010, July 13). Ethnic minorities to make up 20 % of UK population by 2051. *Guardian.* Available at http://www.guardian.co.uk/uk/2010/jul/13/uk-population-growth-ethnic-minorities, accessed July 2015.

Wallace, W. (2002). American hegemony: European dilemmas. *The Political Quarterly, 73*, s1 105–118.

White House. (2002). *United States National Security Strategy.* Washington.

White House. (2015). *United Stated National Security Strategy.* Washington.

Worley, C. (2005). 'It's not about race. It's about the community': New Labour and community cohesion. *Critical Social Policy, 25*(4), 483.

Farzana Shain is Professor of Sociology of Education at Keele University. Her research and writing focuses on educational inequalities and social justice and on young people's experiences of schooling. She is the author of *The New Folk Devils: Muslim Boys and Education* and *The Schooling and Identity of Asian Girls*. Her most recent book is the co-edited (with Kalwant Bhopal) *Neoliberalism and Education: Rearticulating Social Justice and Education* (Routledge). Farzana has also researched and written about the politics of educational change in the further education sector in England.

CHAPTER 3

Late-Modern Muslims: Theorising Islamic Identities Amongst University Students

Paul Bagguley and Yasmin Hussain

INTRODUCTION

In this chapter we develop a series of theoretical reflections conceptualising Muslim identities in contemporary British universities. Given the securitised nature of dominant discursive constructions of Muslim identities in Britain today and the recent (2015) Prevent duty placed on universities, this chapter focuses considerable attention on these which are transforming the Muslim experience of university in Britain.

Firstly, we discuss Muslim identity in the context of debates around late-modernity (Giddens 1990, 1994). Despite the Eurocentric nature of such approaches, they do recognise how many of the broader long-term social changes that are in play with Muslim identity claims. For Archer (2012) late-modernity has created an imperative to be reflexive, and people now have to make more decisions about their lives. For our purposes this is imposed upon Muslims from outside by wider social changes as well as the securitising effects of counter-terrorism (Hussain and Bagguley 2012) to reflect upon their identity and the wider impacts of their actions as Muslims.

We then examine the state's counter-terrorism strategy Prevent which has recently been extended to universities. This exemplifies features of late-modernity – fluid identities, the challenge of the transnational

P. Bagguley (✉) · Y. Hussain
University of Leeds, Leeds, UK
e-mail: p.bagguley@leeds.ac.uk; Y.Hussain@leeds.ac.uk

© The Author(s) 2017
M. Mac an Ghaill, C. Haywood (eds.), *Muslim Students, Education and Neoliberalism*, DOI 10.1057/978-1-137-56921-9_3

35

character of Muslimness, how Muslim identities resist traditional modernist forms of racialisation, issues of trust, risk and unease (Giddens 1994). Next, we examine Prevent's objectification (Nussbaum 1995) of Muslim identities. Drawing on Nussbaum we show how Prevent treats Muslims instrumentally, denies their autonomy and agency, treats them homogenously, treats Muslim identities as violable and as commodities and denies the value of their subjectivities and experiences. These effects operate, we suggest, through Prevent exercising power in the form of a synopticon (Mathieson 1997) where the many watch the few. Prevent seeks to mobilise the majority watching for signs of terrorism amongst Muslims. The overall effect is to undermine or threaten the ontological security (Giddens 1994) of Muslims, a generalised feeling of 'anxiety of being'. It is this we surmise is increasingly characteristic of the Muslim experience of university.

LATE-MODERNITY AND REFLEXIVE IDENTITIES

Giddens sees modernity's main characteristic as being incessant social change and the constant restructuring of social institutions. This is a global system of markets, culture, communications and politics. Historically unique, this modernity is open-ended, unpredictable and uncontrollable (Giddens 1990: 151–54). These societies are post-traditional with no uniformly accepted core values and norms that provide clear guidelines for action. Modernity's detraditionalisation means that people now live and act in different segmentalised social settings. This produces a world where people have to constantly create new social bonds. However, we believe Islam and Muslims sit in a rather odd place in relation to such claims. Superficially, it seems to us that they are mere 'remnants of the past' from Giddens' perspective. This belies his reliance upon a version of traditional secularisation theory, but we suggest that Muslims, certainly in the West, do live late-modern lives, and that this is especially so for university students. Muslim students face numerous opportunities and dilemmas, and Islam is for them one amongst many decentred authorities. Furthermore, Islam is not simply 'inherited from the past', but rather subject to a localised and contextualised application in the late-modern present. For Giddens, globalisation links local social relations across great distances where events in one place have diverse consequences in many other locations. Muslim identities exemplify this by combining a global religious identity – the umma – with Britishness (Lynch 2013) expressing what we have termed reflexive ethnicity (Hussain and Bagguley 2015). These national combined with trans-local identities create 'unease' for nation-states providing the rationale for counter-terrorist strategies such as Prevent (Archer 2009).

Detraditionalisation means that knowledge and belief are both contingent and contextual. Since there are numerous segmentalised settings for producing new, different forms of belief and culture, there are no longer any universally accepted absolute truths for cultural, political and moral questions. These claims by Giddens are clearly from a global perspective, and Islam sits as one amongst many belief systems. This in part, we think, accounts for the interest in formalised religious instruction amongst young Muslims in the West (Lynch 2013: 252).

In late-modernity our everyday experiences are increasingly mediated, rather than based on face-to-face interaction. We experience many other cultures, events, ideas through the global mass media. These processes construct new identities, and new bases for social differences (Giddens 1990: 86–7). Late-modernity is profoundly disembedding. Beliefs and social relations used to be embedded in particular places, in particular times and rooted in local cultures. Social relations and culture are spread to different times and different places, and global Islam and the global Islamophobia are no exception to this in our view. Reflexivity has become a chronic feature of late-modernity so that:

> the self as reflexively understood by the person in terms of his or her biography. Identity here still presumes continuity across time and space: but self-identity is such continuity as interpreted reflexively by the agent. (Giddens 1990: 53)

In contrast to this, Archer (2012) sees reflexivity in a generic feature of all human actions, but identifies several different forms of reflexivity. Crucially for her the recent social changes in the West have created an imperative towards what she terms meta-reflexivity, where people feel that they have to routinely evaluate themselves and the effectivity of their actions in society (Archer 2012: 13). Archer thus differs from Giddens who sees reflexivity as the consequence of individualisation produced by the social structural changes of 'late-modernity', by seeing different social circumstances as being conducive for different forms of reflexivity. Of importance for the discussion here is her claim that conditions of 'contextual discontinuity', where people experience new and challenging social situations, characterise most people's circumstances in the West and that this produces an imperative towards 'meta-reflexivity'. Elsewhere we have suggested that Archer's conceptualisation of different forms of reflexivity is a fruitful way of approaching the theme of reflexivity in relation to ethnic identities (Hussain and Bagguley 2015).

In late-modernity one can no longer simply be born a Muslim, rather one is forced to reflect upon and decide what kind of Muslim one might wish to be. Religion has increasingly replaced ethnicity as the principal source of self-identification for many Muslims in Britain (Ahmed and Donnon 1994; Samad 1996). The re-imagining of Islam as a global religion is seen to be offering an important mode of being for young Muslims in Britain within the context of their British identities (Ahmed and Donnon 1994). Undergoing education within the diaspora enables them to access modernist interpretations of the religion (Samad 1996). Such tendencies are not unique to Islam, but are found more widely amongst diasporic communities, and pose a challenge to conceptions of hybridity framed in terms of ethnicity. The distinctiveness of religious as opposed to ethnic identity arises from the belief in the universally applicability of Islam, whilst ethnic identities are seen as particularistic. Within Islam anyone can become a Muslim, but ethnicity remains productive of difference and boundary making. Furthermore, Islam brings a sense of belonging to a global community – the umma – and provides detailed rules for everyday life (Jacobson 1997). In addition, the development of the assertion of an Islamic identity as the outcome of a complex political process operating locally, for example the Satanic Verses affair, the first Gulf War and the current war on terror. The response of the wider society was to demonise all Muslims, thus ignoring the complex set of different identities of the first-generation migrants (Samad 1996). This has been exacerbated by the development of Muslims as a 'suspect community' and subject to various securitising discourses and practices (Hussain and Bagguley 2012; Abbas 2005; Modood 2005). There is then in late-modernity a long dialectic of external objectification of Muslim identities by the state and various dominant discourses, and internal reflexivity of ethnicity (Hussain and Bagguley 2015) where its meaning is re-created and re-thought in current conditions of contextual discontinuity.

PREVENT AND THE CONSTRUCTION OF MUSLIM IDENTITIES

Underlying the policy and practices of Prevent is the idea of 'radicalisation', which is central to how it constructs Muslim identities. This concept has emerged relatively recently in official security policy circles and political and media debates. For instance, it was not used with reference to the conflict in the North of Ireland in the latter decades of the last century (Richards 2011: 144). Radicalisation was rarely referred to before 2001, and 'took off' as a key theme of public media discourse in relation to terrorism around 2006–07 (Sedgewick 2010: 480), and others have noted how its conceptualisation in official discourse draws upon themes which were only previously present in American neo-conservative debates (Spalek and McDonald 2009: 129). Radicalisation discourse is seen by many as a product of counter-terrorism policy, and the rise of academic interest in radicalisation is evident from 2004 onwards in terms of peer-reviewed journal articles using the term (Kundnani 2012: 5–7).

It has been argued that there is no policy or academic consensus on what radicalisation means in this context (Richards 2015: 373). The incoherence of Prevent's underlying conception of radicalisation has led some to conceptualise it as an 'assemblage' of governance (De Goede and Simon 2013: 317) rather than a logically coherent policy framework. However, this has not prevented the idea from being challenged from a variety of perspectives by academic critics. Government policy has implied a pre-emptive counter-radicalisation strategy, hence called 'Prevent', but this has vacillated between addressing violent extremism, on the one hand, and promoting broader community cohesion and shared values on the other (Richards 2011: 143). This originates in the view of some commentators in the refusal of the Government to recognise and accept that British foreign policy was a primary source of grievances, and their preferred option of seeing domestic factors as the drivers of 'radicalisation' (Richards 2011: 147). The discourse of radicalisation thus enables the state and its academic advisors to treat terrorism as something that can be subject to internal 'governance', facilitating practices that seek to control the future behaviour of individuals (Heath-Kelly 2013: 396). There is also the suggestion that the radicalisation discourse provides an easy to follow narrative about how otherwise 'ordinary' Muslims become terrorists (Githens-Mazer and Lambert 2010). It also fits with a wider narrative about 'dysfunctional' Muslim communities that do not share 'British values', a theme that emerged especially after the 2001 riots, and one that informed the community cohesion agenda (Bagguley and Hussain 2008).

Initial Prevent funding focused on local authorities with sizeable Muslim communities (Husband and Alam 2011; Thomas 2012), and early activities were focused on developing discussions amongst Muslims about violent extremism and cultural and sports activities (Heath-Kelly 2013: 403–4). Prevent, from its outset, clearly targeted Muslims, especially younger age groups, as in the early years of Prevent between 2007 and 2010, 1120 individuals were identified as liable to radicalisation, of whom over 90 percent were Muslims, 290 were under 16 and 55 under 12 (Kundnani 2012: 20). Prevent and Contest have a 'pre-emptive logic' that 'denies young British Muslims social and political agency' (Coppock and McGovern 2014: 253).

In the revised 2009 version of the Prevent strategy, radicalisation was understood to refer to 'the process by which people come to support violent extremism and, in some cases, join terrorist groups' (quoted in Richards 2011: 145). Hence there was a move towards defining extremism in terms of people's ideas and beliefs, rather than actions. This is underscored by the focus on becoming a radical rather than becoming a terrorist (Richards 2011: 145). The discourse around radicalisation shifted from the grievances, ideas and strategies of terrorist groups to the individual's beliefs (Sedgewick 2010: 480–1). This has entailed a clear move away from the political context of terrorism to a focus on psychological factors, which reflects a broader contemporary cultural concern with psychological dysfunction as an explanation of all kinds of social and political phenomena. Consequently, otherwise normal ideas, thoughts and behaviours become framed as potential security risks and signs of vulnerability to radicalisation (Coppock and McGovern 2014: 250). This reflects a broader increase in societal concern with and use of the 'Psy-disciplines' that sociologists have related to the emergence of late-modernity (Giddens 1994) and related processes of individualisation.

A strategically significant change in the 2011 version of Contest, the overall counter-terrorism strategy of which Prevent is a part, was to define radicalisation to include 'non-violent' extremism such as a desire for fundamental social change. This was explicitly borrowed from the Danish Security and Intelligence Service (Coppock and McGovern 2014: 245), which also illustrates how Prevent is part of a global network of similar initiatives in other Western countries. Blurring the distinctions between 'terrorism', 'radicalisation' and 'extremism' and the distinction between extremist ideas and extremist has led to Prevent's renewed focus on ideas which themselves are non-violent (Richards 2015: 373). Radicalisation discourse has become distinct from previous official terrorism discourses by virtue of its focus on religious belief and psychology (Kundnani 2012: 10). This has apparently continued with the Counter-Terrorism and Securities Act 2015 which has extended Prevent to universities (Abbas and Awan 2015).

Underlying the Prevent programme is the assumption of the 'vulnerability' of those susceptible to 'violent extremism' (Richards 2011: 150). This securitises institutions and practices such as education and health care. Young British Muslims in particular are constructed as 'vulnerable', as both suspects and 'in need of being saved' (Coppock and McGovern 2014: 243). These assumptions distract attention from the idea of terrorism as a calculated collective political strategy (Richards 2011). In terms of Prevent discourses Muslim identities are seen as 'risky', where '...risk is understood as "performative," in that it "produces" the effects it names' (Heath-Kelly 2013: 395). Risk and trust are, of course, key themes identified by leading theorists of late-modernity, again illustrating how several of the characteristics of Prevent reflect the wider late-modern social condition. Constructing Muslims as vulnerable also has the effect of securitising them so that radicalisation is a discourse that: '... actually produces (discursively) the threats it claims to identify for the performance of governance, rather than as reacting to the existence of such risks' (Heath-Kelly 2013: 408). Around 2010–11, the scope of Prevent was revised so that local authorities have to integrate Prevent work into all aspects of their work (Coppock and McGovern 2014: 246). This has enabled the state to exceptionally enlist civil society in counter-terrorism work aimed at: '...the regulation of social lifeworlds and the production of intimate, personal and situated interventions' (De Goede and Simon 2013: 328). Such 'care-based interventions' and discourses seek to mobilise the ethical motivations of professionals. Hence the discourse of vulnerability mobilises an ethic of care, which also has the effect of depoliticising Prevent work.

However, early Prevent work was considerably modified in practice (Husband and Alam 2011; O'Toole et al. 2016; Thomas 2012). This has led some to suggest that Prevent has been both ineffective and counter-productive (Thomas 2012), whilst others suggest that local authority staff have had an important role in mediating the effects of an inherently flawed policy imposed from above (Husband and Alam 2011; O'Toole et al. 2016). Whilst much of this work has focused on local authorities' Prevent work and hence the earlier 'softer' versions of the policy, circumstances have changed with both a 'harsher' less community cohesion-led version with the revisions of the coalition Government with their focus on individual beliefs (Richards 2011) and its extension into all areas of local authorities' work, the NHS, schools (Coppock and McGovern 2014) and most recently universities (Abbas and Awan 2015). In comparison there are relatively few studies that focus on the implementation of Prevent in an educational context (Sian 2015). In primary schools it seems that Prevent training has been given priority over race equality training (Sian 2015: 184), and it seems to be targeted at schools with large numbers of Muslim students (Sian 2015: 192). Furthermore, despite the concerns with vulnerability (Coppock and McGovern 2014) and the manner in which Prevent seeks to draw upon the ethic of care of professionals (De Goede and Simon 2013), those working with young Muslims put in a difficult position, and are trained to try and apply an unrealistic list of 'signs' of extremism (Sian 2015: 190).

At this stage it is quite unclear how Prevent will be implemented in universities. Despite the highly prescriptive nature of the Prevent Duty Guidance, universities are institutions that are immensely protective of their traditional autonomy and legal immunities. Formally at least this is a battle which they have lost in the case of Prevent. However, we suspect there will be considerable diversity of response not only due to local institutional, political and contextual factors, but also due to organised resistance, which has not been seen to the same extent in the other sectors where Prevent has been implemented.

PREVENT, OBJECTIFYING MUSLIM IDENTITIES AND THE PRODUCTION OF ONTOLOGICAL INSECURITY

In this section we want to suggest that Prevent has the effect of objectifying Muslim identities with the ultimate effect of producing ontological insecurity for Muslims in contemporary universities in the UK. Whereas there are frequent references to the negative effects of Prevent on Muslims in the general literature on the programme, these tend to be rather superficially conceptualised. Here we try to conceptualise more rigorously what exactly is negative about Prevent and how it has negative effects on Muslim identities. We suggest that drawing upon wider conceptions of objectification (Nussbaum 1995) and ontological security (Giddens 1990, 1994) is a fruitful way towards addressing these issues.

Nussbaum (1995) identifies seven aspects of objectification and we can see that these apply to how Prevent treats Muslims. Firstly, Muslims are treated instrumentally by Prevent; they are treated as the tool for its purposes.

If we see Prevent as a discourse concerned with producing a governable population of Muslims (Heath-Kelly 2013), then this implies they are being treated instrumentally. Prevent attempts to give the impression of controlling terrorism, and ordinary Muslims are the tools to achieve this. Secondly, objectification denies people's autonomy, and this is evident in Prevent's discourse of vulnerability. By constructing Muslims as vulnerable to radicalisation, their autonomy is denied and they are assumed to be powerless in the face of the process of radicalisation. This is also related to Nussbaum's third aspect which is where objectification entails treating the objectified as not being capable of agency. Thus Muslim populations have to be 'saved' by the forces of the state from radicalism, which they are assumed to be incapable of resisting (Coppock and McGovern 2014). Fourthly, objectification constructs people as interchangeable with others of the 'same type'. Prevent discourse and practices essentially treat all Muslims as the same, and there appears to be no way of discriminating between 'real terrorists' and ordinary Muslims despite this being a familiar theme of much counter-terrorism discourse. Any Muslim student, for example, could be a 'suspect'. Fifthly, objectification renders people violable, and their identities are seen as accessible to manipulation and modification. Prevent interventions are assumed to be legitimate violations of, and interventions in, Muslim communities and individuals' lives (De Goede and Simon 2013). Prevent thus seeks to render Muslims 'governable' to 'modify their conduct' (Heath-Kelly 2013: 396). Prevent seeks to control Muslim bodies as if they were owned and controlled, and only when they are deemed to be no longer at risk of or vulnerable to radicalisation are those bodies released. Finally, objectification involves a denial of subjectivity, where the objectified person's experiences and feelings are not taken account of. This is also evident in the case of Prevent, which has proved remarkably resilient to the experiences and critical views of it amongst the majority of Muslims who have encountered it (Husband and Alam 2011; O'Toole et al. 2016; Thomas 2012). Over time, Prevent has become more extensive across a range of institutions, and has shifted its focus from violence to support for extremist ideas and has become a legal duty on hospitals and universities. The new Prevent duty enshrines in law what was previously a frequent if unorganised practice in many universities, based on advice rather than a legally enforceable duty (Brown and Saeed 2015).

One of the reasons for the character of Prevent and radicalisation discourse is the unpredictability of Muslim identities that is rooted in their being expressions of Muslim reflexivity and agency where they displace racialised forms of identification with religious ones. As Tyrer and Sayyid argue:

> the expression of Muslim identities interrupts the processes by which racialized minorities are subjectified in western states, since by choosing their preferred modes of categorization they express an agency not generally afforded to racialized populations within the logics of the racial imaginary, and since by supplanting ascribed racial labels with religious identification they reveal the limits of that imaginary as the basis for governing racialized populations. (Tyrer and Sayyid 2012: 353)

One implication of this insight is that securitising discourses and practices such as Prevent cannot readily latch onto racialised identities, practices or symbols, although they frequently attempt to do so. Rather we want to suggest that Prevent recognises the fluidity (Bauman 2000) of Muslim identities and constitutes this fluidity as the object of its interventions, treating it as pathological and as a symptom or sign of potential radicalisation, involvement in clandestine violence and therefore as a threat. Apparent changes in the identity practices of Muslims are to be taken as signs of being at risk of radicalisation and violent extremism. Contemporary Muslim students are thus treated as having 'suspect identities'; they are suspect identities not just because they are Muslim but because they are mutable. Prevent is, in this sense, a form of late-modern, liquid counter-terrorism policy aimed at 'risky' Muslim identities. They are risky identities not just because of their Muslimness, but because of their fluidity. Their Muslimness is unfathomable from a Eurocentric perspective, but their liquid, late-modern fluidity is risky from the perspective of a state promoting their securitisation. What is seen by some as a generalised feature of liquid modernity (Bauman) in the case of Prevent and Muslim identities is constructed as pathological and potentially threatening.

The Prevent duty and the associated emerging training materials operate with a limited normalised view of Muslim students. They are assumed to be like White middle class as being away from home for the first time, and experimenting with new identities and practices. However, this overlooks the plurality of Muslim identities in universities. Many will still be living at home with their parents, and enter into complex negotiations with their parents over whether or not to leave home to attend university for complex moral, economic and gendered reasons (Hussain and

Bagguley 2015). Yet others will be international students. Amongst the Muslim student body, then there will be a plurality of ethnicities and nationalities articulated in diverse ways with being Muslim. Prevent discourses and practices have the effect of homogenising, reifying and essentialising Muslim student identities.

Some years ago, Thomas Mathieson (1997) proposed the concept of synopticon as a parallel to Foucault's concept of the panopticon. Mathieson and those who have followed up his suggestions have applied this to the mass media where the control of the many is achieved through their viewing of the few. Mathieson drew the parallel partly through noting how Foucault saw 'traditional punishment' entailing the many watching the public spectacle of the torture of the few. Here we want to suggest a rather different kind of synopticon, where Muslim minorities are subjected to the gaze of the non-Muslim majority in order to police them in the name of counter-terrorism. This synoptical gaze is actively encouraged and promoted, in the UK at least, by the state through Prevent. The state's 'softer' counter-terrorist policies actively promote a constant watch over the Muslim minority not in a panoptical manner, but in a synoptical manner encouraging everyone to look out for signs of 'radicalisation'. Whilst some have used the synopticon to examine tele-mediated social relations, where power is exercised over the many through consumerist seduction (Bauman 2000), we wish to conceptualise synoptical power as characterising the state's management of relations between reified and essentialised ethno-religious groups. Through Prevent institutions of civil society, such as schools, hospitals, universities, mosques, community groups and public spaces more generally, have become the loci of synoptical power. They become places where the many non-Muslims watch the few Muslims for signs of radicalisation.

We suggest that synoptical power depends upon both the generation of a specific kind of subject position that of disciplinary citizenship, and a reflexive relationship between the watched and the watchers. In some respect then it bears some of the characteristics of panoptical power, but differs in crucial aspects. Watching and knowing you are being watched, as well as the watcher knowing that the watched knows they are being watched is central to this form of power. There is no realistic option of 'flight' for the watched. It becomes a condition of citizenship to allow yourself to be constantly observed. Where everyone else, like you, is used to being observed and 'tolerates' this, then you tend to go with the flow and tolerate being watched as well. To do otherwise is to risk drawing attention not just to yourself, but to others like you. In this sense the synopticon exerts its power through the reflexivity of those who are subject to it. Whereas panoptical power crucially depends on the invisibility of the watcher – you can never be sure that you are being watched, and discipline is achieved by subjects having to assume that they are always being observed.

Rather than synoptical power being technologically determined (as implied by Bauman 2000), it is relational and reflexive. It constructs relations between reified groups and demands reflexivity amongst those subject to it. For the synopticon to operate the subjects have to be visibly identifiable. Muslims have to be rendered visible, which is why Islamophobia is routinely articulated with processes of racialisation. Visible physical signs of the Muslim become a pre-occupation.

Whilst many, if not all, of the aspects of the objectification and synoptical power inscribed by Prevent's discourses and practices are morally objectionable in and of themselves, it is still legitimate to pose the question as to the effects of objectification. We want to suggest that Prevent through its objectifying practices has the effect of undermining the ontological security of Muslims. Prevent has the effect of undermining the ontological security (Giddens 1990) of Muslim students. Central to ontological security are relations of trust, especially with professionals and experts and the predictability of everyday interactions in institutionalised settings. If these are thrown into question, anxiety is the result. Anxiety arises from a more or less perceived threat to the ontological security of self-identity (Giddens 1990: 42–7). Anxiety is a 'generalised state... diffuse, it is free-floating; lacking a specific object...' (Giddens 1990: 43–4). As Bauman notes, such generalised anxiety is generated by the liquid modern condition, however, we want to suggest that it is more targeted and focused in this present context. Trust is central to the social relations between professionals and clients, and this is no less the case for higher education (HE) professionals and students. Prevent undermines this trust relationship. Although Giddens sees ontological security as a generic consequence of the character of late-modernity, we see it as logically connected to questions of power and inequality. Structural forces produce ontological insecurity for the powerless. One of the gaps in Giddens' analysis is that he does not seem to consider ontological security as an aspect of social inequality whereby the mechanisms producing ontological insecurity are targeted at marginalised groups. Thus in specifying such processes and mechanisms and how they operate through objectification and synoptical power, we are able to uncover the unevenness of ontological insecurity.

CONCLUSION

In this chapter we have argued that the government's counter-terrorism strategy Prevent alongside the wider securitisation of Muslims is now playing a central role in the external construction of Muslim identities in British universities. We began by examining Giddens' conception of late-modern life and identity. From that we concluded that despite its Eurocentric assumptions in many respects, it is a valuable characterisation of the fluidity of contemporary Muslims identities and lives. From there we moved on to critically examine the government's counter-terrorist Prevent programme which has recently been extended to universities. Prevent is focused on the identities of Muslim students and we have drawn out its objectifying consequences constructing a synoptical framework which undermines the ontological security of Muslim students. More specifically, Prevent treats Muslim students instrumentally, denies their autonomy and agency, homogenising them, seeking to govern their conduct and deny their subjectivities. Prevent has constructed a synoptical form of power, whereby Muslims are policed on an everyday basis under the gaze of the many. Everyone now in universities are expected to be suspicious of Muslims, constantly vigilant for signs of vulnerability to radicalisation. For Muslim students these 'imaginary identities' constructed within official discourses and practices undermine their 'ontological security' producing a generalised feeling of anxiety and the destruction of trust in those around them.

REFERENCES

Abbas, T. (2005). *Muslim Britain: Communities under pressure*. London: Zed Books.
Abbas, T., & Awan, I. (2015). Limits of UK counterterrorism policy and its implications for Islamophobia and far right extremism. *International Journal for Crime, Justice and Social Democracy, 4*(3), 16–29.
Ahmed, A. S., & Donnon, H. (Eds.). (1994). *Islam, globalisation and identity*. London: Routledge.
Archer, T. (2009). Welcome to the *umma*: The British state and its Muslim citizens since 9/11. *Cooperation and Conflict: Journal of the Nordic International Studies Association, 44*(3), 329–347.
Archer, M. (2012). *The reflexive imperative in late modernity*. Cambridge: Cambridge University Press.
Bagguley, P., & Hussain, Y. (2008). *Riotous citizens: Ethnic conflict in multicultural Britain*. Aldershot: Ashgate.

Bauman, Z. (2000). *Liquid modernity*. Cambridge: Polity Press.

Brown, T., & Saeed, T. (2015). Radicalisation and counter-radicalisation at British universities: Muslim encounters and alternatives. *Ethnic and Racial Studies, 38*(11), 1952–1968.

Coppock, V., & McGovern, M. (2014). 'Dangerous minds'? Deconstructing counter-terrorism discourse, radicalisation and the "psychological vulnerability" of Muslim children and young people in Britain. *Children and Society, 28,* 242–256.

De Goede, M., & Simon, S. (2013). Governing future radicals in Europe. *Antipode, 45*(2), 315–335.

Giddens, A. (1990). *The consequences of modernity*. Cambridge: Polity Press.

Giddens, A. (1994). *Modernity and self-identity: Self and society in the late modern age*. Cambridge: Polity Press.

Githens-Mazer, J., & Lambert, R. (2010). Why conventional wisdom on radicalisation fails: The persistence of a failed discourse. *International Affairs, 86*(4), 889–901.

Heath-Kelly, C. (2013). Counter-terrorism and the counterfactual: Producing the "radicalisation" discourse and the UK prevent strategy. *The British Journal of Politics and International Relations, 15,* 394–415.

Husband, C., & Alam, Y. (2011). *Social cohesion and counter-terrorism*. Bristol: Policy Press.

Hussain, Y., & Bagguley, P. (2012). Securitised citizens: Islamophobia, racism and the 7/7 London bombings. *The Sociological Review, 60*(4), 714–733.

Hussain, Y., & Bagguley, P. (2015). Reflexive ethnicities: Crisis, diversity and re-composition. *Sociological Research Online, 20*(3), 1–11.

Jacobson, J. (1997). Religion and ethnicity: Dual and alternative sources of identity among young British Pakistanis. *Ethnic and Racial Studies, 20*(2), 238–256.

Kundnani, A. (2012). Radicalisation: The journey of a concept. *Race and Class, 54*(2), 3–25.

Lynch, O. (2013). British Muslim youth: Radicalisation, terrorism and the construction of the "other". *Critical Studies on Terrorism, 6*(2), 241–261.

Mathieson, T. (1997). The viewer society: Michel Foucault's "panopticon" revisited. *Theoretical Criminology, 1*(2), 215–234.

Modood, T. (2005). *Multicultural politics: Racism, ethnicity and Muslims in Britain*. Edinburgh: Edinburgh University Press.

Nussbaum, M. C. (1995). Objectification. *Philosophy and Public Affairs, 24*(4), 249–291.

O'Toole, T. et al. (2016). Governing through prevent? Regulation and contested practice in state-Muslim engagement. *Sociology, 50*(1), 160–177.

Richards, A. (2011). The problem with "radicalisation": The remit of "Prevent" and the need to refocus on terrorism in the UK. *International Affairs, 87*(1), 143–152.

Richards, A. (2015). From terrorism to "radicalisation" to "extremism": Counter terrorist imperative or loss of focus? *International Affairs, 91*(2), 371–380.

Samad, Y. (1996). The politics of Islamic identity among Bangladeshis and Pakistanis in Britain. In T. Ranger, Y. Samad, & O. Stuart (Eds.), *Culture identity and politics: Ethnic minorities in Britain.* Aldershot: Avebury.

Sedgewick, M. (2010). The concept of radicalisation as a source of confusion. *Terrorism and Political Violence, 22,* 479–494.

Sian, K. (2015). Spies, surveillance and stakeouts: Monitoring Muslim moves in British state schools. *Race, Ethnicity and Education, 18*(2), 183–201.

Spalek, B., & McDonald, L. Z. (2009). Terror crime prevention: Constructing Muslim practices and beliefs as "anti-social" and "extreme" through CONTEST 2. *Social Policy and Society, 9*(1), 123–132.

Thomas, P. (2012). *Responding to the threat of violent extremism: Failing to prevent.* London: Bloomsbury.

Tyrer, D., & Sayyid, S. (2012). Governing ghosts: Race, incorporeality and difference in post-political times. *Current Sociology, 60*(3), 353–367.

Paul Bagguley is Reader in Sociology at the University of Leeds. His main interests are in the sociology of protest, social movements, racism and ethnicity economic sociology, urban sociology and sociological theory. In the fields of protest and racism and ethnicity studies, he has worked most recently on the 2001 riots, South Asian women and higher education, and the impacts of the 7/7 London bombings on different ethnic and religious groups in West Yorkshire.

Yasmin Hussain is Associate Professor of Ethnicity and Racism Studies. Her main interests are in ethnicity, gender and terrorism. She carried out research on the urban 'riots' in 2001 and a Joseph Rowntree Foundation-funded project entitled, 'The Role of Higher Education in Providing Opportunities for Young South Asian Women'. She has also worked on a project analysing the impact of the London bombings, and she is currently writing up research on the South Asian diaspora in New Zealand.

CHAPTER 4

Education of Muslim Students in Turbulent Times

Saeeda Shah

Schooling of Muslim students is currently subject to intense debates in many countries. From being construed as a pedagogical challenge during the early phases of immigration in the 1960s, 1970s and 1980s, this phenomenon is now being deliberated as a highly complex issue with political and sociological overtones, moving beyond the concerns regarding educational achievement to issues of national security, socio-political integration and hostile identity formations. Muslims, particularly Muslim youth, are being constructed by the media and political discourses as a major socio-political problem for the state (Mac an Ghaill and Haywood 2015), posing threats to societal cohesion and state security. In this increasingly turbulent context, schools are faced with the challenge of managing a complex and sensitive phenomenon they have not been appropriately prepared for, while on the other hand, the Muslim community and parents are expressing grave concerns over racism, Islamophobia, religious hatred and other forms and expressions of discrimination in schools and the wider society targeting the Muslim community in the UK and elsewhere (Garner and Selod 2015; Mac an Ghaill and Haywood 2015; Richardson 2004).

S. Shah (✉)
University of Leicester, Leicester, UK
e-mail: sjas2@leicester.ac.uk

© The Author(s) 2017
M. Mac an Ghaill, C. Haywood (eds.), *Muslim Students, Education and Neoliberalism*, DOI 10.1057/978-1-137-56921-9_4

As I argue elsewhere (Shah 2009), the Muslim/non-Muslim divide is underpinned by numerous factors including historical and political legacies, such as the Muslims in Spain/Jerusalem, the Crusades, Western Imperialism and then, more recently, the plight of Muslims in Palestine, Kashmir and in other parts of the world, the role of the West, particularly of the USA and the UK in the Gulf War, the Iran/Iraq War and the Afghan *Jihad* against Russia are just a few examples. In addition to these, the Middle East oil, the economic war and the struggle for control over international resources further fuelled the tensions and conflicts (Esposito 2002). Against this backdrop, the events of 9/11 changed the world for most nations, organisations and individuals setting off an avalanche of policies, programmes, actions and activities that affected the global dynamics in multiple complex ways. The turbulence resulting from this one event unleashed hatred and anger against Muslims, impacting on their lives not only in the political, social and economic spheres, but also affecting Muslim youth and their experiences in educational institutions. The very term 'war on terror' created the sense of an inevitable conflict between the West and the world of Islam, and Muslims became the target of the prevention of terrorism and counter-terrorism activities. Events such as military actions in Iraq and Afghanistan to eliminate the Taliban, the role of USA and its Allies in the Arab Spring 'in the name of humanitarian intervention' (Kissinger 2012) and more recently, the Daesh phenomenon further contributed to mutual mistrust between the West and Muslims, promoting a perceived clash of civilisations and intensifying the 'us' and 'other' divide.

After the tragic events of 9/11, state powers were unleashed against Muslims causing a global turbulence. They were subjected to processes such as special registration, police raids, interrogations, profiling and 'stop and search' (MPA 2004), making them feel alienated, insecure and even paranoid. The London bombings of 7/7 and the failed attempt of 21 July 2005 escalated paranoia and tension, leading to the unfortunate shooting the next day by police of a Brazilian who looked Asian. Media played a significant role in the negative portrayal of Muslims, highlighting their association with terrorist activities and thus making ordinary Muslims targets of hatred in social spaces including educational institutions. Many parents became worried for the safety and well-being of their children and were reluctant to send them to schools, while in schools, Muslim students became targets of Islamophobic expressions (Shah 2009).

Government policies and activities added to Muslims' sense of alienation and insecurity. The first general Terrorism Act was passed by the UK
Parliament in 2000 and was already in place before 9/11, giving the police
wide-ranging powers. Muslims became the targets of these powers after
9/11 and 7/7 bombings. The Forest Gate raid of 2 June 2006 when a
police force of about 250 officers raided two houses of Muslim families on
the basis of 'specific intelligence', which proved to be baseless, is just one
example. Although the police apologised to the families but such incidents
not only damaged wider societal cohesion but also added to the resent-
ment among the Muslim community and in particular among its youth, as
reflected in the response of a young student saying, 'After the police raid
lots of people in East London do hate them. Police wouldn't go after
White people like this if allegations of bomb-making were made' (Shah
2009: 528).

Furthermore, a perceived failure of the British education system (MCB
2007) in attending to the educational needs of Muslim youth is seen as
leading to frustration, disaffection and alienation as well as a major factor
in the drive towards alternate identity formations (Esposito 2002; Sen
2006; Shah 2015). Concerns over educational provision in the state
schools, growing demand for Muslim faith schools over the last three
decades (Shah 2012), the recent Trojan Horse Episode (Shah 2015) and
the reported joining of young Muslim boys and girls in Daesh activities
(Cameron 2015) are some of the elements signalling ongoing concerns
and apprehensions on both sides intersecting with the schooling of
Muslim students.

Unfortunately, the schooling of Muslim youth has mostly been dealt
with in a reactive mode, resulting in rather ad hoc approaches and measures (Shah 2009, 2015). Lack of sufficient knowledge on the part of
policy-makers and fragmentation among the Muslim community regarding the educational needs of their youth have added to confusion, ambivalence and misperceptions. This chapter attempts to explain education as a
concept from within Islamic world view, drawing on Islamic religious texts
and relevant sources, to help explicate and conceptualise the education
and educational needs of Muslim students. It will explore the underlying
assumptions, discourses and frameworks that may impact in 'acknowledged or unacknowledged ways' (Pring 2007: 319) on the education of
Muslims and the resulting conceptualisations, expectations and practices.
The first section discusses education from an Islamic perspective, followed
by a discussion of the Muslims' expectations from education in the UK

context. The third section will debate the perceived failure of state schools in attending to the needs of the Muslim community, leading to a growing demand for religious education and faith schools.

EDUCATION: AN ISLAMIC PERSPECTIVE

Islam makes it incumbent upon every Muslim male and female to seek *ilm* (knowledge). The first word of the first revelation to the prophet Mohammed was *Iqra* (read/learn), which signifies the emphasis on *ilm* and *ta'lim* (education) in Islam. According to the Quran, God is *Alim*, the ultimate knower (2:32) and seeking knowledge is the way to God. In Islam knowledge is associated with high status and *taqwa* (righteousness/ Godliness) and is declared the legacy of prophets. Adam, the first human being in Islamic theology, was made vicegerent on earth because God had 'taught Adam the nature of things' (the Quran, 2:31). To this Adam the angels were asked to perform '*sajda*' (the Quran 2:34), which is the ultimate act of prostration and submission. The question is forcefully and clearly raised in the Quran:

> Are those who possess knowledge and those who do not on equal footing?
> (The Quran: 39:9)

Knowledge occupies a central position in Islam and is a distinctive feature of Islamic philosophy and civilisation. The prophet Mohammed himself taught men and women in the mosque of Medina to emphasise the message. There have been variations in the interpretations of the concepts of *ilm* and *ta'lim* over times, and different Muslim scholars have disagreed significantly over the range and scope of these concepts. However, the essential message where all agree is that *ilm* and *ta'lim* are for the holistic development of the individual, including the moral, intellectual, spiritual, material and social aspects. From an Islamic philosophical position, education is not just to prepare the individual for life in this world of matter but for all phases and aspects of life including even the life hereafter, which is part of the Islamic faith:

> For Muslims an ideal Islamic education would insist on knowledge that supports life in this world, but also takes into account the life in the hereafter. (Hussain 2010: 238)

This added dimension of the aims of education within Islamic ideology widens the role of education for Muslims. Education is expected to guide learners to become good Muslims, enabling them to live and act according to the teachings of Islam so as to win God's favour in this world and in the world hereafter. A common critique of Western education is that it fails to appreciate this dimension of the aims of education, focusing on the worldly gains and employability, and ignores Muslims' religious and ideological needs that are essential for developing their Muslim identity or *Muslimness*. Another difference between Western philosophies of education and Islam is that the West sees civic life as end in itself, while Islam sees civic life as means to an end with explicit emphasis on the ethical, moral and spiritual. The purpose of education in Islam thus extends beyond the utilitarian functions of education for employment or economic gains or for personal development as an end in itself, or even for religious rituals and *ibadah* (prayers/worship).

Muslim scholars emphasise the inseparable nature of knowledge and the sacred (Nasr 1989) where the spiritual and material, sacred and secular, the revealed and the acquired, all form a whole, defying fragmentation. This philosophical approach underpins the Islamic concept of education and gives it an ideological unity. From an Islamic perspective, life is an indivisible whole, and therefore, the compartmentalisation of education into religious and secular is artificial. Both types of knowledge contribute to the strengthening of faith, the former through a careful study of what is viewed as the revealed 'word of God' and the latter through a study of the 'world of people' and 'nature' (Sabki and Hardaker 2012: 344–5). This ontological wholeness, rooted in the Islamic world view of *tawhid*, underpins the Islamic concept of *ilm* and *ta'lim* and their role in human life. The underlying assumption is that acts of learning would ultimately lead to knowledge which would then lead to God, as explained by Rahman:

> In Islam there is no division of sacred and profane knowledge, and consequently, the pursuit of physical science is an act of *ibadah* (worship). It is true that the highest level of knowledge is the knowledge of *din* (religion), but the process of knowledge is such that one cannot understand the highest level of knowledge unless one builds up the lower. (2002: 31)

Although education in Islam ideologically aims for the development of the 'self' (Shah 2015), but the focus is not merely at the moral edification of the individual but to serve society more broadly. The philosophical approach is to develop humans through knowledge to enable them to follow the path of righteousness and to become useful members of the *Ummah* and the society, thus combining the personal and the social. The argument is that education in Islam should aim to prepare human beings for leading a life of 'righteousness' *in a social context*, but 'The purpose of education in Islam is not merely to produce a good citizen, or a good worker, but a good person' (Daud 2007: 1). These perceptions ideologically underpin the expectations of Muslim learners and communities from education in diverse contexts. However, in spite of drawing upon shared sources of the Quran and the *Sunnah* that provide a basis for similarities of concepts and practices within the Muslim *Ummah*, processes and practices of education and even interpretations of the terms associated with education have varied across Muslim societies because of subjective and situated understandings of education. The debates are further complicated when engaged from within Western frameworks because of the conceptual polarisation between the world views that makes it difficult for those outside an Islamic world view to appreciate the philosophy that may inform Muslims' expectations from education.

MUSLIMS IN THE UK AND THEIR EXPECTATIONS FROM EDUCATION

Discussing education, Halstead acknowledges that 'the central meaning of the term in Arabic does not correspond very closely with the central meaning of "education" as expounded by liberal philosophers of education in the west' (2004: 519). Although Waghid (2014) highlights some commonalities between a liberal concept of education and Islamic education, however, the aims of Islamic education extend beyond these commonalities to encompass the spiritual and metaphysical, where liberal education is perceived to be falling short of Muslims' expectations, posing the question regarding how to accommodate the needs of Muslim citizens within a framework of liberal education. An extension of the aims of education beyond the individual, material and corporeal informs the conceptualisations of and expectations from education within an Islamic world view that can be, and often are, problematic in fitting within non-Islamic paradigms.

In the UK, the complexities surrounding the education of Muslim students are emerging as a serious challenge. According to the UK census data (NSO 2011), the Muslim population has increased from 1.6 in 2001 to 2.7 in 2011, which is the highest increase in any religious group. Muslims also have the youngest age profile with more than half of them under 25 and mostly British born. The growing tendency among the Muslim youth in particular to identify with religion and its teachings marks a shift among the British-born 'away from ethnicity and homeland, [is] not towards national majority identity but towards alternative, less locally specific and more global identities' (Platt 2014: 49). They are increasingly looking towards faith as a source of identification. Davidson et al. (2010) claim that 'In considering the identity of ethnic communities and Muslims in the UK research has revealed a very clear generational difference. It is that the day-to-day interaction of first generation migrants takes place mostly within ethnic boundaries, whereas interaction among young Muslims in the UK is far more complex and reveals a shift away from ethnic divisions towards a more pan-Muslim (global) identity' (p.12). The South Asian Muslim males who migrated to Britain in response to a demand for labour and arrived penniless and single in the 1960s have become active citizens within the diasporic public sphere (Kalra 2000), and are increasingly engaged in 'maintaining a hold on culture and religion' (Geaves 2005: 68–9). The desire to retain their culture, belief systems and associated identity, not only for themselves but also for their coming generations (Shah 2015), has influenced their expectations from educational institutions, particularly at compulsory education level. Attributing this phenomenon to religious resurgence will be simplistic as many complex interacting factors including political, economic and socio-cultural are responsible for the increasing engagement with religion, which have contributed to the rising expectations among the Muslim community that educational institutions should attend to their children's educational and religious needs and make appropriate provisions (MCB 2007; Shah 2012). The concerns are not only about the lower educational achievement of Muslim students but also about schools' cultural environment, curriculum, discrimination and Islamophobia.

The schooling experiences of their children in the British state education system have made the parents and the community sensitive to the perceived threat of the British-born/educated generations moving away from their cultural heritage with the risk of disrupting the social fabric of their community life (Shah 2015). The concerns about low educational achievement and marginalisation of Muslim students in schools, as well as about the dress-code, swimming, physical education (PE) or sex-education were reflective of their educational and socio-cultural apprehensions. The co-educational environment of the state schools providing free mixing of sexes was also seen by the Muslim community as a threat to maintaining cultural and religious norms and practices (Shah 2015). Islamic moral values and the concept of chastity in conjunction with the cultural concept of izzat or honour with specific reference to females further add to Muslim parents' concerns about the un-welcome effects of the host culture. In this context, events such as the Satanic verses and 9/11 resulting in international political and economic targeting of Muslims enhanced the level of threat.

The perception among Muslims, particularly among the youth, of being 'targeted' (Esposito 2002) post 9/11, and the subsequent processes and practices targeting Muslims contributed to a sense of alienation and rejection, sending these young people in search of alternate identities. A heightened engagement with religion and religious identity post-9/11 can be a response to imposed 'otherness', offering a sense of belonging to a powerful global identity in opposition to feelings of otherness (Shah 2006). The dynamics involved in this re-positioning had implications for the education of Muslim students. Compared to the first generation of immigrants, the second and the subsequent generations born and being brought up in the UK have expectations of equal treatment. They are not only more intensely aware of discrimination but also resent it more strongly. This has contributed to a growing association with *Muslimness*. Young Muslims' experiences of discrimination and Islamophobia in educational institutions and the wider society contributed to their distancing from the host society (Tomlinson 2008), encouraging association with religion, religious identity and a desire to learn about religion, reflected in a growing demand for Muslim faith schools and for the accommodation of their religious and cultural needs in the state system (Shah 2012). Today's context has moved on from the early 1980s and 1990s when measures such as language, dress, single-sex PE, *halal* food, prayer-rooms etc., were top priority to facilitate schooling for the Muslim children. The expectations now include recognising faith as a category of difference and making appropriate provisions in the school environment, curriculum and different services to improve Muslim students' educational engagement without any threat to their faith identity, values and practices.

EDUCATION OF MUSLIMS IN THE UK

Education of diverse groups of students from different cultural, religious and ethnic backgrounds is a complex, controversial and problematic challenge across the world. In the case of British-born young Muslims, a sense of marginalisation, deprivation and alienation has been growing stronger (MCB 2007). The enhanced desire among Muslim youth to become informed about their faith identity signifies their dissatisfaction with the racialised identity and experiences of discrimination and marginalisation in a politicised anti-Muslim climate. Complaints of absence of appropriate provisions within the education system breed further dissatisfaction. The Muslim community, specifically of Pakistani and Bangladeshi origin, are of the view that Muslim learners educated through the British state system are suffering emotionally, culturally, linguistically and academically (MCB 2007). Records and statistics of their low educational achievement (Shah 2006) are offered as evidence. The debate becomes more complex when Muslim students appear to perform better in schools with larger populations of Muslim pupils even when these are poorly resourced Muslim Faith Schools (Lawson 2005; Meer 2007).

Muslim students in state schools are often exposed to various expressions of Islamophobia. Literature and archives abound in records of negative media constructions of Muslims. Studies recognise religious discrimination or/and Islamophobia as leading to disaffection and underachievement among Muslim students (Richardson and Wood 2004; MCB 2007). Parents and Muslim community leaders tend to blame the state education sector for not making enough effort to cope with these challenges. They argue that schools and the staff have a responsibility not only to deal with racist and religious hatred incidents but also to prepare pupils for life in a multi-cultural and multi-faith society in addition to improving their own knowledge and understanding of the communities of students they are responsible for (Shah 2009). However, many schools and their staff are either not fully aware or not doing enough to combat prejudiced attitudes towards Muslims:

I'm the only Asian teacher at my school. During the war in Iraq a pupil who's also Asian told me that she was being teased by other pupils. 'We killed hundreds of your lot yesterday...Saddam's your dad, innit...we're getting our revenge for what you Pakis did to us on 11 September...' I asked her if she had told her class teacher. Yes, she had told her teacher, and her teacher had said: 'Never mind, it's not serious. It'll soon pass. You'll have to expect a bit of teasing at a time like this'. (Richardson and Wood 2004: 64)

This is evidence of not only a lack of knowledge, understanding and sensitivity but also of professional expertise to respond to these challenges. In fact, many teachers themselves knowingly or unknowingly become instruments of discrimination by having low expectations of the academic potential of ethnic minority pupils. Gillborn (1998) maintains that 'even where teachers are conscientious and committed to equality of opportunity as an ideal, they may nevertheless *act* in ways that unwittingly reproduce familiar racial stereotypes, generate conflict...and perpetuate existing inequalities of opportunities and achievement' (p.35). The sense of alienation and disaffection generated by negative experiences of schooling not only impacts on the young learners' self-esteem, aspirations, educational engagement and achievement (Shah 2006) but also has negative implications for integration. As I discuss elsewhere (Shah 2009), individual schools do make efforts to enhance the black and minority ethnic engagement and performance and to 'fight racism' but the overall environment is generally hostile to Muslims. Being at the receiving end of marginalisation, discrimination and racism, the absence of appropriate opportunities and provisions within the education system to attend to their needs and support their sense of self, and more recently being singled out as targets of 'Prevent' policies and processes as a community do not promote inclusion.

Besides a hostile environment, the mainstream curriculum in the UK state schools is also critiqued for not incorporating cultural, ethnic and faith diversity (Shah 2015). It is often criticised for lacking a balance of perspectives, affecting minority students' self-esteem and educational engagement (Shah 2015). Muslim parents expect from the state schools to provide a culturally and religiously coherent learning environment for their children, where more faith-based principles are incorporated into an integrated education system, so that the 'whole person' can be educated in an Islamic environment (Meer 2007). They expect schools to promote respect for Muslim identity and for Islamic social and moral values that are considered essential for their social structure, and to enhance awareness of Islamic history and teachings through the curriculum to promote inclusion and educational engagement. The recent inclusion of a module on the history of Islam in the curriculum was welcomed by the Muslim community (Mansell 2014) as a positive step in a multi-faith society. However, the ensuing debates and critique following these revisions point to the highly complex and politically challenging nature of these issues.

CONCLUSIONS

State policy and apparatus fail to take into account the changing nature of the sociology of Muslim youth, born and brought up in a proclaimed democracy. The contemporary schooling and racialisation as experienced by the British-born generations of Muslims (Gilroy 2004) demand new theorisation to capture the nuances and complexities. For the first generation of deprived and often persecuted immigrants, Britain was a heaven of rights and facilities as compared to life in their countries of origin. For the British-born generations, rights and facilities need to be equal to other British citizens. Experiences of marginalisation and discrimination contribute to othering and alienation, promoting the very phenomenon of disengaged and frustrated communities that the government complains of. Muslims appear to be a political problem for the West, but are they also a social problem for the state and, more specifically, an educational problem for schools?

The initiatives and strategies adopted over the last few decades to achieve inclusion in educational institutions have lacked full cognisance of ethnic cultures and their value systems (Shah 2012). In the case of Muslims, in view of a perceived vacuum left by mainstream schools, Muslim faith schools have been gaining popularity (Meer 2007). Muslim learners in these schools are achieving higher scores and studies claim that Muslim faith schools are developing high-achieving, more confident and well-informed students, prepared better for integration through a confidence in personal identity (Lawson 2005). It might be useful for the state schools with high numbers of Muslim students to engage with the Muslim faith schools to explore how state schools can improve educational achievement of Muslim students. They need to recognise the desire among the Muslim community to retain their faith identity and also to pass these to succeeding generations 'who may come under increasing pressure to adapt to the hostland's demands' (Rai and Reeves 2009: 7–8). Cush (2014) points to the need to discuss religious education for 'a society where diversity is respected' (p.122). The Trojan Horse episode, at one level of analysis, can be explained as an expression of desire on the part of some members of the Muslim community to ensure that their children are educated in an environment congruent with their religious values even if the processes were not appropriate. However, in the backdrop of the Daesh phenomenon in recent years and involvement of some very young Muslim boys and girls in its activities, the government went for hard-line policies. Miah (2014) claims that the Trojan Horse controversy led to the embedding of a particular secularisation agenda in Britain's schools, arguing for locating it within a broader sociological and historical context of the functioning of the racial state. What implications does this have for racial and religious minorities? Policy developments following the Trojan Horse episode underline the tensions between a wish on the part of Muslim parents and community to ensure that their children retain their religious values and identity, and the government's 'Prevent' strategy and 'fight against extremism' that is bound to impact on the schooling of Muslim students.

In an atmosphere fraught with tensions and mistrust on both sides, Muslim youth in many schools are suffering educationally, emotionally and socially. An increasing number of very young Muslim students are being reported to the police and/or referred to the Channel programme. According to the National Police Chiefs' Council (NPCC) figures obtained by the BBC, nearly 2000 children under the age of 15 have been referred by schools to the UK government's de-radicalisation programme, Channel (Moore 2016). A look into these cases and the age of the children referred to Channel points to the problematics of these referrals. For example, a recent case, as reported in the Telegraph is that 'A primary school reported a 10-year-old Muslim boy to police on suspicion of extremism after he complained about not having a prayer room' (Telegraph 2015). This school is reported to have a high majority of Muslim children; however, instead of considering the issue of a prayer room as a religious need, it was treated in the context of Islamophobia and radicalisation, leading to the reporting of the child to the police. Then more recently (21 January 2016), another 10-year-old Muslim student living in a terraced house wrote: 'I live in a terrorist house', while writing: 'I live in a "terraced house"' (Independent 2016) and got reported by the school to the police. Although after a detailed investigation the police statement did admit that 'there were not thought to be any areas for concern and no further action was required by any agency', but this certainly raises concerns regarding the damage that this might have done to the child, the family and the community, not ignoring its impact on other Muslim children. These incidents point to the turbulence in schools with substantial numbers of Muslim students, as well as the inadequacy and unpreparedness of schools in dealing with these complex and sensitive issues. School leaders and teachers whether they act out of a sense of responsibility towards 'Prevent duty' or a sense of insecurity, the tensions and conflicts will keep rising, affecting not only the future of individual students referred to police but also the overall fabric of the society as well.

Many questions beg for attention. What impact will these referrals have on the concerned young students' futures and their educational engagement? Why are these referrals increasing? What are the messages being signalled for the Muslim community by government policies and schools' responses to these policies? If the government aims for inclusion and integration of Muslims, will the current policies and measures take that agenda forward? How does the securitisation agenda reconcile with the integration agenda? Will identifying very young people with terrorism and their 'referrals' prevent radicalisation? If scaring or threatening communities/groups into submission or compliance was a long-term solution, then the democracies wouldn't have replaced powerful dictatorships. Perhaps there is a need to move away from negative perceptions and constructions towards positive thinking and accommodation of difference provided there is a will to improve educational provisions and opportunities for Muslims and a desire for what Bauman (2002) suggests as new ways to re-forge human diversity into human solidarity.

REFERENCES

Bauman, Z. (2002). *Society Under Siege*. Cambridge: Polity Press in association with Blackwell Publishers.

Cameron, D. (2015). Tory Party Conference. Online: http://www.independent. co.uk/news/uk/politics/tory-party-conference-2015-david-camerons-speech-in-full-a6684656.html.

Cush, D. (2014). Autonomy, identity, community and society: Balancing the aims and purposes of religious education. *British Journal of Religious Education, 36* (2), 119–122.

Daud, W. M. (2007). Al-Attas' concept of Ta'dib.... In T. Stepanyants (Ed.), Comparative ethics in a global age (pp. 243–258, Series IVA, Vol. 30). Washington, D.C. https://books.google.co.uk/books?id=QRZ-P7VOqAQC&pg=PT5&lpg=PT5&dq=Comparative+Ethics+in+a+Global +Age&source=bl&ots=mqKFexr_FQ&sig=IXpi-GiPHGD4Thr5xmom

O9RMrN0&hl=en&sa=X&ved=0ahUKEwia57-j28rQAhUkB8AKHdc4BHkQ
6AEIJTAC#v=onepage&q=Comparative%20Ethics%20in%20a%20Global%
20Age&f=false.

Davidson, J., Huq, R., Seetzen, H., & GroveHills, J. (2010). *Towards engaging with and understanding three BME communities in Kingston: Identity, interaction, belonging and belief; final report*. London: Kingston University. http://eprints.kingston.ac.uk/23597/1/Davidson-J-23597.pdf.

Esposito, J. L. (2002). *Unholy war: Terror in the name of Islam*. Oxford: Oxford University Press.

Garner, S., & Selod, S. (2015). The racialization of Muslims: Empirical studies of Islamophobia. *Critical Sociology, 41*(1), 9–19.

Geaves, R. (2005). Negotiating British citizenship and Muslim identity. In T. Abbas (Ed.), *Muslim Britain: Communities under pressure* (pp. 66–77). London: Zed Books.

Gillborn, D. (1998). Racism and the politics of qualitative research.... In P. Connoally & B. Troyna (Eds.), *Researching racism in Education: Politics, theory, and practice*. Buckingham: OUP.

Gilroy, P. (2004). *After empire: Multiculture or postcolonial melancholia?* London: Routledge.

Halstead, J. M. (2004). An Islamic concept of education. *Comparative Education, 40*(4), 517–529.

Hussain, A. (2010). Islamic education in the West: Theoretical foundations and practical implications. In K. Engebretson, M. De Souza, G. Durka, & L. Gearon (Eds.), *International Handbook of Inter-religious Education* (Part 4) (pp. 235–248). London: Springer.

Independent. (2016). Lancashire police say 'terrorist house' incident not about spelling mistake. Online: http://www.independent.co.uk/news/uk/home-news/lancashire-police-say-terrorist-house-incident-not-about-spelling-mis take-a6824481.html.

Kalra, V. S. (2000). *From textile mills to taxi ranks: Experiences of migration, labour, and social change*. Aldershot: Ashgate.

Kissinger, H. (2012). *Defining U.S. role in the Arab Spring*. http://www.henrya kissinger.com/articles/iht040212.html.

Lawson, I. (2005.) Leading Islamic schools in the UK: A challenge for us all. NCSL report: http://webarchive.nationalarchives.gov.uk/20130401151715/http://www.education.gov.uk/publications/eOrderingDownload/RASLAW05.pdf.pdf.

Mac an Ghaill, M., & Haywood, C. (2015). British-born Pakistani and Bangladeshi young men: Exploring unstable concepts of Muslim, Islamophobia and racialization. *Critical Sociology, 41*(1), 97–114.

Mansell, W. (2014). Michael Gove redrafts new history curriculum after outcry. http://www.theguardian.com/education/2013/jun/21/michael-gove-his tory-curriculum.

MCB. (2007). Towards greater understanding: Meeting the needs of Muslim pupils in state schools. Muslim Council of Britain.

Meer, N. (2007). Muslim schools in Britain: Challenging mobilisations or logical developments? *Asia Pacific Journal of Education, 27*(1), 55–71.

Miah, S. (2014, November 14). Trojan Horse and the racial state: Race, religion and securitisation. BERA SIG seminar, University of Huddersfield.

Moore, A. (2016). Figures for channel programme are rising. http://alicemooreuk.blogspot.co.uk/2016/01/figures-for-channel-programme-are-rising.html.

MPA. (2004). A report by the metropolitan police authority. *BBC News* World Edition. http://news.bbc.co.uk/1/hi/england/london/3732169.stm

Nasr, S. H. (1989). *Knowledge and the sacred*. Albany: State University of New York Press.

NSO. (2011). National statistics. http://www.ons.gov.uk/ons/rel/census/2011-census/key-statistics-for-local-authorities-in-england-and-wales/stb-2011-census-key-statistics-for-england-and-wales.html#tab-Religion.

Platt, L. (2014). Is there assimilation in minority groups' national, ethnic and religious identity? *Ethnic and Racial Studies, 37*(1), 46–70.

Pring, R. (2007). Reclaiming philosophy for educational research. *Educational Review, 59*(3), 315–330.

Rahman, F. (2002). Islam to the modern mind. In Y. Mohamed (Ed.), *Lectures in South Africa (1970–1972)*, 2nd ed. Oosterland Street, Paarl, South Africa: Paarl Print.

Rai, R., & Reeves, P. (2009). Introduction. In R. Rai & P. Reeves (Eds.), *The South Asian diaspora: Transnational networks and changing identities* (pp. 1–12). New York: Routledge.

Richardson, R. (2004). *Islamophobia: Issues, challenges and action*. Stoke-on-Trent: Trentham Books Limited.

Richardson, R., & Wood, A. (2004). The achievement of British Pakistani learners. RAISE project report. Trentham Books.

Sabki, A. A., & Hardaker, G. (2012). The madrasah concept of Islamic pedagogy. *Educational Review, 65*(3), 342–356.

Sen, A. (2006). *Identity and violence: The illusion of destiny*. London: Allen Lane.

Shah, S. (2006). Leading multiethnic schools: A new understanding of Muslim youth identity. *Educational Management, Administration and Leadership, 34*(2), 215–237.

Shah, S. (2009). Muslim learners in English schools: A challenge for school leaders. *Oxford Review of Education, 35*(4), 1–18.

Shah, S. (2012). Islamic schools in the West: Persistence or resistance. *British Journal of Religious Education, 34*(1), 51–65.

Shah, S. (2015). *Education, leadership and Islam. Theories, discourses and practices from an Islamic perspective*. London: Routledge. http://www.amazon.

com/Education-Leadership-Islam-discourses-perspective-ebook/dp/B010 VJ8VQO.

Telegraph. (2015). Teachers' extremist fears over boy 10. http://www.telegraph. co.uk/news/uknews/terrorism-in-the-uk/11927303/Teachers-extremist-fears-over-boy-10-after-he-complains-about-lack-of-prayer-room.html.

Tomlinson, S. (2008). *Race and education: Policy and politics in Britain.* Maidenhead: OUP.

Waghid, Y. (2014). Islamic education and cosmopolitanism: A philosophical interlude. *Studies in Philosophy of Education, 33*, 329–342.

Saeeda Shah is Reader in Education at the University of Leicester and Visiting Professor of Education at the University of Derby. Previously, she has worked in higher education in Pakistan, holding senior positions, her last post being Professor and Dean at AJK University Pakistan. Her research interests include leadership with a focus on diversity, cultural and belief systems, gender and power issues. Saeeda is on editorial boards of many journals and has published in highly prestigious journals about educational leadership, gender, social justice, comparative education, Islam and society and the issues of identity/ethnicity. She also works with charities and community groups for educational and social uplift.

CHAPTER 5

Factoring-in Faith Fairly: A Contribution from Critical Realism to the Authentic Framing of Muslims-in-Education

Matthew Wilkinson

INTRODUCTION: YOUNG MUSLIMS CAUGHT IN A PARADIGM CLASH

Classical sociology does not have a good track record in taking religious faith and communities of religious faith seriously. The founding father of contemporary sociology Auguste Comte (1798–1857) was so set against the metaphysical claims of traditional religions that he founded his own humanist religion called Religion de l'Humanité with its own Postitivist Church (Église Positiviste) which would expound humanistic principles in a God-free world. The pioneering social scientist, Émile Durkheim (1858–1917), famously reduced the sacred to 'collective effervescence' which, although regarded as an important and necessary component of a healthy human group, was in and of itself merely the product of human needs rather than representative of any transcendent reality.

Sociology, as a child of the Enlightenment (Hallaq 2012), is usually premised on the nature of the world as fundamentally observable and measureable and the ability of human reason to explain both the nature

M. Wilkinson (✉)
University of London, London, UK
e-mail: mw66@soas.ac.uk

© The Author(s) 2017
M. Mac an Ghaill, C. Haywood (eds.), *Muslim Students, Education and Neoliberalism*, DOI 10.1057/978-1-137-56921-9_5

and dynamics of the human experience, whilst dispensing with the 'crutches' both of metaphysics – including the Divine – and of religious scripture.

Religious faith and its academic cognate – theology – are often premised on the relative *inability* of human reason to give a fully adequate explanatory account of human and social life without understanding it as in some way indicative of the Presence and Acts of God (or equivalent(s)) and His (her/their) relationship with humanity through representatives, scripture and mediated by acts (not just thoughts) of human worship.

Given some apparently incommensurable assumptions underpinning the contemporary disciplines of academic sociology and academic theology, it is hardly surprising that contemporary accounts of young Muslims (Archer 2003; Alexander 2000; Hopkins 2004; Ipgrave forthcoming; Shain 2011; Wilkinson 2015), a social group(s) that self-defines theologically, have tended to occupy two apparently incommensurable and dichotomised epistemological positions in the academic and, particularly, policy literature.

Accounts from the Right of the political spectrum have tended to emphasise the *presence* of faulty Islamic theology and the faith-saturation of Muslim identity as an obstacle to the healthy attachment of young British Muslims to Britain and 'British values' and as *the* significant causal factor in the failure of young British Muslims to integrate successfully into British life and take full advantage of educational opportunities (Cameron 2011; May 2015).

The Left has tended to identify the absences of socio-economic opportunity (unemployment, poor housing and poor maternal English language skills) (Hussain 2008) and the toxic impact of the absence of solutions to festering geopolitical problems involving Muslims such as Israel–Palestine (1947–present), Afghanistan (2001–present), Iraq (2003–present) and Syria (2011–present) as obstacles to Muslim educational and civic engagement, whilst minimising the causative impact of the Muslim faith or related Islamic/-ist ideologies (Hassan 2013).

In the shadow of this often dichotomised and highly politicised intellectual context, this chapter aims to do two related things:

1. To propose a robust and flexible ontological framework for thinking systematically and coherently about young Muslims in education derived from the philosophy of critical realism, in a way that includes *inter alia* the spiritual dimension.

2. Using this robust theoretical framework, to provide an account of young Muslims in education as existing on laminated, articulated levels and to suggest by reference to some recent empirical research around Muslims in history education in the UK that the spiritual dimension of Muslim young people in education cannot be ignored if we are to represent young Muslims accurately in research and cater for their educational needs.

This theoretical framework and accompanying illustrative account is intended to enable researchers to factor both the effects of the *presence* of faith and, crucially, the effects of the *absence* of considerations of faith into their research on young Muslims.

THE SUITABILITY OF CRITICAL REALIST THEORY TO FRAME MUSLIMS-IN-EDUCATION

Factoring-in the Presence and Absence of Faith: Original and Dialectical Critical Realism

Original critical realism (OCR) (e.g. Bhaskar 1975/2008), which emerged as a philosophy of natural and then social science in the 1970s, asserts as its theoretical fulcrum (Wilkinson 2015) the relationship of three necessarily inter-related principles: ontological realism, epistemological relativism and judgemental rationality. This fulcrum states that both natural and social phenomena exist either independently (in natural science) or relatively independently (in social science) of the knower/researcher (ontological realism), and that the multiplicity of ways in which existent things can come to be known (epistemological relativism) must be subject to rigorous critical analysis and assessment according to criteria of truth, accuracy and plausibility (judgemental rationality) if the nature of phenomena is to be made apparent in an accurate and useful way (Little 1993).

Within this fulcrum, central to the critical realist science of being (ontology) in OCR are two ideas: (1) that reality is 'stratified' and (2) that most events (outside the laboratory) occur in 'open systems'. To say that reality is 'stratified' is to say that phenomena at one level of reality are scientifically to be explained in terms of structures or mechanisms located at a deeper level that generate or produce these phenomena from which they are 'emergent' (Bhaskar 1975/2008: 119) but to which they are irreducible (Bhaskar 2002).

To say that most events occur in 'open systems' is to say that they are determined by and, therefore, require explanation in terms of a multiplicity of such structures and mechanisms. For example, the learning of a child at school or the rehabilitation of an offender in prison will be determined by a multiplicity of personal(-ity), inter-personal, natural/physical, institutional and socio-cultural factors that are operating simultaneously and are in interaction with each other, both directly and with 'feedback-loops'.

Emergence

To give a simple example of the principle of *emergence* in the natural world, water (H_2O) is dependent on the 'lower order' existence of hydrogen and oxygen atoms and yet has causal properties and a relationship to the rest of living things that are irreducible to hydrogen and oxygen (Smith 2010). Emergence in the human and social worlds typically comprises stratified, laminated, articulated layers of being that are closely connected but also differentiated one from another (Bhaskar 2002).

To put this more concretely, the mind at the psychological level is dependent on the chemistry of the body at the level of biology; it could not operate without it. But the mind as cause or category is not reducible to chemical reactions and the physical activity of neurons at the chemical level. To couch this in legal terms, 'intent' as existential cause and a legal category cannot be reduced either causally or taxonomically to chemical reactions in the brain – the law would be a nonsense if this were the case – nevertheless, 'intent' is dependent on those chemical reactions.

This idea of emergence has also been applied by Brown (2009) to education. Slightly expanding Brown's schema (to include socio-economic mechanisms), this emergence in education entails and comprises a formation, including:

- **physical mechanisms**, e.g. size and quality of classrooms;
- **biological mechanisms**, e.g. adequate nutrition;
- **psychological mechanisms**, e.g. student motivation and parental expectation;
- **socio-economic mechanisms**, e.g. class and wealth;
- **socio-cultural (including moral and political) mechanisms**, e.g. language and peer-group attitudes;
- **normative mechanisms**, e.g. as determined by curricula and 'official' bodies of authorised knowledge (Apple 1993).

With reference to the above schema, the metaphor of 'articulation' is also useful. It suggests that changes at one level may have either intended or unintended 'knock-on' effects at a different level or levels of being. To give a concrete example of the system above applied to a Muslim child in education, an overheated classroom at the physical level may have a 'knock-on', articulated effect at the psychological level on a child's concentration and at a cognitive level in his/her ability to remember 'the facts'; poverty at the level of class as well as a lack of socio-cultural resonance of Muslim parents with aspects of Britain may reduce a child's ability to engage with the normative level of the history curriculum by diminishing *inter alia* his/her chances of travel to places of historical interest.

Laminated Systems in Humanities Education

As well as this useful non-reductive heuristic of emergence, Bhaskar (1979/2008) has provided the ontological metaphor of the 'laminated system' of four-planar social being, which can be applied neatly to frame meta-theoretically the Muslim child in an educational setting. The education of the Muslim child in History education, for example, can be theorised to exist in at least four social planes and involves simultaneously:

1. **material transactions with nature** or artefacts ultimately derived from nature – textbooks, PCs, school buildings, food, transport, heating, electricity, etc.;
2. **formative inter-personal relations with peers**, teachers, family members and community figures by which formal and informal learning will be transmitted to the child;
3. **indirect involvement via, for example, the level of school management with other institutions and policy-making organisations** – the government, local authority, museums, historical sites, publishers, etc. – which will produce powerful regimes of knowledge (Foucault 1980); e.g. school subjects, into which the child's learning will, at least to a certain extent, be bound;
4. all of which will be brought to bear on the **emergent stratified personality of the child.**

Critically for an adequate ontological model of the Muslim child/young person, in such 'stratified, articulated, laminated' accounts, faith and the dimension of the spirit can be plausibly said to be 'emergent' from the dimension of the mind as described by psychology, and yet, neither taxonomically nor causally reducible to it. Moreover, according to the critical realist idea of 'demi-reality', whereby even false ideas can be admitted to have real effects in the world,[1] faith and the dimension of the spirit can be allowed to have real causative effects in the transitive world even if the researcher does not believe that the realities of faith have alethic intransitive (Bhaskar 1975/2008) existence.

Factoring-In Absence

Finally, it is also axiomatic to critical realist theory in its dialectical phase (Bhaskar 2008) that 'absence' and what is missing from being is understood as 'real determinate absence' (Norrie 2010). Absence is not indeterminate nothingness; it is causally efficacious, effecting real, natural, social and trans-cendental outcomes. According to this theoretical position, one would expect curricular elements that were missing in the spiritual dimension, theorised by me elsewhere as the absent curriculum (Wilkinson 2014a), also to affect the learning outcomes of the Muslim young person.

In other words, the philosophy of critical realism can provide the types of multi-dimensional, non-reductive theoretical framework that account for both the presence and absence of faith in young Muslims' lives and learning relatively independently of the beliefs (or lack of them) of the researcher.

An Empirical Application of Critical Realism to Framing Muslims in History Education

Theoretical considerations such as those described earlier made in conversation with the multi-dimensional situation of Muslim young people in Britain as described empirically by previous research, which typically showed the significance of their faith for 90 % of young Muslims both as a praxis and as the performance of identity (Archer 2003; Alexander 2000; Hopkins 2004; Ipgrave forthcoming; Shain 2011; Wilkinson 2015), led me to develop a laminated ontology of the educational success of young Muslims in a variety of different dimensions for my own educational research.

This research focused on the impact of the National Curriculum for History (NCH) on the holistic development of 307 representative Muslim young people (Year 9; i.e. 13–14-year-olds) in education in four English state secondary schools: one in Birmingham, one in Leicester, one in North London and one in East London (Wilkinson 2011, 2015).

All these schools had a high proportion of Muslim students. Out of the students at each school:

- Technology School – (*n*) 52 – was 63.4 % Muslim.
- Faith School – (*n*) 67 – was 100 % Muslim.
- Community School – (*n*) 49 – was 63.6 % Muslim.
- Specialist School – (*n*) 139 – was 98.6 % Muslim.

From the total sample of Muslim young people who completed a quantitative attitudinal survey about their history provision, 23 young people were sampled for interview using a sampling strategy that took into account the history class/set that they were in, their interest in the subject of history and their measured NCH level. These factors had been shown by the statistical data of a pilot study to be significant predictors of success with the subject (Wilkinson 2007).

History was selected as the subject focus due to the documented power of school History as a crucible of both national (Barton and McCully 2005; Wegner 1990) and personal identity (Cronon 2000) and for the exploration of citizenship and the power of school History both to include and exclude national groups (Ahonen 2001).

My Theoretical Model

The dimensions of my theoretical model were multiple, and 'articulated' and loosely emergent from/with each other. Empirically, these dimensions were to be substantiated extensionally (Scott 2010), i.e. in national breadth, through the Muslim young peoples' responses to attitudinal surveys about the effects of NCH and 'filled in' intensively with an understanding of the causal relationships between these 'articulated' dimensions through analysis of the interview data, non-participant observations and the interviewees' diaries.

Thus, I conceived of the dimensions of the success and potential success of the Muslim learner as constituted by:

- **The intellectual dimension of success (IDS).** This was success understood both as 'objective' academic *attainment* as assessed by the sample of Muslim boys' teachers according to NCH levels and interpretatively in terms of pupils' own assessment of their *basic historical understanding* of the history of England, Britain and the rest of the world. It was also the dimension of success delineated by the ability of the Muslim young people to understand and *articulate* the understandings of the history that they had learnt in relation to their own lived experiences.[2]

- **The spiritual dimension of success (SDS) – the focus of this chapter.** This was the dimension of success at which the Muslim young people reflected on changing historical values and apprehended *ethical, moral and religious significance*. This was a vital level given the importance of religiosity and strong religious identifications for Muslim boys recorded in all the literature and exemplified in the sample, **89 %** of whom strongly agreed that 'my religion is very important'.[3]

Using the 'laminated' categorisations outlined above, both the intellectual and spiritual success related primarily, although not exclusively, at the level of biography to the emergent embodied personality of the individual child (4, above in four social planes).

- **The affective-cultural dimension of success (ADS).** This was an emotional, identity-related and motivational dimension of success that was connected to the level at which NCH helped/did not help the pupils reflect upon and understand their home cultures and their relationships with majority British culture. It was also related to the types of negotiations of masculinity and femininity within the peer-group identified by researchers into Muslim-in-education through the prism of gender (Archer 2001; Shain 2003). The dimension of *affective-cultural success* related to the embodied personality of the child and formative inter-personal relations with peers (2 and 3 in the laminated four-planar model cited earlier).[4]

- **The instrumental dimension of success (InDS).** This was the dimension at which NCH did/did not provide life skills that Muslim young people recognised would be useful in post-school contexts of work. This was also a vital dimension given the heightened instrumentalised attitudes to schooling of Muslim boys, in particular, identified in previous research and the general perception noted in the literature that Muslim male pupils, in particular, tend not to regard the humanities subjects as useful for their chances of gaining employment (Adey and Biddulph 2001).

It was also related to levels of uptake of General Certificate of Secondary Education (GCSE) history.[5] This dimension of *instrumental success* is related to all the levels in the laminated four-planar model cited earlier.

- **The civic dimension of success (CDS).** This was the dimension at which NCH nurtured/did not nurture Muslim pupils' desire and ability to participate socio-politically and belong emotionally to British society and to relate to the international community, including the Muslim-majority world. This was important given the significance of the political context of history education and its connection with the Britishness agenda that was established by former UK Prime Minister Gordon Brown and continued by the recent Conservative–Liberal Democrat Coalition Government (2010–2015) during the period of research.[6]

- **The overall holistic dimension of success (OHDS).** This corresponded to pupils' overall assessment of the impact of history on their complete development as a human being which was measured as a factor called *awareness of myself and my world*. The OHDS took into account the successful emergence of the embodied personality of each individual child (4, above in four social planes) considered as a whole. It was the most important facet of success which was used as a dependent variable in statistical regressions. It was meant to correspond to feelings of deepening integration, both internally related to self and externally related to society, for each child through the process of history education.[7]

This model enabled me to investigate the impact of history education on Muslim young people holistically and at multiple, discrete ontological levels and it helped me to avoid reducing success to measurable academic attainment, which was nonetheless accounted for as an important component of *the intellectual dimension of success.*

The Significance of Spiritual Success

While all the dimensions of success identified earlier were significant explanatory factors of the *overall holistic dimension of success* (see Table 5.1) and have been considered by me in detail elsewhere (Wilkinson 2014b, 2015), it is germane to this chapter that the dimension of *spiritual success* was a surprisingly significant predictor of both the

Table 5.1 Significant factors in different types of Muslim success with National Curriculum History (Ordinal Logistic Regression)

Success factors	Intellectual success (R² = 0.410)	GCSE uptake (R² = 0.302)	Overall holistic success (R² = 0.431)
Overall attitude to history	ß = 0.266***	ß = 0.366***	
Civic success	ß = 0.246***	ß = 0.385**	ß = 0.370**
Spiritual success	ß = 0.270***		ß = 0.345***
Teaching		ß = -0.171**	ß = 0.141**
Out-of-school history			ß = 0.170***

NB *$p < 0.10$, **$p < 0.05$, ***$p < 0.01$

intellectual success (ß = 0.270***; R^2 = 0.410) and of the *overall holistic success* of the sample (ß = 0.345***; R^2 = 0.431) (Table 5.1).

Interviews and observations confirmed that the spiritual and moral domain (Hallaq 2012) was, to varying degrees, intrinsic to the development of the historical understanding of the majority of my sample. These made it clear that *the more the NCH had challenged the boys to examine ethical or moral issues, the more historical facts and information they remembered.* This was particularly the case with lower-achieving pupils. For example, for one lower-achieving boy from the Technology College, who by his own admission had very little taste for history, a process of ethical reflection about the Holocaust – 'How could a civilised nation have done this?' – was complemented by a surprisingly detailed recollection of Nazi racial policy and the grisly technology of the Holocaust.

The ethical and moral benefits in the spiritual dimension of success that the Muslim young people consistently said that they enjoyed deriving from the study of history included:

- Gratitude for the social, medical and technological privileges of the present through acknowledgement of the achievements and the sacrifices of people in the past.

For Ahmad (Technology School, middle-achieving, Afghan-British) this feeling of gratitude was connected to awareness that the technological and medical progress of the past 100 years meant people lived longer, which he had found 'inspirational'.

Samir (Specialist School, middle-achieving, Bengali-British) compared and contrasted the hardships endured by child labourers in the past with his own privileged situation of receiving an education compared to some children in the world who still do not.

Amir (Community School, high-achieving, Pakistani-British) reflected on the necessity of not taking things for granted due to the fragility of present gains and the often unexpected nature of war.

> AMIR: ... [history] made me a bit grateful that it (war) doesn't happen anymore but in some situations it might come up [...] Might repeat itself if things get out of hand.

- Challenging stereotypes and countering discrimination, including challenging anti-Semitic and anti-Western/Christian prejudice amongst their Muslim peers.

Five of the Muslim young people interviewed thought that history in school had a significant role to play in the spiritual dimension of success by challenging the Manichean 'Us' vs. 'Them', Muslim (good)/non-Muslim (bad) (or vice versa) world views:
Ahmad cited a critical role for history in combating Islamophobia if the achievements of Islamic civilisation and the Muslim contribution were a feature of classroom learning. He also recognised the value to Muslims of acknowledging the achievements of notable Westerners/Christians to the general patrimony of humankind.

> MATTHEW: And how about the other way round? Do you think if Muslims knew more of the History of Western countries they might show more respect for Western countries as well?
>
> AHMAD: Yeah, it would be like some Muslims, yeah, the extremism and the terrorism they would, it's more like good, but if they know about Western people like [Isambard] Kingdom Brunel, they wouldn't do that stuff [terrorism].

- **Providing lessons in teamwork and serving others.**

For Waleed (Community School, middle-achieving, Pakistani-British), the pre-eminent lesson that he had taken from his study of the English Civil War and the mistakes of Charles I was the need 'to listen to advice' and to work with other people.

Uthman (Faith School, middle-achieving, British-Indian) thought that NCH in general could contribute to people wanting to work together as part of 'Team England'. In a related way, the life of William Wilberforce had impressed on Amir (Community School, high-achieving, Pakistani-British) the value of having empathy for other people's situations and the importance of looking beyond the trappings of wealth and status to observe and respect people's true character.

MATTHEW: *You said something very nice here [in your diary]: 'I think he was a good man because he had feelings for others rather than for himself....'*

AMIR: *Yeah, because I seen... in the film that we watched it gave me a decent opinion of why, how he felt, because he was just looking at the slave being sold to rich people and he wanted to buy it, buy the slave, to free him from his sadness [...] He was different. He was unique to others because people that have money think about themselves only. It's better to be poor and look at other people.*

- **Making more sophisticated, autonomous, moral decisions.**

Three of the interview sample cited the role of NCH for stimulating autonomous moral decision-making. For example, Benyamin (Technology School, middle-achieving, British-Algerian) eloquently cited the crucial general role of history in developing the ability to make autonomous moral judgements eloquently using the specific example of the Treaty of Versailles (1919):

MATTHEW: *So do you think [...]history does have a...purpose for helping young people to make their mind up about things, decide, and make moral judgements?*

BENYAMIN: *Yeah, I think it is. [...] you have to make moral judgements; you can't just make judgements like what you hear*

> *or like you can't just follow other people; you have to be*
> *yourself and you have to think about what you're going to*
> *do, what's your decision, what's your conscience telling you*
> *to do [...] when there was the Treaty (of Versailles)*
> *between the French, the British and the Germans and*
> *the French [...] wanted revenge but the British wanted*
> *peace and the Americans wanted them to be punished but*
> *not too harshly and I decided that peace was like, would be*
> *the best option...*

- Becoming a better, more reflective person.

In short, nearly half the sample of boys reckoned that the study of history in general and their NCH provision in particular had the power in some way to help them and others become better people and lead 'better' lives at the level of SDS.

> *AHMAD:*   *It's like [...] it can actually help... 'cause if you're*
> *learning, if you're learning about the history, what's*
> *good, what happened in the world, you might change the*
> *way you live or help like how the way you treat people*
> *around you [...] if you think of that, it actually helps*
> *you like live as a better person.*

The Significance of the Absence of Spiritual Success

Conversely, if *spiritual success* was not achieved and the spiritual dimension was not adequately addressed by teachers, the *intellectual success* and the absorption of core historical knowledge as well as the *affective-cultural* and *civic dimensions* of success of some pupils also suffered in a 'knock-on' way. These negative 'knock-on' effects led to both a decreased engagement with the history curriculum and to a decrease in reflection on citizenship and their status as both Muslims and young British citizens.

For Pervez (Faith School, high-achieving, British-Pakistani), for example, the absence of the history of the formation of Pakistan as an Islamic Republic from the curricular account of Indian Independence and the exclusive curricular focus on the role of Gandhi was a source of disappointment and confusion.

PERVEZ: To learn about Gandhi is not exactly something that's very exciting. If it was more like how the Pakistan started then it would be exciting but Gandhi... I don't mind learning it but it would be better about... I'm not exactly excited about it.

MATTHEW: So would I be right in saying that if, let's say, Gandhi... you were learning about Gandhi and Mohammed Jinnah and the whole sort of movement to start Pakistan... as sort of together... then that might be more interesting?

PERVEZ: Yeah [...]'cause I wasn't even aware of that, you know, because we haven't learn it, I haven't even heard of that, so yeah, that's quite new to me so it would be better if we can learn things like that.

The Absent Curriculum

In fact, none of the schools, despite their high intake of Muslim pupils, taught any of the modules of the history of Islam that were available on NCH at the time of research. The history of the Muslim contribution constituted an absent, unenacted curriculum (Wilkinson 2014a) that had detrimental effects across the sample. Out of the sample of 23 students (48 %), 11 noted unprompted the absence of the history of the Muslim contribution from their curricular learning. All 11 boys alluded in some way to the real determinate, negative impact of this absent curriculum (Wilkinson 2014a), which ranged from its generating 'boredom' and frustration to more keenly felt feelings of alienation and rejection.

For Haider (Faith School, Pakistani-British, low-achieving), for example, the absence of history of the Muslim contribution at school contributed to his 'boredom' with the subject, to his finding it unimportant and to the feeling that he was 'not learning the right stuff'.

Pervez (Faith School, Pakistani-British, high-achieving) said that without the history of the Muslim contribution, history at school was 'a complete waste of time'. Notwithstanding the adolescent hyperbole of this statement, Pervez's testimony suggested that something that would have been seminal to Pervez's potential engagement with the subject was missing. This was reinforced by the fact that both Pervez and

Haider said that the inclusion of some element of the history of the Muslim contribution in their learning would have rendered other topics, such as the compulsory study of the changing relationship between the British Monarchy and Parliament, more interesting. Even, said Haider, '... *all those Henries!*'

This absence of the engagement of Haider's and Pervez's faith-based identities in the *spiritual and affective-cultural dimensions of success* had prompted negative 'knock-on' effects on both the *intellectual* and *civic* dimensions of their development.

CONCLUSION: FACTORING-IN FAITH FAIRLY

My data about the impact of the history curriculum on British Muslim young people's holistic development would have made much less sense had I not factored-in both the presence and the absence of the spiritual dimension in their educational experience and being.

Success in the spiritual dimension was a significant predictor, both of *intellectual success* ($ß = 0.270***$; $R^2 = 0.410$) and of *overall holistic success* ($ß = 0.345***$; $R^2 = 0.431$), and interviews corroborated the fact that the more that the Muslim young people were engaged to reflect ethically, morally and religiously about the past, the more historical facts they remembered and the more engaged they were with the subject of History as a whole. Conversely, when the Muslim young people were *not* engaged to reflect ethically, morally and religiously about the past, they learnt less and were less engaged with the subject of History as a whole, sometimes to the point of boredom and even alienation.

This research strongly suggests that contemporary theoretical models used to frame research on Muslims-in-education need to be multi-dimensional, non-reductive models that factor in the faith and faith-based identities of young Muslims as at least partially determinate of their life choices and chances.

These models need to factor-in faith fairly in articulation with other 'laminated' dimensions, without swamping research with faith-based explanatory accounts or naïvely obliterating other explanatory elements such as class, 'ethnicity' and gender and the way that young people tend to form and perform identity in innovative and hybrid ways.

NOTES

1. Two obvious examples of demi-reality are Nazi ideology and the Indian caste system, both of which are false ideological accounts of the world that have/had real effects on peoples' lives.

2. This was measured through each pupil's National Curriculum Level and survey independent variables: **3a**, The history I have studied at Key Stage 3 (KS3) has given me a good understanding of the history of England, **3b**, The history I have studied at KS3 has not given me a good understanding of the history of the rest of Britain, **3c**, The history I have studied at KS3 has helped me understand the history of other countries, and **8d**, The history I have studied in Years 7, 8 and 9 has helped me think more deeply about the world I live in, and related Principal Component Factor Analysis (PCFA). Intellectual Success further explored in interview data and through classroom observations.

3. It was measured by independent variables: **5d**, The history I have studied at KS3 has helped me think about my own religion, **5e**, The history I have studied at KS3 has not helped me to think about what is right and what is wrong, and **5f**, The history I have studied at KS3 has taught me important Lessons-for-Life, and related PCFA.

4. It was measured by independent variables: **5c**, The history I have studied at KS3 has not helped me to think about my own cultural background, and **9 k**, I talk about history with my family at home and related Regressions and PCFA.

5. It was measured by independent variables: **7a**, I am going to take history at GCSE and an open-ended variable: **7b**, I am going to take history at GCSE because… and related PCFA.

6. It was measured by independent variables: **4a**, The history I have studied at KS3 has helped me understand how Parliament developed, **4b**, The history I have studied at KS3 has not helped me to understand the changing role of British Kings and Queens, **4c**, The history I have studied at KS3 has helped me understand what a democracy is, **4e**, The history I have studied at KS3 has helped me think about what it means to be a British citizen, and **4f**, I am more likely to vote when I am old enough, as a result of the history I have learnt and **5b**, History lessons have helped me feel more at home in England.

7. This was derived as an aggregated factor from *dependent* variables: **8c**, The history I have studied in Years 7, 8 and 9 has helped me think more deeply about myself, and **8d**, The history I have studied in Years 7, 8 and 9 has helped me think more deeply about the world I live in, and explored more deeply in the interview data.

REFERENCES

Adey, K., & Biddulph, M. (2001). The influence of pupil perceptions on subject choice at 14+ in geography and history. *Educational Studies, 27*(4), 439–447.

Ahonen, S. (2001). Politics of identity through history curriculum: Narratives of the past for social exclusion – or inclusion? *Journal of Curriculum Studies, 33*(2), 179–194.

Alexander, C. E. (2000). *The Asian gang*. Oxford: Berg.

Apple, M. W. (1993). The politics of official knowledge: Does a national curriculum make sense? *Teachers College Record, 95*(2), 222–241.

Archer, L. (2001). Muslim brothers, black lads, traditional Asians: British Muslim young men's constructions of "race", religion and masculinity. *Feminism and Psychology, 11*(1), 79–105.

Archer, L. (2003). *Race, masculinity and schooling: Muslim boys and education*. Maidenhead, Berkshire: Open University Press.

Barton, K. C., & McCully, A. W. (2005). History, identity, and the school curriculum in Northern Ireland: An empirical study of secondary students' ideas and perspectives. *Journal of Curriculum Studies, 37*(1), 85–116.

Bhaskar, R. (1975/2008). *A realist theory of science*. Abingdon: Routledge.

Bhaskar, R. (1979/2008). *The possibility of naturalism*. London: Routledge.

Bhaskar, R. (2002). *From science to emancipation*. New Delhi: Sage Publications.

Bhaskar, R. (2008). *Dialectic: The pulse of freedom* (2nd ed.). Abingdon: Routledge.

Brown, G. (2009). The ontological turn in education. *The Journal of Critical Realism, 8*(1), 5–34.

Cameron, D. (2011). Muslims must embrace our British values. In Munich Security Conference 2011. *The Telegraph*. Available at: http://www.telegraph.co.uk/news/newstopics/politics/david-cameron/8305346/Muslims-must-embrace-our-British-values-David-Cameron-says.html.

Cronon, W. (2000). Why the past matters. *Wisconsin Magazine of History*, Autumn, pp. 2–13.

Foucault, M. (1980). Two Lectures. In C. Gordon (Ed.), *Power/Knowledge: Selected Interviews*. New York: Pantheon.

Hallaq, W. (2012). *The impossible state: Islam, politics, and modernity's moral predicament*. New York: Columbia University Press.

Hassan, M. (2013). Extremists point to Western foreign policy to explain their acts. Why do we ignore them? Available at: http://www.newstatesman.com/politics/politics/2013/05/extremists-point-western-foreign-policy-explain-their-acts-why-do-we-ignor [Accessed 20 November 2015].

Hopkins, P. (2004). Young Muslim men in Scotland: Inclusions & exclusions. *Children's Geographies, 2*(2), 257–272.

Hussain, S. (2008). *Muslims on the map*. London: Tauris Academic Studies.

Ipgrave, J. (Forthcoming). Multiculturalism, communitarianism, cohesion, and security: The impact of changing responses to British Islam on the nature of English religious education. In R. Heffner & A. Seligman (Eds.), *Civic enculturation and citizenship in North America and Western Europe*.

Little, D. (1993). Evidence and objectivity in the social sciences. *Social Research*, *60*(2), 363–396.

May, T. (2015). Theresa May set to urge UK's Muslims to help fight extremism. *The Guardian*. Available at: http://www.theguardian.com/politics/2015/mar/23/theresa-may-muslims-fight-extremism-uk [Accessed 20 November 2015].

Norrie, A. (2010). *Dialectic and difference*. London: Routledge.

Scott, D. (2010). *Education, epistemology and critical realism*. London: Routledge.

Shain, F. (2003). *The schooling and identity of Asian girls*. Stoke-on-Trent: Trentham.

Shain, F. (2011). *The new folk devils: Muslim boys and education in England*. Stoke on Trent: Trentham Books.

Smith, C. (2010). *What is a person?* Chicago: University of Chicago Press.

Wegner, G. (1990). Germany's past contested: The Soviet-American conflict in Berlin over history curriculum reform, 1945–1948. *History of Education Quarterly*, *30*(1), 1–6.

Wilkinson, M. L. N. (2007). *The national curriculum for history: Is it failing Muslim boys?* MRes London: King's College London.

Wilkinson, M. L. N. (2011). *History curriculum, citizenship & Muslim boys: Learning to succeed?* London: King's College London.

Wilkinson, M. L. N. (2014a). The concept of the absent curriculum: The case of the Muslim contribution and the English National Curriculum for history. *Journal of Curriculum Studies*, *46*(4), 419–440.

Wilkinson, M. L. N. (2014b). Helping Muslim boys succeed: The case for history education. *The Curriculum Journal*, *25*(3), 1–36.

Wilkinson, M. L. N. (2015). *A fresh look at Islam in a multi-faith world: A philosophy for success through education*. Abingdon: Routledge.

Matthew Wilkinson is Research Fellow in Islam in Education and Law at SOAS, University of London. He researches theological philosophy of Islam with a focus on its application to understanding the presence (and absence) of Islam and Muslims in processes of education and law. He is known for originating an educational philosophy of Islam called Islamic Critical Realism designed to help young people flourish in multi-faith contexts. This philosophy has been published in '*A Fresh Look at Islam in a Multi-faith World: A Philosophy for Success Through Education*', which was awarded the Cheryl Frank Memorial Prize (2014).

Towards Multi-cultural, Multi-religious European Societies? Schooling Turkish Students in Britain and Germany

Daniel Faas

Introduction

Processes of European integration, globalisation and migration are currently challenging national identities and changing education across Europe. Politicians and academics have been debating intensively the reasons underlying tensions between national majorities and Muslim minorities across a range of European societies and what should be done to develop and promote civic cohesion models in European societies (Faas 2013; Triandafyllidou 2010). This chapter sheds light on the educational experiences of Turkish Muslim students in Germany and Britain. Drawing on mainly qualitative data, it argues that when the concept of Europe is allied to multi-culturalism, there is the possibility of including minority ethnic groups, like the Turkish Muslims, and giving them the opportunity of relating to the European project and identity in a positive way. If, however, Europe is framed as a white Christian concept, then Turkish Muslim students will struggle to relate positively to Europe as a political identity. The chapter theorises the education of Muslim students in European societies and, in so doing, it contributes to ongoing academic

D. Faas (✉)
Department of Sociology, Trinity College, Dublin, Ireland
e-mail: faasd@tcd.ie

© The Author(s) 2017
M. Mac an Ghaill, C. Haywood (eds.), *Muslim Students, Education and Neoliberalism*, DOI 10.1057/978-1-137-56921-9_6

and political debates about the challenges of constructing and promoting inclusive, multi-religious models of Europe and the nation-state, addressing the issue of marginalised Muslim communities and promoting multicultural alongside traditional European and national values.

The question of Muslim integration is interesting in the current European integration process. Old and new European Union (EU) member states strive to accept diversity within Europe as well as to define their geopolitical and cultural position within the ever-enlarging EU. National identities are under pressure by the Europeanisation process – especially the former communist countries that joined the EU in 2004 and 2007 (see Kuus 2004). The question of Turkey's accession into the EU has given rise to new debates about the Christian (or not) roots of Europe, about the compatibility of a predominantly Muslim, albeit secular, country within the EU, and about the borders of Europe – where does Europe end effectively (for more on this, see Triandafyllidou and Gropas 2015)? In this process of identity negotiation and geopolitical reorganisation within the EU, the challenge of Islam comes as one more complexity in the management of diversity in Europe, which, if anything, is less desirable and more alien than intra-European diversity. Although the EU indirectly, and sometimes even directly, supports minority protection and combats discrimination, the overall Europeanisation process has certainly not made the integration of Muslims in specific member states any simpler. On the contrary, long-term Muslim residents fully integrated in their country of settlement discover that they are sometimes at a disadvantage in EU member states compared with other newcomers who gain European citizenship. These debates are also played out in schooling systems across Europe that are facing challenges of managing increasing migration-related cultural and religious diversity.

Germany has the largest Muslim population (3.8 to 4.3 million, nearly half of whom have German citizenship) in Western Europe after France, being home to around 2.6 million Turkish economic migrants, mostly Sunnis, from an avowedly secular country which has experience with democratic norms and has been in EU membership negotiations since 2005. Unlike in Britain where Pakistani and Bangladeshi (Sunni) communities, and men in particular, tend to define their identities along religious lines (Archer 2003), 'Muslimness' does not figure prominently in the multi-dimensional hybrid identities of either young Turks in Germany or Britain (Faas 2009, 2010). Germany's 2.4 million Turks (almost 500,000 Turkish students in German schools in 2001–2) form the country's largest minority ethnic community, and in Britain, the Turkish community comprises around 200,000 people and is thus one of the smaller minority ethnic communities. The Turkish community is relatively under-researched and disadvantaged. Enneli et al. (2005), for instance, argue that Britain's young Turkish Muslims are even more disadvantaged in housing, employment and education than the Bangladeshi population (who are widely regarded as the least integrated community in Britain; see Modood and Werbner 1997).

The Turkish community within Europe has always had a very complex history. Turkish Muslims were physically brought into the European project as 'guest workers' (*Gastarbeiter*) by the Germans who increasingly needed labour after the construction of the Berlin Wall in 1961. The bilateral agreement between Germany and Turkey made on 31st October 1961, which Şen and Goldberg (1994: 10) referred to as 'one of the most important milestones in the history of German-Turkish relations', stated that Turkish workers should return to their home country within two years. However, because of the need of workers beyond the initially agreed date, many of these young men continued to stay in Germany and were joined by their families in subsequent decades (Königseder 2001). By 1980, Turkish Muslims formed the largest minority ethnic community in Germany (1,462,000) and, because of family reunions, their number increased to more than 2 million by the late 1990s. Many 15-year-old Turkish youths in Germany are now in their second generation.

In Britain, however, it was mainly for political reasons that mainland Turkish people, Turkish Cypriots and Kurds sought refuge. As a result of the British occupation of Cyprus between 1878 and 1959, the Turkish community is much more heterogeneous and some of the refugees had British passports. The first wave of migration, mainly male Turkish Cypriots, fled from their increasingly politically unstable island to seek refuge in Britain in the 1950s and 1960s, when the National Organisation of Cypriot Fighters fought for union with Greece (Sonyel 1988). The wave of migration from mainland Turkey only gained momentum after the military coup by General Evren in 1980 (Mehmet Ali 2001). In the late 1980s and early 1990s, most of the Kurds arrived in Britain as refugees. As a result of this migration, many young Turkish Cypriots are now in their second generation whereas most first-generation mainland Turkish people were born in Turkey. Despite different histories of migration, Turkish Muslims have faced enormous conflict and marginalisation in both European countries in terms of employment and education (Kagitçibasi 1991) and have often been the victims of racism and Islamophobia (Piper 1998; Archer 2003; Wilpert 2003; Dodd 2005). Neither research on the Turkish community in Germany (e.g. Auernheimer 1990; Şen and Goldberg 1994; Şen 2002) nor Britain (e.g. Sonyel 1988; Küçükcan 1999; Enneli et al. 2005) has hitherto explored the responses of Turkish students to Europe and the factors affecting their identity formation processes. The question of how Turkish students in Britain and Germany relate to notions of Europeanness and a European identity is an intriguing one, which the remainder of this chapter aims to address.

Schooling Turkish Students in Germany and Britain

The predominantly ethno-cultural conception of citizenship in Germany, together with the understanding of German society as monocultural, would have made it difficult for the country's minority ethnic communities, and Turkish 'guest workers' in particular, to relate positively to German society. They were being positioned as 'others' by successive post-war governments and, once Germany's economy was in recession, were seen by many white Germans as a threat to job opportunities. Until the late 1990s, politicians did not acknowledge that Germany was a multi-cultural society despite the presence of more than 7 million immigrants (in 1998), and the 'guest workers' only had limited rights to citizenship. Successive governments had hoped that the 'guest workers' would one day return to their country of origin and, when their hopes were not met, they adopted exclusionary policy approaches (e.g. 'foreigner' pedagogy; 'foreigner' law). Today, schools are first and foremost expected to deliver a European agenda through cross-curricular teaching units. There is no coherent message for schools as each of the 16 federal states delivers the relationship between national, European and multi-cultural agendas in different ways. For example, Baden-Württemberg recently introduced legislation banning teachers from wearing headscarves and thus sent a strong message to schools that concepts of 'being German' and 'being Muslim' may not be compatible. This was further fuelled by senior Conservative politicians who took the view that Turkey should only be offered a 'privileged partnership' instead of full EU membership (Faas 2008).

The policy approaches and messages sent to schools are quite different in Britain, particularly in inner-city and industrial areas. Britain had to develop approaches to migration-related diversity after the 1948 arrival of the Empire Windrush from the Caribbean, whereas this was not an issue in

Germany until well into the 1960s given that migrant labourers were recruited on a temporary basis only. Concerns were expressed in Britain about how to address the wide range of ethnic groups, and successive governments had protected and reinforced the concept of Britishness, for instance, through conservative and monocultural educational initiatives (1950s–1970s). The assumption during those years was that immigrants should integrate as quickly as possible with the English way of life. Initiatives included a dispersal policy (also known as *busing*), introduced for the first time in 1965, to avoid undue concentration of minority ethnic communities in any particular school. The Thatcher era had seen a major shift back to a more exclusive notion of 'Englishness', which perceived minority ethnic groups as a threat to the English way of life and national identity. For example, the 1981 Nationality Act constructed a national identity and thus boundaries of belonging by reinforcing the differential citizenship status between white and minority ethnic people. And the 1988 Education Reform Act largely removed the concept of multi-culturalism from the National Curriculum.

Schools had been encouraged to adopt a neo-liberal agenda based on principles of marketisation and individualisation, thus facing the dilemma of having to integrate an increasingly heterogonous population into an exam-orientated, market-driven education system. New Labour (1997–2010), in contrast, promoted race equality and sent out a different message to schools. New Labour administrations tried hard to ally the concept of cultural and ethnic diversity with Britishness (Meer et al. 2015). However, the terrorist atrocities in New York (2001), Madrid (2004) and London (2005) undermined this inclusionist agenda and brought to light deep societal divisions along religious lines and a subsequent focus in schools on community (social) cohesion.

Germany was a founding member of the European integration project, and as a result, schools and the curriculum throughout the 1980s and 1990s were used to construct a Europeanised national identity. Britain, in contrast, experienced Europe very differently. There was little reason why the country should reconceptualise her national identity in European terms and the processes of Europeanisation have not seriously affected British schools. The politics of Europe, initiated by Germany and France, were undercut by the special relationship with the USA; the geographical detachment from continental Europe; and Britain's post-war role in the Commonwealth. Consequently, Britain engaged little with the European project until the 1960s when Prime

Minister Macmillan realised that his country needed to reorientate as the Empire was rapidly falling apart. However, it was extremely difficult for politicians to promote a sense of European identity in Britain where, arguably, the level of national pride was much higher than in post-war Germany because of the fact that the country had won the war. Unlike Germany, Britain's relationship with Europe was largely based on economic reasons and politicians increasingly faced the dilemma of having to engage with an entity they felt only loosely attached to and that had been led, for most of the time, by joint Franco-German initiatives (e.g. Franco-German Brigade).

These different historical engagements with cultural diversity and with Europe have had enormous implications for schools. As early as 1978, attempts were made to include a European dimension in German schools. The task for schools was to convey insights into geographical diversity, political and social structures, formative historical forces and the history of the European idea. Some federal states, such as Baden-Württemberg in 1994, specifically overhauled their curricula to include a European cross-curricular dimension. Subjects such as Geography or History devoted an entire academic year on European issues (for more on this, see Faas 2011). The danger with promoting a European curricular dimension was that it could potentially marginalise all those immigrants in Germany coming from non-Europeanised countries such as Turkey. Faas (2010) conducted a comparative case study of the experiences of 15-year-old ethnic majority and Turkish students in two German and two British secondary schools, respectively. The empirical data in this chapter refers to this study. The data set included 24 student focus groups, 32 individual student interviews, 16 teacher interviews and school policy documents. This study demonstrated that the Eurocentric approach adopted by some of the teachers in a local German school (Tannberg Hauptschule) made it difficult for both ethnic majority and Turkish youth to relate positively to Europe as a political identity. In Britain, in contrast, the European dimension received little attention and, unlike multi-cultural education, did not specifically appear amongst the cross-curricular themes and dimensions of the 1988 National Curriculum. Even under New Labour, the processes of Europeanisation received little attention in the development of citizenship education which reasserted the concept of Britishness. The 'non-European' students like the Turkish Muslims were, therefore, hardly threatened by this dimension in Britain.

However, the non-European students in both countries might have gained if it had been provided with both multi-cultural and European education – a concept I call *multi-cultural multi-religious Europeanness*. This approach, which was well developed in another German school (Goethe Gymnasium), combines the notion of multi-culturalism with social inclusion in order to construct a multi-ethnic, multi-religious model of Europe; in other words, it embraces plural ways of belonging to Europe. Turkish students in such an environment were able to relate positively to Europe; for example, they engaged in discussions about European political issues and made Europe part of their hybrid identities. The school prospectus stated that:

> The ethos of our school is characterised by mutual respect, confidence and tolerance towards other people. Our students, which come from diverse backgrounds, practice intercultural tolerance and community; they learn the manifoldness of European languages, cultures and mentalities and can thus develop their own identity within our school. The internationality of our school community alongside its location next to libraries, museums, opera houses, archives, theatres and galleries characterise our profile. Europe as a cultural area is one of our guiding principles. (School brochure; translated from German)

The concept of 'multi-cultural Europeanness' promoted at Goethe Gymnasium shaped Turkish students' political discourses and the ways in which they perceived their identities. Unlike in the other schools in this study (Faas 2010), where young people preferred national governments, a majority of Turkish respondents argued for more European integration (e.g. 'national laws would be subordinated to the European Constitution which would be good'). Nerhim alluded to the notion of a family arguing that 'I find the EU, the unification of all these countries, a good thing. It's just the same within a family; for example, when you have a problem then you discuss that amongst four or five people and so; and I find it good that Europe is doing the same generally speaking'. Other examples which were suggestive of Turkish students' positioning within national and European discourses emerged from the discussions I had with Melik and the group of four Turkish boys. Melik argued that if there was further European integration, 'the language would have to be the same too', thus alluding to the status of English as a 'lingua franca' for Europe.

The school's interpretation of 'Europeanness' to include multi-culturalism (coupled with students' privileged backgrounds) allowed many Turkish students to relate positively to Europe, to think of Europe as being part of their multi-dimensional political identities. Most students made identification with Europe dependent on stays abroad (e.g. 'I only know Germany; if I was living in Spain for a few years, then I'd more say that I'm European cos I'd be familiar with different countries'), parental influence (e.g. 'my parents experienced a lot and tell me a lot about other countries and culture; Europe plays an important role for me too cos I'm interested in getting to know these other countries') and the school curriculum (e.g. 'we learn a lot of European languages here in school and talking in Italian, English and French makes me feel partly European'). The following excerpts indicate that the young people felt positive about Europe:

DF (Daniel Faas):	To what extent do you see yourself as European?
ALI:	Erm, of course I'm European. Europe is very big and is getting bigger and bigger. And when Turkey joins the EU it'll be even bigger. Europe is getting more and more important to me cos of Turkey. […]
MARIAM:	I feel European because of the Euro. The Euro impacts on your life and that's why Europe is important. I mean, in the newspaper they always talk about the Euro, Eurozone, Europe and I've noticed that the countries are getting closer and closer and not every country has its own policy. And the economy has grown together too. And you can travel to other countries without any problems at the borders.

These statements were suggestive of the fact that the processes of European integration, be it the expansion to include countries like Turkey (e.g. Ali) or deeper political and economic cooperation (e.g. Mariam), seemed to contribute to students' identification with Europe.

In contrast, as a result of the policy approach of the British government, Europe was a relatively low priority in the London schools included in my study. Like the Goethe Gymnasium in Germany with its high performance and multi-cultural intake, the school celebrated similarity rather than diversity. This similarity was not based on Europe – instead the school encouraged its students to think of themselves as liberal democratic British citizens living in a global multi-ethnic international community. In so doing, this school was much closer to New Labour's model of 'multi-cultural

Britishness' and, like Goethe Gymnasium, allied the concept of multiculturalism with social inclusion. The ethos of Darwin School in London, for example, suggested that young people were encouraged to think of themselves as liberal democratic British citizens living in a multi-ethnic international community. These messages were highlighted in the school prospectus:

> The school strives to be a high-performing inclusive community school, fully committed to active citizenship and academic excellence. We value all who learn and work here; promoting a strong sense of community within and beyond the school. (...) Bilingualism is actively encouraged and supported and opportunities offered to be examined in community languages. (...) All students are of equal concern and the school promotes self-discipline and empathy for others, both within the school and the wider community. (...) The teacher cannot be neutral towards those values which underpin liberal democracy. Values such as freedom of speech and discussion, respect for truth and reasoning, the peaceful resolution of conflicts, are the means whereby indoctrination is combated and prevented.

Despite this inclusive approach, or perhaps because of it, Darwin School made little effort to integrate students on the basis of common European membership. The promotion of national agendas (i.e. Britishness) in a school which celebrates similarity made it difficult for most Turkish students to relate to Europe. As a result of Britain's lukewarm approach to the EU, young people's Turkish British identities did not easily fit with Europe so that this political identity played a less important role in the lives of students I interviewed. However, (first-generation) mainland Turkish and (second-generation) Turkish Cypriot students were able to identify with Europe so long as Turkey was included in the notion of Europe. Typically, respondents argued that 'if Turkey was in the European Union, then I would see myself as more of a European' and 'I see myself wherever Turkey belongs in Asia or whatever'. A number of Turkish Cypriot interviewees, such as Mustafa and Safak, referred to British insularity and separateness from Europe arguing that 'I am European 'cos I'm in Europe, and I'm in Britain which is in Europe and part of the European society; but I don't see myself as a European because Britain is separate from Europe'. Here, Mustafa and Safak tried to position themselves within the British national discourse. These discourses were suggestive of students' Turkish British identities.

DF:	To what extent would you see yourself as European?
MUSTAFA:	I don't really see myself as European, because, erm, I don't know, I just, erm, I'm not sure because I'd sort of be like failing my argument now if I said that, erm, I don't count myself as European because if I was born in Europe, I'd count myself as European, but I'm not born there so I guess I call myself British, cos I was born here and, like growing up here, since day one. That's it.
DF:	That's interesting that you are saying that, because you were born in England, and England has been part of the EU for decades, and now you were just saying 'I'm not born in Europe'?
MUSTAFA:	But the thing is, I don't see England being a strong... I know they're quite strong in Europe, but I guess like I think like Europe's sort of latching onto England, and I think England's more distant from Europe, even though they're quite strong contenders in the European Union. Now if you've seen the news, they're actually thinking to vote not to be key contenders in the European Union, so they'll be more of the people that's on the marginal lines of Europe, instead of the core players like Germany or France.

Conceptually, these interviews are very intriguing as they underline the potential of both the nation-state and Europe to act as a cohesive bond or society if defined and constructed along multi-cultural multi-religious lines. The extracts are also revealing in the current British context following the Brexit vote on 23 June 2016 as it appears to be the case, at least for Turkish students in my sample, to identify with the nation-state and Europe if these opportunities are promoted by governments and schools and thus salient as identities. For a fuller discussion of the school dynamics, teacher interpretations of macro-political agendas, student–teacher interactions and responses of ethnic majority students, see Faas (2010).

CONCLUSION: TOWARDS MULTI-CULTURAL, MULTI-RELIGIOUS EUROPEAN SOCIETIES

The broader study (Faas 2010) revealed that ethnic majority students in German and British schools formed, what could be called, a *chain of identities* meaning that local, regional and (supra)national spheres were all integrated within the other and not competing. In particular, ethnic majority youth in the German schools forged their political identities by linking the local, regional, national German and supranational European citizenship levels. However, as a result of the different prioritisation of European agendas at German and British government level, these chains of identities generally did not include supranational levels in the case of ethnic majority student interviewees at the British secondary schools. Turkish 15-year-olds, in contrast, had developed different forms of hybrid identities so that the image of a chain of identities could not be easily used with regard to Turkish Muslims in either country. One of the most notable differences between ethnic majority and Turkish youths was that ethnic majority youths, in both Germany and Britain, generally also had a regional identity whereas virtually none of the Turkish students I interviewed saw themselves as having a regional identity. In other words, the Turkish youth in the study broke the chain by linking, for example, the local with the supranational levels or the local with the national levels. This suggests that 15-year-old Turkish students positioned themselves within, what could be called, a *triangle of identities*. In such a triangle, it is possible to combine all the different political identities (e.g. local, regional, national, supranational) without seeing one sphere as being integrated within the other.

The politics of multi-culturalism appears to be successful when allied with the concept of social inclusion – which I call *inclusive multi-culturalism*. This allows young people to relate positively to the British/German or European societies and develop hybrid identities. Faas (2010) demonstrated that German schools successfully included students on the basis of 'multi-cultural Europeanness' by promoting multi-cultural and European agendas whereas some British schools included students into a multi-ethnic concept of nationhood. The fact that the German schools drew upon the concept of Europe whereas the British schools encouraged students to think of themselves as liberal democratic British citizens living in a multi-ethnic community had to do with the different prioritisation and focus of European agendas in the two countries. Also, most minority ethnic communities in Germany originate from other European countries including Turkey whereas Commonwealth immigration produced a rather different picture in British schools. Consequently, a school-like Goethe Gymnasium in Germany could mobilise the European agenda as a means of including students in the school community whereas this might be more difficult to achieve in a British school. Since the politics of multi-culturalism can be successfully combined with notions of social inclusion, so too can the European agenda work in an inclusive school context.

There are also dangers associated with promoting a strong European dimension in education. Some teachers I interviewed in Germany constructed a white European national identity and, in so doing, privileged a Eurocentric educational approach which made it extremely difficult for students, and Turkish Muslims in particular, to relate positively to Europe. At the same time, there is potential for the concept Europe to be a source for cultural and linguistic enrichment and a common ground, for both ethnic majority and Turkish Muslim youth, to negotiate their political identities. Both ethnic majority and Turkish Muslim youth seemed to be able to gain from the opportunities associated with Europe (e.g. knowledge, identity) if Europe is reconceptualised in multi-cultural terms. It is therefore worth considering the potential of a multi-cultural political and educational approach to European citizenship and identity (i.e. *multi-cultural European citizenship*) as a common bond which may hold together the different racial and ethno-religious communities in Europe at a time of increasing societal fragmentation and globalisation in the twenty-first century. Rather than global citizenship *per se*, or any of its associated approaches such as cosmopolitan citizenship (Osler and Starkey 2003), global citizenship education (Walkington 1999) and world citizenship (Heater 1996), the notion of a multi-cultural Europe and education for multi-cultural European citizenship, with an incorporated global and international dimension, has a variety of benefits for people already living in, or migrating into, the EU. It might help prevent Eurocentric education and help a new generation of youth forge a loyalty to Europe as a political identity.

At a theoretical and policy level, this then suggests that when schools construct an inclusive multi-ethnic concept of Europe, Turkish youth engage with Europe as a political identity and develop national-European identities. If, however, Europe is conceptualised as an exclusionary mono-cultural (i.e. white, Christian) concept, then Turkish students will struggle to relate positively to Europe as a political identity. Politicians, policy-makers and educators are therefore presented with the challenge of constructing and promoting an inclusive, multi-religious model of Europe – one which addresses the issue of marginalised Muslim communities and promotes multi-cultural alongside traditional European values. There is potential for the concept of Europe to be a source for cultural and linguistic enrichment and minority ethnic youth like the Turkish Muslims seemed to be able to gain from the opportunities associated with the European knowledge economy if Europe is reconceptualised in multi-cultural terms. This might not only help prevent Eurocentric education but could also help Turkish and other teenagers forge a loyalty to Europe.

REFERENCES

Archer, L. (2003). *Race, masculinity and schooling: Muslim boys and education.* London: Open University Press.

Auernheimer, G. (1990). How black are the German Turks? Ethnicity, marginality and interethnic relations for young people of Turkish origin in the FRG. In L. Chisholm et al. (Eds.), *Childhood, youth, and social change: A comparative perspective.* Basingstoke: The Falmer Press.

Dodd, V. (2005). Muslim women advised to abandon hijab to avoid attack. Retrieved 4 August 2005, from the World Wide Web: http://www.guardian.co.uk/attackonlondon.

Enneli, P., Modood, T., & Bradley, H. (2005). *Young Turks and Kurds: A set of 'invisible' disadvantaged groups.* York: Joseph Rowntree Foundation.

Faas, D. (2008). From foreigner pedagogy to intercultural education: An analysis of the German responses to diversity and its impacts on schools and students. *European Educational Research Journal, 7*(1), 108–123.

Faas, D. (2009). Reconsidering identity: The ethnic and political dimensions of hybridity among majority and Turkish youth in Germany and England. *British Journal of Sociology, 60*(2), 299–320.

Faas, D. (2010). *Negotiating political identities: Multiethnic schools and youth in Europe.* Farnham: Ashgate.

Faas, D. (2011). The nation, Europe and migration: A comparison of geography, history and citizenship education curricula in Greece, Germany and England. *Journal of Curriculum Studies, 43*(4), 471–492.

Faas, D. (2013). Ethnic diversity and schooling in national education systems: Issues of policy and identity (Introduction thematic section). *Education Inquiry, 4*(1), 5–10.

Heater, D. (1996). *World citizenship and government: Cosmopolitan ideas in the history of Western political thought.* Basingstoke: Macmillan.

Kagitçibasi, C. (1991). Türkische Migranten aus der Sicht des Herkunftslandes. In P. Bott, H. Merkens, & F. Schmidt (Eds.), *Türkische Jugendliche und Aussiedlerkinder in Familie und Schule.* Hohengehren: Schneider.

Königseder, A. (2001). Türkische Minderheit in Deutschland. *Informationen zur Politischen Bildung 271.* München: Franzis' print & media.

Küçükcan, T. (1999). *Politics of ethnicity, identity and religion: Turkish Muslims in Britain.* Aldershot: Ashgate.

Kuus, M. (2004). Europe's eastern expansion and the re-inscription of otherness in East Central Europe. *Progress in Human Geography, 28*(4), 472–489.

Meer, N., Mouritsen, P., Faas, D., & De Witte, N. (2015). Examining 'postmulti-cultural' and civic turns in the Netherlands, Britain, Germany and Denmark. *American Behavioral Scientist*, 59(6), 702–726.

Mehmet Ali, A. (2001). *Turkish speaking communities and education: No delight*. London: Fatal Publications.

Modood, T., & Werbner, P. (Eds.). (1997). *The politics of multiculturalism in the New Europe: Racism, identity and community*. London: Zed Books.

Osler, A., & Starkey, H. (2003). Learning for cosmopolitan citizenship: Theoretical debates and young people's experiences. *Educational Review*, 55(3), 243–254.

Piper, N. (1998). *Racism, nationalism and citizenship: Ethnic minorities in Britain and Germany*. Aldershot: Ashgate.

Şen, F. (2002). Türkische Minderheit in Deutschland. *Informationen zur politischen Bildung*, 277, 53–62.

Şen, F., & Goldberg, A. (1994). *Türken in Deutschland: Leben zwischen zwei Kulturen*. München: Verlag C.H. Beck.

Sonyel, S. R. (1988). *The silent minority: Turkish Muslim children in British schools*. Cambridge: The Islamic Academy.

Triandafyllidou, A. (Ed.). (2010). *Muslims in 21st century Europe: Structural and cultural perspectives*. London: Routledge.

Triandafyllidou, A., & Gropas, R. (2015). *What is Europe?* London: Palgrave Macmillan.

Walkington, H. (1999). *Theory into practice: Global citizenship education*. Sheffield: The Geographical Association.

Wilpert, C. (2003). Racism, discrimination, citizenship and the need for anti-discrimination legislation in Germany. In Z. Layton-Henry & C. Wilpert (Eds.), *Challenging racism in Britain and Germany*. Basingstoke: Palgrave Macmillan.

Daniel Faas is an associate professor, head of the department of sociology and a member of the University Council at Trinity College, Dublin. His research interests are in the sociology of migration with specific emphasis on the intersection of migration and education. His work focuses on youth identities in relation to immigrant integration, national identity, multi-culturalism and social cohesion in Europe, diversity management in educational sites and work places, curriculum design and development, as well as comparative case study methodologies. He has published widely on these topics in high-impact peer-reviewed international journals, as well as a sole-authored monograph. In 2015, he was elected to Fellowship at Trinity College, Dublin, in recognition of his research achievements.

CHAPTER 7

'Uncivil' Activism: Arab, South Asian, and Afghan American Youth Politics after 9/11

Sunaina Maira

The attacks of 11 September 2001 led to a heightened racialization, or re-racialization, of Muslim, Arab, and South Asian communities in the USA. This re-codification of race was driven in part by the attempt to find new categories for classifying populations seen as 'suspect' of being threats to national security, accompanied by community-led efforts to create coalitions among those targeted by the state in the US-led War on Terror. My research examines the significance of these new and shifting racial formations in the post-9/11 era and the implications they have for Muslim American youth who have come of age in this moment. In the book on which this chapter is based (Maira 2016), I discuss the ways in which coalitional categories such as AMSA (Arab, Muslim, and South Asian) or AMEMSA (Arab, Middle Eastern, Muslim, and South Asian) have been produced by campaigns that challenge anti-Muslim and anti-Arab racism but may also participate in a politics of disciplinary inclusion. One of the major tensions in this negotiation of post-9/11 racial politics is the complicated and sometimes uneasy relationship between religious and racial or national categories and the racialization of the category of 'the Muslim'. The scrutiny of Muslim Americans as the 'enemy within' rests on

S. Maira (✉)
University of California-Davis, Davis, CA, USA
e-mail: smaira@ucdavis.edu

© The Author(s) 2017
M. Mac an Ghaill, C. Haywood (eds.), *Muslim Students, Education and Neoliberalism*, DOI 10.1057/978-1-137-56921-9_7

sedimented associations with violent and deviant Blacks and Latinos, alien Asians, and uncivilized Natives. However, the figure of 'the Muslim' as reified in dominant discourses about terrorism obfuscates the racial and imperial histories that underlie these intersecting racial imaginaries.

This ethnographic study, conducted in Silicon Valley in northern California between 2007 and 2011, examines what it means for young people targeted in the War on Terror to be 'political' in the context of neo-liberal multi-culturalism and permanent surveillance. It examines how Arab, South Asian, and Afghan American youth (Muslim as well as non-Muslim) have turned to rights, especially civil rights and human rights, to respond to Islamophobia, racism, and imperial wars, and also how they grapple with the limits of rights-based activism. Under the PATRIOT Act and with the expanded powers given to law enforcement and intelligence agencies to hunt down potential terrorists and 'pre-empt' terrorism, Arab, South Asian (particularly Pakistani), Afghan, Iranian, and Muslim Americans in general have been subjected to surveillance as well as detention and deportation, hence the increased mobilization in defence of 'Muslim civil rights'. Muslim, Arab, and Middle Eastern youth, who are defined as objects of the domestic as well as global War on Terror, have come of age in a moment when the question of political engagement for Muslim youth is not only extremely urgent but also incredibly fraught. This essay draws on my research in the greater San Jose area and in Fremont/Hayward, where there are significant Arab, South Asian, and Afghan immigrant and refugee populations, and is based on participant observation at community and political events and interviews with college-age youth, community activists, and religious leaders. The questions stemmed in many ways from my own experiences of organizing in these communities and in the anti-war movement after 9/11.

From San Jose and Syracuse to London and Lahore, the US-led war on terror is now a globalized regime of biopolitics. Muslim and Arab American youth have become primary objects of the counter-terrorism regime which views them as susceptible to 'radicalization' and violent extremism based on generational, racial, and religious categorizations. This focus on 'home-grown terrorism' has occurred in tandem with shifts in USA wars and counter-terrorism operations in Afghanistan, Pakistan, Yemen and other sites which are mapped onto a transnational jihadist network (Kundnani 2014). The homeland war on terror has become an increasingly central part of the planetary war and in the decade since 9/11, increasingly focused on monitoring and prosecuting ideological and religious *beliefs*, not just terrorist activities. The strategy of pre-emptive prosecution thus mirrors the doctrine of 'pre-emptive war'. In all these debates, the figure of the young (especially males) Muslim or Arab American is particularly central, given the notion that youth, as a liminal category, are presumably vulnerable to indoctrination or radicalization. The 'new order of War on Terror' established under the Obama regime has relied on mass surveillance, clandestine cooperation between various arms of law enforcement and intelligence, and a counter-radicalization programme to police political and social lives and monitor the 'enemy within' (Kumar 2012: 158). In response, young people have engaged in cross-racial alliances and global justice movements based on pan-Islamic solidarity as well as on anti-imperial and anti-racist paradigms, vectors of politicization that are overlapping but that generate tensions in some cases.

In this chapter, I will focus on not only how solidarity activism related to Palestine is the threshold of 'radicalism' and object of intense repression, but also the site of cross-racial, pan-Islamic, and transnational solidarities, for Muslim, South Asian, and Arab American youth. Palestine activism is a key site of political pedagogy for Muslim and Arab American youth in the post-9/11 era. In the first section of this chapter, I focus on the turn to human rights as a discourse that young activists hope will make legible the violence against and suffering of Palestinians, which is often suppressed in the US mainstream media. I discuss how the inadmissibility of Palestinian rights as human rights forces youth to confront the limitations of liberal human rights as a racialized regime embedded in Western colonial modernity. The youth I spoke to struggled with the censorship and demonization of Palestine solidarity activism, due to the intense racialization in the USA of the figure of 'the Palestinian', and by association, of those in solidarity with the Palestinian national struggle, who are deemed automatically anti-American, anti-Semitic, militant, and racist. The condensation of all of these attributes in representations of what it means to support Palestinian liberation has made Palestine solidarity activism the third rail of campus activism in the USA, or what Edward Said (2000) famously called 'the last taboo'. In the second section, I argue that the encounter with the exceptional silencing of the Palestinian narrative in the USA produces what I call 'Palestinianization', for Palestinian/Arab and Muslim as well as non-Palestinian/Arab American and non-Muslim American youth. This pedagogical process of Palestinianization exposes the limitations of rights talk and campus multi-culturalism and animates an ongoing 'dissensus' against the War on Terror (Ranciere 2004).

GOT RIGHTS?

I am interested in the ways in which the engagement with human rights, including organizing for Palestinian or Muslim rights, is a 'social process of producing norms, knowledge, and compliance', that shapes political subjectivities and produces political critiques of forms of collective suffering and political justice denied by the existing, institutionalized human rights and humanitarian discourse (Merry 2006: 109). Human rights activism, as Wendy Brown (2004: 453–454) observes, has come to represent '*the* progressive international justice project', a moral-political project that offers 'protection against pain, deprivation, or suffering'.

Human rights was invoked by Arab, South Asian, and Afghan American youth in Silicon Valley in two major arenas of mobilization, both grounded in notions of cross-racial, transnational solidarity: pan-Islamic activism, on the one hand, and the Palestine solidarity and anti-war movement, on the other. These movements are overlapping and some youth had been involved in protests organized by the anti-war campaigns – for example, national Left groups such as ANSWER or South Bay Mobilization in Silicon Valley – but also in events with mosqued communities and Muslim civil rights organizations focused on 'Muslim rights'. Muslim Student Association (MSA) chapters and other Muslim activist groups have engaged in advocacy for the human rights of Muslims suffering in zones of war and conflict such as Kashmir, Chechnya, Afghanistan, Iraq, Pakistan, or Palestine, participating in some instances in coalitions with non-faith identified anti-war, Palestine solidarity, and civil rights groups. However, these two strands of human rights organizing – issue-based and faith-based – did not always converge and there were often distinct idioms of political protest.

Many students I spoke to were involved with both MSA and Students for Justice in Palestine (SJP) groups on their campuses, and attempted to connect post-9/11 concerns regarding civil rights violations with global politics. Marwa, an Egyptian American woman, was actively involved in the Islamic Society and the Muslim Student Awareness Network at Stanford University, both of which were ethnically and racially mixed and included students from Pakistan, Nigeria, Syria, Egypt, and Kazakhstan. She commented: 'We've done things, like, about Africa, all around the world because there are Muslims everywhere.' Pan-Islamic internationalism, in her view, anchors mobilization against military interventions and occupation affecting Muslims around the globe. In the Bay

Area, Nadine Naber (2012: 147–148) observes there was a shift in the 2000s to faith-based organizing among Arab Muslim Americans, based on the notion of 'global Muslim social justice', and an increasing 'centrality of religion as an organizing framework for Palestine solidarity activism', evident in mass prayers organized by Muslim Americans in San Francisco during the second Intifada. During the Israeli War on Gaza in summer 2014, the African American imam Zaid Shakir and Palestinian cleric and scholar Hatem Bazian organized a similar mass Friday prayer in downtown San Francisco, followed by a march to the Israeli consulate, sponsored by American Muslims for Palestine.

Some youth I spoke to straddled activism based on a 'transnational, coalitional concept of Islam' and non-faith-based political solidarity (Naber 2012: 148). Marwa, for example, was also involved with the Palestine solidarity movement and in a divestment campaign, launched by the Student Coalition against Israeli Apartheid at Stanford University in 2007, becoming a part of a cross-ethnic coalition including Arab Americans, African Americans, and Jewish Americans. Other youth argued that human rights trumped Muslim rights; for example, Aisha, a Palestinian American woman, thought that organizing in solidarity with Palestinians had to transcend pan-Islamic solidarity. She reflected on activism in support of Palestine: 'I have been thinking about this a lot and I think it needs to be framed as an issue of human rights, a something that affects all of humanity. That is the way we can connect to other people and to different groups.' Many young activists echoed Aisha's observations and turned to human rights as a potentially universalist framework that they believed would make legible the suffering generated by US imperial violence and US-backed regimes of warfare and occupation to a larger public.

Interestingly, some Muslim and Arab American youth noted that the Israeli War on Lebanon in 2006 was a catalysing event that shaped their awareness of global politics, even more than the attacks of 9/11 since they were only in middle school in 2001, but in high school or college during the assault on Lebanon. For many youth, the Israeli assault on Gaza in winter 2008–09 was also a turning point in their political involvement in international human rights campaigns, as also for many youth across the nation (Barrows-Friedman 2014: 38). For example, in Silicon Valley and Fremont, there were many large demonstrations in winter 2009 protesting the Israeli massacre in Gaza in which Arab, South Asian, and Afghan American youth were visibly involved. On 11 January 2009, I went to a rally in Santa Clara held on near an upscale outdoor mall, Santana Row, which was attended by a very diverse, multi-generational crowd of Arabs, Afghans, Iranians, and South Asians, as well as white Americans. Many protesters were carrying signs protesting the deaths of Palestinian children in Gaza; at least 1400 Palestinians had been killed in the massacre, and more than 300 of them were estimated to be children.[1] The previous weekend there had been a rally at the same location where the protestors, many of them youth, had blocked the entrance to Santana Row and marched through the manicured streets of the mall and past the elegant boutiques and cafes. Sabina, a young Pakistani American from Santa Clara, who attended the rally described it as 'very intense. I was at the end of a huge crowd and there were actually police following us. . . . [I]t was interesting going around Santana Row because it was very rich people who have no idea what's going on around the world. They were probably thinking, "Who are these crazy people screaming?"' At the rally I attended, a young woman in hijab was standing at the intersection, in the middle of the busy street, waving a large Palestinian flag. Another young woman in hijab, with a kaffiyeh (Palestinian scarf) around her shoulders, was shouting vigorously through a bullhorn: 'Free, FREE Palestine! Stop bomb-ing Ga-za!'

While the outrage of the crowd was palpable at the rally I attended, I sensed some internal disagreements about how to express the critique of US-backed violence. One South Asian girl at the protest complained about the young Arab American men at the protest who had their faces wrapped in kaffiyehs, concerned that they looked like 'terrorists' – given that the image of militant Islamism has largely been conflated with the iconic image of Palestinian fedayeen (fighters). She said, 'This is supposed to be a peaceful protest. I am going to tell the organizers to ask them to take it off!' The comment emerges from a political landscape where the performance of 'moderate'/good and 'angry'/bad Islam has shaped the expressions of public protest for Muslim American youth, as I have discussed elsewhere (Maira 2009). Solidarity is a structure of political feeling and can be infused with sentiments of anxiety, anger, frustration, fear, happiness, and empathy (Williams 1977). These emotions are variously expressed and translated into or borne out of political actions, producing the affective, moral and political registers of proper subjecthood for Muslim, Arab, South Asian, and Afghan American youth.

Aisha, for example, was frustrated with the absence of interest by others in the dispossession, displacement, and violence experienced by Palestinians. She became aware at an early age of the erasure of Palestine in the US mainstream media due to her own, invisibilized family history. She reflected: 'As a child, I was hanging out with my grandpa who was beaten by Israeli soldiers and his leg was injured, his front tooth was broken. . . . I was left wondering why this wasn't on the news, why people weren't talking about it. I felt I was growing up as a second-class citizen, I couldn't engage politically. These issues were real to me, but there was no place in society to talk about it'. Aisha's sense of exclusion from citizenship, and from participation in the body politic of the nation, was not just due to the denial of the Palestinian narrative in the USA but also the lack of a space to enter politics related to the Palestine question. In recent years, Palestine solidarity activism in the USA has grown, particularly on college campuses, with the emergence of a new generation of Palestinian and Arab American activists as well as the leadership of non-Palestinian/Arab (and non-Muslim) student activists, making this an increasingly prominent – if also intensely embattled – student movement and contributing to the Palestinianization of a new generation.

PALESTINIANIZATION

Palestine solidarity activism, including the rapidly expanding Boycott, Divestment, and Sanctions (BDS) movement in which many youth and college students have been involved, often relies on human rights discourse, based on the premise that Palestinians do not have the rights that they should and so must assert the right to claim rights (Isin and Ruppert 2015: 180). The Palestine solidarity movement in the USA is a cross-racial human rights movement that extends beyond Arab and Muslim American communities, but it is also a unifying axis for Muslim, Arab, South Asian, and Afghan American politics and a significant crucible for politicization of youth. It is important to consider the Palestine solidarity movement as an *anti-racist* movement that challenges racial violence against Palestinians and racist policies by the Israeli state, one that crosses boundaries of ethnicity, nationalism, religion, and class, though these various axes of mobilization may be variously highlighted or downplayed depending on the particular group or campaign. While faith-based groups might approach the Palestine issue primarily as an issue of 'Muslim rights', which generates an internationalist but not a universalist rubric, Palestinian solidarity campaigns also cross religious boundaries and generate alliances opposed to militarism, dispossession, apartheid, and colonialism. There is also a flourishing interfaith project that has drawn many youth into Jewish-Muslim and interfaith dialogue programmes since 9/11, including programmes focused on

Palestine-Israel that portray the issue as one of 'religious conflict' and 'tolerance'. As I discuss in the book, a liberal interfaith or cross-cultural approach to Palestinian rights uses a depoliticized model of 'co-existence' that evades political realities of colonialism and militarism through 'faithwashing' these structural realities and reducing them to a primordial, intractable conflict (Saeed 2014).

National, racial, and religious politics are variously negotiated in both faith and non-faith-based forms of organizing in support of Palestine by youth. Less attention, in fact, has been paid to the politicization of Christian Arab American youth whose experiences are often lost in the post-9/11 discourse that is heavily invested in the experiences of young Muslim Americans. While the War on Terror compelled some youth to focus on combating Islamophobia and turn to pan-Islamic solidarity, I found for some Arab Christian youth there was a turn to Arab nationalist politics, in addition to solidarity with Muslim Americans and civil rights activism. In general, the resurgence of Palestinian activism since 2001 has occurred as a new generation of Arab and Palestinian Americans has come of age, including many whose families are part of the old, well-established Palestinian Christian community in the Bay Area. During the second Intifada in Palestine that began in 2000, solidarity groups and SJP chapters were launched on college campuses, and Palestinian, Arab, and Muslim American youth began mobilizing in coalition with others, as the events of 9/11 precipitating an intensified focus on the Middle East. These two historical events, in Palestine and in the USA, converged to galvanize Palestine activism and the focus on human rights in the last decade of the old millennium.

It is striking that the Palestine issue is, according to many I spoke to, a focal point for Muslim American political identity. Bashir, a young Pakistani American man, observed: 'It's the single most important issue. And sometimes it's not realized how important it is, especially by certain governments. And again and again people say that if this is resolved, many things will be resolved.' As Bashir points out, concern about Palestine underlies much of the oppositional politics among Muslims (and Arabs) within the USA as well as globally, who are frustrated and outraged at the consistent US support and funding for the Israeli occupation. The issue of justice in Palestine is a political thread that also links older and younger generations of Muslim and Arab Americans. Furthermore, solidarity with the Palestinian struggle in Arab and Muslim American communities animates a pedagogy of political protest for youth as they confront the embargo on criticism of Israel in the USA. Marwa reminisced about her early encounters with anti-Palestinianism in school:

> One of the turning points of my life was . . . one of our teachers was . . . saying stuff about Palestine and suicide bombers, which I don't support, but like he made it sound like Palestinians are crazy and are terrorist. So I was only in 8th grade and I spoke out–because I am crazy–and I was like, 'Uhhh I think your wrong!' And then we kind of battled him out in class and then he was like . . . 'I'll give you twenty minutes in class next week to do a presentation'. And I was like, 'Okay!' And I started doing the presentations which really started my activism.

This early experience of being catapulted into political debate and activism due to racist and Orientalist assumptions of Palestinian/Arab irrationality and violence is common for many Arab and Muslim American youth (Salaita 2006). It is the question of Palestine that stands at the threshold of cultural and political assimilation for Arab, and in many cases, Muslim Americans, historically troubling the entry of these groups into easy identification with US imperial nationalism and white middle-class America. Linking the post-9/11 backlash to the Palestine question and the long history of anti-Arab racism situates what is usually glossed simply as Islamophobia in the deeper structure of repression created by the US state's involvement in the Middle East, and in relation to Arabophobia (see Maira and Shihade 2006).

Given this historical context, I argue that we need to consider the process of *Palestinianization*, or politicization around Palestinian identity and struggles, as a site of racialization that is endemic to US national culture due to the enduring alliance between the USA and Israel and the exceptional suppression of the Palestinian national struggle in the USA. Palestinianization is a process that overlaps with the anti-racist and anti-state politics of other groups subjected to racial violence, displacement, and genocide by the USA; it is not an exceptional site of counter-hegemonic race politics, of course, but it is one that has been heavily repressed in the USA and also (as a result) has been much less theorized in US scholarship, including on Muslim American youth. The definition of Palestinians as subjects who cannot have human rights has been consolidated through the permeation of Zionist discourse in US public culture, including in liberal domains such as higher education, which has normalized anti-Arab racism as it bleeds into Islamophobia (Salaita 2011).

REPRESSION AND 'RADICALISM'

Palestine activism is an important site where human rights organizing and discourse, and their slippages, have shaped political subjecthood for Muslim American youth in a climate of policing and surveillance of political movements related to the Middle East. Several young people talked about the hostility, racism, and silencing they encountered while trying to organize in support of Palestinian rights on their campuses or in the larger community. A young Egyptian American man, Abed, recalled that one of the few incidents of 'intolerance' that he had experienced in the Bay Area was, in fact, after a protest in San Francisco during the 'bombings in Gaza' in winter 2008–09. He was carrying a Palestinian flag and someone hit him and pushed him over in the street. Bashir talked about the backlash against MSA organizing in solidarity with Palestine at San Jose State University: 'We have events for Palestine. Unfortunately, these events have led some people to conclude that these Muslim groups are a terrorist front. It's sad because those people get their news from Fox News and they have strong racism and Islamophobia.' Bashir touched on an important aspect of anti-Palestinianism, that is, the moral panic whipped up about the 'radicalization' of Muslim and Arab American youth – especially in the right-wing media – is often accompanied by the charge that they are automatically anti-Semites if they are critical of the Israeli state's policies:

> We're not anti-Jewish or anti-Israel as we're called. . . . Even the left are called radical. Sometimes we're called terrorist sympathizers. I mean you have to be a strong person to stand up against these people, so there is discouragement.

Many young Muslim and Arab Americans worry about the real threat of vilification and intimidation if they publicly support Palestine and some distance themselves from a politics defined as 'radical', which has become a dirty word associated with 'bad' Muslim and Arab subjects. Bashir also pointed out that this defamation of radicalism targets not just the Palestine solidarity movement but the Left at large in a post-9/11 moment. As Ali Abunimah (2014: 171) incisively observes, the 'war on critics of Israel' is a 'war on the left more broadly'. This is a crucial issue, for the oppositional politics of Muslim, Arab, South Asian, and Afghan American youth inter-sects (but is not identical) with left movements in the USA, and is in transnational conversation with secular Left politics in the Middle East, yet it is often calibrated exclusively in relation to religious allegiances and politics. The machinery of repression counters the threat posed by transnational solidarities by stripping the category 'radical' of its progressive registers and re-appropriating it through the lexicon of counter-terrorism and 'jihadism'. There is thus an evacuation of the political critique suggested by 'radicalism' – whether for the Left or the Right – which is replaced with the connotation of violence, and also religious fundamentalism, in the security state's vocabulary of 'radicalization' and counter-radicalization of Muslim American youth.

In Palestinian rights activism in the USA, furthermore, the purportedly universalist language of rights operates on highly slippery, if not impossible, ground. Yara, an Iraqi American woman, organized a Middle East film series at Foothill College; however, a member of the Silicon Valley chapter of Hillel complained to her advisor that the films were 'pro-terrorist' and the speakers she had invited were 'anti-Semitic' – including, ironically, the Jewish American speakers. Yara also faced backlash from students who accused her of 'promoting hate' and being 'anti-American'. What is striking about this incident is the ways in which critiques of the violence of occupation and dispossession in Palestine was dismissed and suppressed by casting it as an expression of 'hate', a coded word that suggests an irrational affect that can spill over into a violent 'anti-Americanism', part of the liberal disciplinary discourse of the post-9/11 culture wars that targets selective regions, peoples, and struggles.

A pattern of systematic repression across the USA focused on youth and student activism related to Palestine solidarity and Palestinian rights, often involving the interventions of off-campus pro-Israel groups in campus affairs, is unfortunately by now quite well documented (see Barrows-Friedman 2014; Malek 2009; Salaita 2011).[2] At the University of California (UC)-Irvine, groups such as the Zionist Organization of America and the Jewish Federation of Orange County called for punishment and prosecution of the 11 students who protested the speech of the Israeli ambassador, a former Israeli soldier, after the 2008–09 war on Gaza. The Muslim Student Association at UC-Irvine was suspended, though they did not sponsor the protest, and 10 of the 'Irvine 11' students were convicted under the California Penal Code and disciplined by the university, despite the fact that they had staged an act of civil disobedience by disrupting the speech and then willingly accepting arrest (Abunimah 2014: 197–201). Similar cases of exceptional disciplining by universities of student protests in solidarity with Palestine have happened across the USA. Students attempting to mobilize around Palestine as a human rights issue thus do so in a fraught context of organized hostility to and criminalization of their activism which is viewed as 'uncivil', a deeply racialized term with troubling colonialist implications.

The impact of this demonization and repression enacted by powerful lobby groups, university administrations, and state agencies on youth movements and on Arab and Muslim American political subjecthood reveals the ways in which the neo-liberal university increasingly reflects the agenda of corporate and national interests (see Chatterjee and Maira 2014). The fear that Muslim, Arab, and Palestinian American students at UC campuses have about involvement with Palestinian rights activism and the worry that it will affect their educational and work opportunities was documented in a report to UC President Mark Yudof in 2012 by a cluster of civil rights organizations (including the Centre for Constitutional Rights, the Asian Law Caucus of San Francisco, and CAIR).[3] Furthermore, while post-9/11 profiling may rest heavily on the racialized and gendered imagery of young male terrorists, as the stories by youth here highlight, repression and censorship is felt equally by young women as well as men. I think this is a crucial point, for too often the issue of gender has been linked to the War on Terror by assuming that Muslim and Arab men are the only targets of profiling, and that Muslim and Arab women are only the victims of cultural and religious repression, or within a liberal narrative, of Islamophobia, but not targets of political repression.

Silicon Valley, due to the presence of significant Arab and Muslim American communities that have established major institutions (such as the Council of American-Islamic Relations and the Muslim Community Association) and a new generation of activists, has seen growing Palestine solidarity activism but also repression of this movement. At an event at San Jose State with Jewish American solidarity activists sponsored by the MSA in 2008, in which Bashir was involved, one Jewish American faculty member secretly photographed the activists and students, who were 'petrified' when they found out. After the students organized talks by Robert Fisk, the British journalist and author, and Norman Finkelstein, a Jewish American scholar, the same faculty member 'sent a 16-page dossier to all faculty' including photos, attacking these events, according to Ali, an Indian Muslim community and anti-war activist. Allegations were made to the administration that the event organizers 'were a terrorist organization and supported Hamas'. Bashir observed that Muslim American students felt they were 'being attacked' and discredited as terrorists simply for being 'young idealist people', but he commented thoughtfully, 'It gives us more motivation'. Repression can also fuel the urgency of resistance and greater solidarity but it is a site where the racialization of Muslim and Arab American activism and solidarity movements is acutely visible.

CONCLUSION

Palestinian rights activism in the USA is a site where Muslim and Arab American youth, and also others, confront the limitations of the liberal discourse of human rights, academic freedom, freedom of speech, and multi-cultural tolerance, a discourse bound up with a defence of the Israeli state that has come to define patriotic American-ness in the War on Terror. The mobilization by youth around international human rights issues such as Palestine, Iraq, and Afghanistan is also the link to the infringement of civil rights within the USA, for the demonization of Muslim and Arab American youth and activists as 'terrorist sympathizers' underlies the selective scrutiny of domestic political organizing and 'radicalization' in Muslim American communities.[4] The notion that Palestinian rights are indivisibly *human* rights is not legible within a mainstream, US-based rights framework due to the exceptionalism of USA and Israeli security discourse and a deeply Orientalist narrative about Islam, gender, and violence that continues to obscure US and Israeli colonial violence.

In some cases, in fact, a liberal model of civil rights provides an alibi for the failure of human rights discourse, given that criticism of Israel is deemed uncivil, if not automatically anti-Semitic – an affront to the multi-cultural humanism institutionalized on college campuses that represses critique of Israeli state policies or BDS activism by labeling it 'divisive' and racist (Salaita 2011). Critiques of racial discrimination and violence by Israel, ironically, are suppressed by casting them as expressions of racism. This inversion of racism is consistently produced within a multi-cultural politics, which obscures state racism and imperial violence.

I argue that the Palestinian exception to human rights and academic freedom reveals a crucial critique of the politics of human rights as it has shaped modern governmentality and demonstrates the hinge between imperial sovereignty, democracy, and surveillance. These young people enact what Rancière (2004: 304) describes as the political subjectivization of those who can 'confront the inscriptions of rights to situations of denial; they put together the world where those rights are valid and the world where they are not. The put together a relation of inclusion and exclusion'. It is the exceptions of rights that these young people expose that produce a political dissensus against the War on Terror, and the wars, occupations, and invasions conducted in the name of human rights in Palestine, Iraq, Afghanistan, and Pakistan. In doing so, they also complicate the problematic and racist discourse of counter-terrorism that rests on a reductive paradigm of 'good' (moderate) and 'bad' (militant) Muslims. Challenging these state paradigms that view Muslim American youth through the lens of securitization requires thinking of the conditions of insecurity and vulnerability that young people inhabit every day, as they attempt to demonstrate solidarities with those living in precarity and with violence in other places.

NOTES

1. 'Amnesty: U.S, Europe Shielding Israel Over Gaza War Crimes', *Haaretz*, 27 May 2010. http://www.haaretz.com/news/diplomacy-defense/amnesty-u-s-europe-shielding-israelover-gaza-war-crimes-1.292505.
2. See reports compiled by Palestine Solidarity Legal Support: http://palestinelegalsupport.org/news-and-updates/news-updates-archive/.
3. Ali Abunimah, 'Climate of Fear Silencing Palestinian, Muslim Students at UC Campuses, Rights Groups Warn', *Electronic Intifada*, 4 December 2012. http://electronicintifada.net/blogs/ali-abunimah/climate-fear-silencing-palestinian-muslim-students-university-california-rights.
4. The 1964 Civil Rights Act can now be used to deem illegal criticism of Israel as expressions of the 'new anti-Semitism' on college campuses and deny federal funding to universities (Barrows-Friedman 2014, p. 98).

REFERENCES

Abunimah, A. (2014). *The battle for justice in Palestine*. Chicago: Haymarket Books.

Barrows-Friedman, N. (2014). *In our power: U.S. students organize for justice in Palestine*. Charlottesville, VA: Just World Books.

Brown, W. (2004). The most we can hope for: Human rights and the politics of fatalism. *South Atlantic Quarterly, 103*(2/3), 451–463.

Chatterjee, P., & Maira, S. (2014). *The imperial University: Academic repression and scholarly dissent*. Minneapolis: University of Minnesota Press.

Isin, E., & Ruppert, E. (2015). *Being digital citizens*. London and New York: Rowman and Littlefield.

Kumar, D. (2012). *Islamophobia and the politics of empire*. Chicago: Haymarket.

Kundnani, A. (2014). *The Muslims are coming: Islamophobia, extremism, and the domestic war on terror*. London and New York: Verso.

Maira, S. (2009). 'Good' and 'bad' Muslim citizens: Feminists, terrorists, and U.S. orientalisms. *Feminist Studies, 35*(3), 631–656.

Maira, S. (2016). *The 9/11 generation: Youth, rights, and solidarity in the War on Terror*. New York and London: NYU Press.

Maira, S., & Shihade, M. (2006). Meeting Asian/Arab American studies. *Journal of Asian American Studies, 9*(2), ix–xiii 117–140.

Malek, A. (2009). *A country called Amreeka: U.S. history retold through Arab-American lives*. New York: Free Press.

Merry, S. (2006). Anthropology and international law. *Annual Review of Anthropology, 35*, 99–116.

Naber, N. (2012). *Arab America: Gender, cultural politics, and activism*. New York and London: NYU Press.

Rancière, J. (2004). Who is the subject of the rights of man? *South Atlantic Quarterly, 103*(2/3), 297–309.

Saeed, S. (2014, July 1). An interfaith Trojan horse: Faithwashing apartheid and occupation. *Islamic Monthly*. http://www.theislamicmonthly.com/an-interfaith-trojan-horse-faithwashing-apartheid-and-occupation/.

Said, E. (2000, Nov./Dec.). America's last taboo. *New Left Review, 6*, 45–53.

Salaita, S. (2006). *Anti-Arab racism in the U.S.A.: Where it comes from and what it means for politics today*. London: Pluto Press.

Salaita, S. (2011). *Israel's dead soul*. Philadelphia, PA: Temple University.

Williams, R. (1977). *Marxism and literature*. Oxford: Oxford University Press.

Sunaina Maira is Professor of Asian American Studies at the University of California, Davis. She is the author of *Desis in the House: Indian American Youth Culture in New York City* and *Missing: Youth, Citizenship, and Empire After 9/11*. Maira's recent publications include an edited volume, *The Imperial University: Academic Repression and Scholarly Dissent* (University of Minnesota Press) and *Jil [Generation] Oslo: Palestinian Hip-Hop, Youth Culture, and the Youth Movement*. Her new book project is a study of South Asian, Arab, and Afghan American youth and political movements focused on civil and human rights and issues of sovereignty and surveillance in the War on Terror.

CHAPTER 8

Schooling the Enemy Within: Politics and Pedagogy

Khawlah Ahmed

INTRODUCTION

With the so-called war on terror anything and everything that deals with Muslims and/or Islam has become a threat, even students. Schooling Muslim students in the USA and Europe has seemingly become a challenge. Those who were, just a decade or so ago, some of the top achievers with numbers ranking among the highest percentages of university candidates, competing in the fields of medicine, engineering, and the sciences, coming from some of the most law abiding, productive, and successful communities in society, have now become the new 'challenges', 'suspects', 'problems' and, let's not forget, 'potential jihadists' (see Sensoy and Stonebanks 2009; Shain 2011). Today governments and academic institutions seem confused as to what is going on and are at a loss as to how to deal with Muslim students who are members of communities deemed by powerful political discourse as the new 'enemy within'.

One is left wondering why these students, and the communities they belong to, have become the antagonist in the story on the war on terror. The reasons and interpretations are quite conflicting and just as enigmatic. A great deal of literature shows that this story is not simply a by-product of the 9/11 and 7/7 events. To some it is related to the age-old adage of Orientalism discourse,

K. Ahmed (✉)
American University of Sharjah, Sharjah, United Arab Emirates
e-mail: khawlah@aus.edu

© The Author(s) 2017
M. Mac an Ghaill, C. Haywood (eds.), *Muslim Students, Education and Neoliberalism*, DOI 10.1057/978-1-137-56921-9_8

revamping and reproducing itself (Said 2001) in the twenty-first century. It seemingly has to do with imperialism and globalization, where 'Imperialism is the project, globalization the process, culture the vehicle and the nation-state the political and military agent' (Sivanandan 2004: 34) and deals with 'white governmentality' being replaced with 'white control' in today's neoliberal society (Tyrer 2008: 50). For others it deals with a resurgence of the common evil/threat theory since the panic of the Cold War has come to an end, and new anxieties must be created. From British Member of Parliament Enoch Powell's 1968 speech that maintained there will be 'violent consequences of non-white immigration' to Margaret Thatcher's sympathy with Britons who are being 'swamped by an alien tide', to Jacques Chirac's speech in which he explained how the French worker will go 'crazy' when he sees the house next door 'piled-up' with a 'family with a father, three or four spouses and twenty children' along with 'the noise and the smell', it seems high time that an 'existential threat to a mythological national cohesion' (see Younge in the preface of Lentin and Titley 2011: vii) is created. And who better to fit the bill than the Muslims whose numbers have been increasing in the heart of Western societies at an alarming rate? To a few others, like Australia's Senator Bernardi, it is simple – Islam is the problem (Harvey and Lewis 2011). Whatever the reason, these students and their communities have officially been recognized and deemed the evil enemy of the West.

BEING PART OF THE 'ISLAM PROBLEMATIC':
THE 'MUSLIM PROBLEM'

Muslim students have, by virtue of association, found themselves part of, what has been referred to by many as the 'Islam problematic', the 'Muslim Question' that fervently needs to be dealt with by governments and agencies on international and domestic levels throughout the Western world. Relying on memetic warfare as the principal weapon in the 'war against evil' (see Crane 2012), powerful political discourse attempts to ingrain itself in the hearts and minds of the Western society that Muslims are, without doubt, the new enemy. Powerful governments have directly or indirectly stated that Muslims 'hate' the West because of their 'fear' of Western freedom and their 'envy' of their 'wealth' (see Cobb 2013). Western religious leaders have expressed their concern in regards to Islam trying to enforce its laws on Western democracies, values, and beliefs (see Bano 2008). The media, using the discourse of intolerance and Islamophobia rhetoric as part of a broader profit-making strategy, has gone out of its way to portray these Muslims as the dangerous, violent and angry 'enemy within' (Alexander 2005; Dwyer et al. 2008), and as the untrustworthy citizens who are subject to foreign allegiances with divided loyalties (Fekete 2008). Newspaper headlines confirm, in the UK for example, that 'Britain is becoming a country of ghettos', 'minorities do not want to be integrated', and soon there will be nothing but 'minority whites cities' (see Finney and Simpson 2009). There have been heated debates about ethnic segregation and fear of 'Muslim ghettos' (Carey 2008; Lord 2008) and 'no-go areas' (Nazir-Ali 2008). Even maps have done their part within the debate on race and ethnicity in countries like the UK and USA in portraying the demographic danger of such communities. Brown (2013) shows how 'media interpretations of population growth amongst ethnic minorities' usually rely 'on maps as key evidence for increasing ethnic or racial concentration, segregation or exclusion' (51). Brown (2013) explains that some of these maps are often distorted because they 'privilig[e] ethnic segregating and isolation' (54) and 'tend to visually suggest segregation through their focus on the special distribution of a single ethnic group' (51).

On the academic front, the picture is not much different. Academia is heading in the same direction since the powerful neoliberal ideology is now the most dominant ideology of the twenty-first century on the economic, social, and also on the academic fronts. In education, today's politics has become more pedagogical and education appears quite useful to those who are in power (Giroux 2004; McCafferty 2010). As Giroux (2004) explains:

> Central to the hegemony of neo-liberal ideology is a particular view of education in which market-driven identities and values are both produced and legitimated. Under such circumstances, pedagogy both within and outside of schools increasingly becomes a powerful force for creating the ideological and affective regimes central to reproducing neo-liberalism... [which] feeds a growing authoritarianism... steeped in religious fundamentalism and jingoistic patriotism, encouraging intolerance and hate as it punishes critical thought, especially if it is at odds with the reactionary religious and political agenda. (2004: 494)

Like the media discourse on the 'enemy within', education, from this neoliberal perspective, has also become market-driven. The impact of discourse, such as the discourse on the dangerous Muslim terrorist not integrating in Western societies (Kundnani 2007), has resulted in Western countries involving institutions, including universities, to try to 'identify sleepers of terrorist organizations' and 'track individuals presenting suspects' features', using 'criteria established at the national level', which included being 'Muslim' and 'current or former students' (De Schutter and Ringelheim 2008: 359). In many instances, as De Schutter and Ringelheim explain, 'persons were signaled out by law enforcement officers not because of their individual behavior but rather because of their ethnicity or religion' (2008: 359). Anything and everything that had any connection with being a 'Muslim' became a target, even Muslim community schools (see McCreery et al. 2007; Odone 2008; Halstead 2009). And, of course, a great deal of the wisdom behind these attacks was reflected in politics (Laborde 2008; Caldwell 2009; Thomas 2011). Muslim schools were now described as resisting the liberal West's influences (MacEoin 2009) posing challenges 'to our own educational beliefs and values' (McCreery et al. 2007: 203), social cohesion (Short 2002) and, of course, undermining the process of equipping Muslim students for life in today's modern Western societies (Smithers 2005). Though there were those who defended these schools (Halstead and McLaughlin 2005; Halstead 2005, 2009; Meer 2009) showing that such remarks are based on 'inaccurate and mischievous claims': (Halstead 2009: 50), education and academic curricula became politicized. And so, new educational policy emerged as a result of such discursive positioning, in the last decade, which set out to address the 'Muslim Question' through ethnic integration, segregation, and de-radicalization policies (Miah 2012).

Education became part of the government initiatives targeting communities to help counter-terrorism. Governments, like the UK, began to connect national security with educational policy (Taylor 2009) and using what has been described as 'softer' or more 'community-relations' approaches to fighting terrorism in the hopes of stopping the radicalization of Europe and America (Briggs et al. 2006; Silk 2010). Soon afterwards, some of these programmes, policies, and approaches, like the Prevent Strategy in the UK, even came under criticism for allegedly jeopardizing the integrity of teachers and teaching (Kundnani 2009), using communities and community outreach programmes as infiltration tools and networks to spy on these communities (Hewitt 2010), dividing members of these communities into 'good' and 'bad' Muslims (Aziz 2014), and presenting Muslim communities as 'suspect communities' (McGhee 2008: 8).

POWERFUL DISCOURSE, POWERFUL OUTCOMES

Such powerful discourse has influenced political agendas and policies across Western countries (see Brown 2007; Laborde 2008; Caldwell 2009; Thomas 2011) and has led to calls to 'stop the Islamization' and 'radicalization' of Europe and America (Jackson 2006, 2005). Not only that, in the 2016 presidential campaigns, hopeful US presidential candidates, like Donald Trump, are even calling for a 'ban' on Muslims from entering the USA. 'Islamophobia', which was officially recognized in The Runnymede Trust Report (1997) a decade or so ago as becoming 'part of everyday life in modern Britain' accompanied by a 'dislike' of Islam and Muslims that 'has become more explicit, more extreme and more dangerous', has now become a phenomenon that is 'more natural, more normal and because of this, far more dangerous' (Allen 2008: 32) than it was before 9/11 (Allen 2010). 'Islamofascism', which Marranci (2008) explains was coined in 1978 and brought into the academic world in 1990, has resurfaced again, and even universities in the USA and Europe are celebrating 'Islamo-Fascism Awareness Week'.

Using what Jackson (2005) refers to as the 'myth of exceptional suffering', Patel (2013) shows how the war on terror 'has been articulated in ways which produce a new mode of racism and ethnic discrimination' that has allowed 'discriminatory practices to continue in ever more intensified, state "legitimated" and publicly accepted ways' (34). This 'new popular racism' (Kundnani's 2001), or 'xeno-racism' (Fekete 2001; Sivanandan 2006), within the war on terror discourse has also produced a new mode of discrimination linked with a new approach of control, profiling, racial construction, and categorization (Patel and Tyrer 2011).

According to Younge (in the preface of Lentin and Titley 2011) the intentions behind all of these 'series of edicts, popular, political and judicial' is 'not to erase all differences but act as a filter for certain people who are considered dangerously different', 'pathologiz[ing]' their behaviours 'so that they might then be more easily particularized' (2011: vii). Those 'pathologized', today are the Muslims. And due to the escalation of terrorist acts in the name of Islam, as Younge explains, terror has come to lie in the anticipation of the 'next attack', the 'possibility that anyone may be a soldier in disguise, a sleeper among us, waiting to strike at the heart of our social slumber' (2011: vii). And of course, the orchestrator of the next attack, that soldier in disguise, that sleeper amongst society waiting to strike, is undoubtedly a Muslim. Such politically and culturally powerful discourse has not only officially created a new 'Other' (Razack 2008), but such 'radicalized narratives', presented in 'Public Spaces' have 'creat[ed] the conditions for the expulsion of the Other' (Cobb 2013: 135), that is, the Muslim.

New Identities, New Realities

Muslim students are official members of this new 'Other' which has enforced upon them, and their communities, new realities, and forged identities. Situated within a context where even the old enemies are seen in a much milder and favourable light, they are now the blacks of yesterday, the 'new brown' or 'brown bodies', the new criminals, representative of the 'ethnic deviant behavior', 'illegal bodies' that are posing a problem for 'community cohesion' (Modood 2010), the 'hyper-visible', the 'outsiders', the 'dangerous others', the 'hostile enemies' (Khoury 2009), and the anti 'white bodies' of European heritage and Christian faith (Patel 2013; Patel 2010). They have been initiated, against all odds, as members of a 'new terrorism' or 'Islamic terrorism' which is 'driven by hatred, fanaticism and extremism' (Jackson 2006: 11) where, compared to the 'old terrorism' represented by groups such as The Irish Republican Army (IRA) and Euskadi Ta Askatasuna (ETA), these groups are far more favourable. They are the 'homegrown terrorist' and 'the enemy within', the criminals behind what Gilroy (2006) refers to as the 'death of multiculturalism'. Muslim students, along with their communities, have been, as Fekete (2008, 2009) explains, removed from their social reality in the West and linked to a homogenous and repressive force of a global Islam, which she says is an illusion of unity and power that relates to a strategy for reworking of race in more cultural terms and redefining Muslim identities.

Also incorporated in the newer and more 'softer approaches' is the effort to assimilate and/or integrate Muslims in Western society, creating a new 'moderate Muslim', which according to Abbas (2007) is an example of good Muslim conduct that will be rewarded through patronage and incorporation. This new Muslim will follow the 'legitimate' Islam instead of the 'illegitimate Islam' (see Jackson 2006; Spalek and Imtoual 2007; Haddad and Golson 2007). What may be considered legitimate or moderate Muslims are seemingly what Haddad and Golson (2007: 488) refer to as 'Euro-friendly', 'acceptable' 'loyal Muslim citizens' who 'share European values'.

With the new identities, new realities have also kicked in. The new reality for Muslim students is that they are now part of a community that can be stopped and searched, detained without charge, and deported as a result of the counter-terrorism policies, laws, and bills. Islamophobia is not recognized in existing legislation on racism (Meer 2007), and those who have tried to rectify such state of affairs have not been dealt with kindly (Toynbee 2005).

THE QUESTION REMAINS

So the question for those government officials and academic institutions who are at a loss as to how to deal with the 'new enemy', the Muslim students, is: *Has such rhetoric and powerful political discourse, coming from governments, the media, and reverberating in society at large, including the curriculum and the classroom, had an effect on Muslim students?*

In terms of Muslim communities, in general, research shows that these new realities have taken their toll on Muslim individuals who are part of these 'suspect communities'. This has been reflected in their lives, in their family breakdown, their loss of jobs, and their ostracization in society (Spalek et al. 2009; Murray 2010) where 'even the most normative Muslim practices and beliefs' are seen 'as "anti-social" and "extreme"' leading to 'hard policing tactics' being applied to members of this community, especially young Muslim men who have 'been profiled and categorised as constituting a "problem group" and even a "fifth column enemy within" by media, politicians, the security services and criminal justice agencies' (Spalek and McDonald 2009: 124). As Patel (2012) explains, the "selective nature and suspect marking powers of surveillance" are not only powerful means of creating and strengthening negative labels, but they signal such individuals as "suspicious bodies," or "dirty bodies" which in turn can destroy their social identify and further jeopardizing these individuals to "devaluation, discrimination and disadvantage" (p. 217).

These new realities have increased feelings of fear and insecurity within these communities and within their lives (Staeheli and Nagel 2009). Individuals in these communities have become part of a powerless group in society, with deviant labels, which according to Mathur (2006) have had powerful ramifications, where some of those who were arrested and detained for many years after 9/11, and who were cleared of all links to terrorism, were unable to resume their normal lives, even when they left the West and returned back to their native homelands because "the presumption of guilt followed them" (p. 32). In a study conducted on university Muslim students across the UK, Hussain (2008) shows that the majority of the students surveyed expressed concerns regarding faith issues, anxiety regarding universities spying on them, and some being signalled out by university personnel. Research has shown that many Muslim students have become victims of violence and discrimination within the academic context (see Moore 2009; Merry 2005). From verbal to physical assaults, students have endured their fair share of wrath, as the new scapegoats of society. Mossalli (2009) shows how even teachers have contributed to this abuse, as the second-grade teacher who waved a piece of pork in a Muslim child's face arguing that it is not going to bite him. Some end up distancing themselves from their religious and ethnic identities (Mourchid 2009). Others are forced to adopt coping strategies to navigate the 'volume of dominant societal messages' (Sensoy and Stonebanks 2009: xii) inside and outside the classroom.

In general, research shows the importance of one's 'various self-definitions' being 'recognized and respected in public spaces' because of its importance for 'one's citizenship behaviours' (Blackwood et al. 2015: 123). It also shows that 'othering' and 'misrecognition' problematizes not only a person's national identity but a variety of other identities which 'cannot just be assumed or taken, but must also be conferred' (Blackwood et al. 2015: 164). Heine et al. (2006) say that if a person's 'sense of meaning' is in any way 'threatened' they will reaffirm alternative representations as a way of regaining meaning. Davydov's (1995) interpretation of Vygotsky's psychological development theory shows that the development of human personality takes place during a person's upbringing and teaching where the social milieu and healthy psychological development are crucial foundations. According to Vygotsky, every function in the cultural development leading to individual consciousness appears twice: The first is on the social plane, the second on the psychological plane; that is first between people and then inside the individual.

Now, if in the West, as Younge (see preface of Lentin and Titley 2011) shows, 'The combined effect' of all these 'flawed distinctions and sweeping demonization has unleashed a series of moral panics', resulting in national referendum banning the building of minarets in countries that had only four (as is the case in Switzerland in 2009), calls for bans on sharia law even though Muslims comprise less than 0.1 per cent of the population (as in Oklahoma in the USA in 2010), and parliaments seriously considering banning the burka worn by fewer than 50 women in the entire country of the Netherlands (p. vii), and within this atmosphere of fear and the 'permission to hate' (Perry 2001: 179), need we ask *what or how has all of this affected young Muslim students?* I leave that to the bewildered governments and academic institutions to answer.

CONCLUSION

Many, whether in governments and academic institutions, or society at large, fail to realize that if there are to be any spaces of hope (Phillips 2009) for Muslim students and their communities in the West, or today's multi-cultural societies in general, solutions are needed that are going to heal societies and not divide them further apart, like the demonizing political discourse and distorted media representation and information. These solutions may be sought whether in social contact theories (Cantle 2008; Thomas 2011) or through integration processes (see Hewstone 2006, 2009). But in doing so, what needs to be understood is that if the relationship between, for example, education and citizenship is to be considered, then inclusive communication and collective problem-solving rather than 'shared values' (Diwan 2008) need to come into the equation, instead of the residential 'white flights' (Dench et al. 2006), 'white terror' (Abbas 2013) or 'othering' and ethnic segregation.

There is a great deal of media and political rhetoric which has stigmatized Muslim students and their communities describing them as 'the enemy within', the 'homegrown' terrorists, as if this is a given, but not many have seriously addressed or attempted to approach the topic of how or who has placed them in such positions, and study the effects that such a position has had on them. Despite the abundance of rhetoric on 'terrorism' and a so-called 'enemy', there is very little discussion in the curriculum or classroom on such topics (see Al-Jaber 2012).

There is a great deal of inequality and double standards when dealing with Muslims, whether it is at the level of governments, society at large, or, in classrooms. Even the term 'Muslim', according to Appleton's study (2005), has come to be used as a 'code word' for 'terrorist', or 'Muslim fundamentalist', or 'Al Qaeda sympathizer'. But as Appleton explains, only the term 'Muslim terrorist' has become commonly used, whereas other 'terrorists' who have 'misused' other religions, such as apocalyptic cults in the USA or Japan, are not similarly labelled with terms such as 'Christian terrorists'.

There is a great deal of information presented on Muslims and Islam that has been distorted by political discourse, media, and even those who claim to be Muslims, yet have nothing in common with Islam. Such distortion and demonization has worked in favour of these so-called Muslim groups that go by the name of Islam, and who have interpreted Islam based on their own whims and political agendas. There are many injustices that have been done to a world religion that deems the killing of one person as the killing of all of mankind.

Finally, I end with Cobb (2013) who says 'In symmetry with the destructive force of what this narrative affords or makes possible in terms of violence, it is equivalently violent in terms of what it constrains – we in the West are disabled from exploring the Other(s) in all their complexity, doomed in a very tragic sense, to create the enemy we then seek to destroy' (2013: 4).

REFERENCES

Abbas, T. (2007). *Islamic political radicalism: A European perspective*. Edinburgh: Edinburgh University Press.

Abbas, M. (2013). White terror in the 'war on terror'. *Critical Race and Whiteness Studies*, 9(1). [Online] Available from http://www.acrawsa.org.au/files/ejour nalfiles/195Abbas20131.pdf. [Accessed: 6th December 2015].

Alexander, C. (2005). Embodying violence: 'Riots', Dis/order and the private lives of the Asian Gang. In C. Alexander & C. Knowles (Eds.), *Making race matter: Bodies, space and identity* (pp. 199–217). Basingstoke: Palgrave.

Al-Jaber, H. (2012). *Terrorism and counter-terrorism: Young people's perspectives*. *Arches Quarterly*, 5(9), 146–152.

Allen, C. (2008). K.I.S.S. (Keeping Islamophobia Simple & Stupid). Centre for Ethnicity and Racism Studies (CERS), University of Leeds. [Online] Available from: http://www.sociology.leeds.ac.uk/assets/files/research/cers/Islamophobia%20Symposium%20Papers%20e-working%20paper%20%283%29.pdf#page=48. [Accessed: 10th November 2015].

Allen, C. (2010). Contemporary Islamophobia before 9/11: A brief history. *Arches Quarterly*, 4(7), 14–22.

Appleton, M. (2005). The political attitudes of Muslims studying at British universities in the post-9/11 world. *Journal of Muslim Minority Affairs*, 25(3), 299–316.

Aziz, S. F. (2014). Policing terrorists in the community. *Harvard National Security Journal*, 5, 147–224.

Bano, S. (2008). Islamophobia and the law. Thinking Thru' Islamophobia Symposium Papers. *Centre for Ethnicity & Racism Studies* (CERS). Available from: http://www.sociology.leeds.ac.uk/assets/files/research/cers/Islamophobia%20Symposium%20Papers%20e-working%20paper%20%283%29.pdf. [Accessed: 15th September 2015].

Blackwood, L., Hopkins, N., & Reicher, S. D. (2015). Critical race and whiteness studies. *Journal of Social and Political Psychology, 3*(2), 148–170.

Briggs, R., Fieschi, C., & Lownsbrough, H. (2006). *Bringing it home: Community based approaches to counter terrorism.* London: Demos.

Brown, G. (2007). Making ethnic citizens: The politics and practice of education in Malaysia. *International Journal of Educational Development, 27*, 318–330.

Brown, L. (2013). The role of technology: 'Mapping ethnic segregation and diversity in a digital age'. *Ethnicity and Race in a Changing World, 4*(1), 51–57.

Caldwell, C. (2009). *Reflections on the revolution in Europe: Immigration, Islam, and the West.* London: Allen Lane.

Cantle, T. (2008). *Parallel lives – the development of community cohesion.* Retrieved from http://tedcantle.co.uk/pdf/Parallel%20lives%20Ted%20Cantle.pdf. [online]. [Accessed: 3rd December 2015].

Carey, J. (2008). A cultural approach to communication. In J. W. Carey (Ed.), *Communication as culture: Essays on media and society* (pp. 11–28). New York: Routledge.

Cobb, S. (2013). *Speaking of violence: The politics and poetics of narrative in conflict resolution.* Oxford and New York: Oxford University Press.

Crane, D. (2012). A grand American strategy of counter-terrorism. *Arches Quarterly, 5*(9), 28–38.

Davydov, V. V. (1995). The influence of L.S. Vygotsky on education: Theory, research, and practice. *Educational Researcher, 24*(3), 12–21.

De Schutter, O., & Ringelheim, J. (2008). Ethnic profiling: A rising challenge for European human rights law. *Modern Law Review, 78*(3), 358–384.

Dench, G., Gavron, K., & Young, M. (2006). *The new east end: Kinship, race and conflict.* London: Profile Books.

Diwan, K. (2008). *Education for inclusive citizenship.* London: Routledge.

Dwyer, C., Shah, B., & Sanghera, G. (2008). From cricket lover to terror suspect – challenging representations of young British Muslim men. *A Journal of Feminist Geography, 15*(2), 117–136.

Fekete, L. (2001). The emergence of xeno-racism. *Race and Class, 43*(2), 23–40.

Fekete, L. (2008). Islamophobia: Europe's new McCarthyism. Thinking Thru' Islamophobia Symposium Papers. Centre for Ethnicity & Racism Studies (CERS). Available from: http://www.sociology.leeds.ac.uk/assets/files/research/cers/Islamophobia%20Symposium%20Papers%20e-working%20paper%20%283%29.pdf

Fekete, L. (2009). *A suitable enemy: Islamophobia and Xeno-racism in Europe*. London: Pluto Press.

Finney, N., & Simpson, L. (2009). *Sleepwalking to segregation: Challenging myths about race and migration*. Bristol: Policy Press.

Gilroy, P. (2006). Multiculture in times of war: An inaugural lecture given at the London school of economics. *Critical Quarterly, 28*(4), 27–45.

Giroux, A. (2004). Public pedagogy and the politics of neo-liberalism: Making the political more pedagogical. *Policy Futures in Education, 2*(3). Retrieved from http://www.cws.illinois.edu/iprhdigitalliteracies/girouxpublicpfine2004.pdf [Accessed 5th December 2015].

Haddad, Y., & Goldson, T. (2007). Overhauling Islam: Representation, construction, and cooption of "moderate Islam" in Western Europe. *Journal of Church and State, 49*(3), 487–515.

Halstead, J. M. (2005). Islam, homophobia and education: A reply to Michael Merry. *Journal of Moral Education, 34*(1), 37–42.

Halstead, J. M. (2009). In defence of faith schools. In G. Haydon (Ed.), *Faith in education: A tribute to Terence McLaughlin*. London: Institute of Education.

Halstead, J. M., & McLaughlin, T. (2005). Are faith schools divisive? In J. Cairns, R. Gardner, & D. Lawton (Eds.), *Faith schools: Consensus or conflict?* London: Routledge.

Harvey, M., & Lewis, S. (2011). Islam's the problems, not Muslims, says Senator Cory Bernardi. *Herald Sun*. [Online]. Available from: http://www.news.com.au/national/islams-the-problems-not-muslims-says-senator-cory-bernardi/story-e6frfkvr-1226008540417. [Accessed: 12th November 2011].

Heine, S. J., Proulx, T., & Vohs, K. D. (2006). The meaning maintenance model: On the coherence of social motivations. *Personality and Social Psychology Review, 10*(2), 88–110.

Hewitt, S. (2010). *Snitch! A history of the modern intelligence informer*. London: Continuum.

Hewstone, M. (2006). Living apart, living together? The role of inter-group contact in social integration. *British Academy*. doi:10.5871/bacad/9780197264584.003.0009

Hewstone, M. (2009). *Living apart, living together? The role of intergroup contact in social integration*. [Online] Available from: http://www.mmg.mpg.de/fileadmin/user_upload/documents/wp/WP_09-12_Hewstone_Intergroup-contact.pdf [Accessed: 3rd December 2015].

Hussain, S. (2008). *Muslims on the map: A National Survey of Social Trends in Britain*. London: International Library of Human Geography. IB Tauri.

Jackson, R. (2005). *Writing the war on terrorism: Language, politics and counter-terrorism*. Manchester: Manchester University Press.

Jackson, R. (2006). Religion, politics and terrorism: A critical analysis of narratives of 'Islamic terrorism'. *Centre for International Politics Working Paper Series No. 21.* [Online]. Available from: http://www.socialsciences.manchester.ac. uk/disciplines/politics/about/themes/cip/publicatio9s/documents/ Jackson_000.pdf. [Accessed: 10th November 2015].

Khoury, L. J. (2009). *Racial profiling as dressage: A social control regime! African Identities,* 7(1), 55–70.

Kundnani, A. (2001). *In a foreign land: The new popular racism. Race and Class,* 43(2), 41–60.

Kundnani, A. (2007). *The end of tolerance.* London: Pluto Press.

Kundnani, A. (2009). *Spooked! How not to prevent violent extremism.* London: Institute of Race Relations.

Laborde, C. (2008). *Critical republicanism.* Oxford: Oxford University Press.

Lentin, A., & Titley, B. (2011). *The crises of multiculturalism: Racism in a neoliberal age.* London: Zed Books.

Lord, C. (2008). Are we promoting harmony or Muslim ghettos? Retrieved from: http://www.telegraph.co.uk/news/uknews/1578216/Are-we-promoting-harmony-or-Muslim-ghettos.html.

MacEoin, D. (2009). *The Hijacking of British Islam: How extremist literature is subverting mosques in the UK.* London: Policy Exchange, 2007.

Marranci, G. (2008). A wolf in sheep's clothing: The neologism 'Islamofascism.' Retrieved from http://www.sociology.leeds.ac.uk/assets/files/research/ cers/Islamophobia%20Symposium%20Papers%20e-working%20paper%20% 283%29.pdf#page=8. [Retrieved on 10 November 2015].

Mathur, S. (2006). Surviving the Dragnet: 'Special interest' detainees in the US after 9/11. *Race and Class,* 47(3), 31–46.

McCafferty, P. (2010). Forging a 'neoliberal pedagogy': The 'enterprising education' agenda in schools. *Critical Social Policy,* 30(4), 541–563. [Online] Retrieved from http://www.sagepub.com/sites/default/files/upm-binaries/ 52409_Forging_a_neoliberal_pedagogy___The_enterprising_education_ agenda_in_schools.pdf [Assessed: 3rd December, 2015].

McCreery, E., Jones, L., & Holmes, R. (2007). Why do Muslim parents want Muslim schools? *Journal of International Research and Development,* 27(3), 203–219.

McGhee, D. (2008). *The end of multiculturalism: Terrorism, integration and human rights.* Berkshire: Open University Press.

Meer, N. (2007). Less equal than others. *Index on Censorship,* 36(2), 112–126.

Meer, N. (2009). Identity articulations, mobilisation and autonomy in the movement for Muslim Schools in Britain. *Race, Ethnicity and Education,* 12(3), 379–398.

Merry, M. S. (2005). Social exclusion of Muslim youth in Flemish- and French-speaking Belgian schools. *Comparative Education Review,* 49(1), 19–36.

Miah, S. (2012). Muslim discourses on integration and schooling. Doctoral thesis, University of Huddersfield. Retrieved from http://eprints.hud.ac.uk/17536/.

Modood, T. (2010). Still not easy being British: Struggles for a multicultural citizenship. *Trentham Books.*

Moore, J. R. (2009). Why religious education matters: The role of Islam in multicultural education. *Multicultural Perspectives, 11*(3), 139–145.

Mossalli, N. N. (2009). The voice of a covered Muslim-American teen in a southern public school. In O. Sensoy & C. D. Stonebanks (Eds.), *Muslim voices in school: Narratives of identity and pluralism* (pp. 55–70). Rotterdam: Sense Publishers.

Mourchid, Y. (2009). Left to my own devices: Hybrid identity development of religion and sexual orientation among Muslim students in the United States. In O. Sensoy & C. D. Stonebanks (Eds.), *Muslim voices in school: Narratives of identity and pluralism* (pp. 99–116). Rotterdam: Sense Publishers.

Murray, N. (2010). Profiling in the age of total information awareness. *Race and Class, 52*(3), 3–24.

Nazir-Ali, M. (2008). Extremism flourished as UK lost Christianity. *Telegraph.*

Odone, C. (2008). *In bad faith: The new betrayal in faith schools.* London: Centre for Policy Studies.

Patel, S. (2010). Where are the settlers of colour? Upping the Anti 10. http://uppingtheanti.org/journal/article/10-where-are-the-settlers-of-colour/

Patel, T. (2013) Ethnic Deviant Labels within a Terror-Panic Context: Excusing White Deviance. *Ethnicity and Race in a Changing World. 4*(1), 34–49. doi: 10.7227/ercw.4.1.3.

Patel, T. G. (2012). Surveillance, suspicion and stigma: Brown bodies in a terror-panic climate. *Surveillance & Society, 10*(3), 215–234. Retrieved from http://ezproxy.aus.edu/login?url=http://search.proquest.com/docview/1314733034?accountid=16946

Patel, T. G., & Tyrer, D. (2011). *Race, crime and resistance.* London: Sage.

Perry, B. (2001). *In the name of hate: Understanding hate crimes.* New York: Routledge.

Phillips, R. (Ed.). (2009). *Muslim spaces of hope: Geographies of possibility in Britain and the West.* Zed: London.

Razack, S. (2008). *Casting out: The eviction of Muslims from Western law and politics.* Toronto: Toronto University Press.

RUNNYMEDE TRUST. (1997). *Islamophobia: A challenge for us all.* London: Runnymede Trust.

Said, E. W. (2001). *Orientalism: Western conceptions of the orientalism.* London: Penguin Group.

Sensoy, O., & Stonebanks, C. D. (Eds.). (2009). *Muslim voices in school: Narratives of identity and pluralism.* Rotterdam: Sense Publishers.

Shain, F. (2011). *The New folk devils: Muslim boys and education in England.* Stoke-on-Trent: Trentham.

Short, G. (2002). Faith-based schools: A threat to social cohesion? *Journal of Philosophy of Education, 36*(4), 559–572.

Silk, P. D. (2010). Planning outreach between Muslim communities and police in the USA and the UK. (Unpublished doctoral dissertation). University of Georgia, Athens, Georgia.

Sivanandan, A. (2004, October 29). Racism in the age of globalisation. *Institute of Race Relations.* [Online] Available from: http://www.irr.org.uk/news/racism-in-the-age-of-globalisation/http://www.irr.org.uk/2004/october/ha000024.html. [Accessed: 12th September 2015].

Sivanandan, A. (2006). Race, terror and civil society. *Race and Class, 47*(1), 1–8.

Smithers, R. (2005). Anger at Muslim schools attack claims by education chief 'derogatory'. *Guardian,* [Online] Available from: http://www.guardian.co.uk/uk/2005/jan/18/schools. faithschools [Accessed: 15th September 2015].

Spalek, B., & Imtoual, A. (2007). "Hard' approaches to community engagement in the UK and Australia: Muslim communities and counter-terror responses'. *Journal of Muslim Minority Affairs, 27*(2), 185–202.

Spalek, B., & McDonald, L. Z. (2009). Terror crime prevention: Constructing Muslim practices and beliefs as 'anti-social' and 'extreme' through CONTEST 2. *Social Policy and Society, 9*(1), 123–132.

Spalek, B., El Awa, S., & McDonald, L. Z. (2009). *Police-Muslim engagement and partnerships for the purposes of counter terrorism: An examination.* London: Arts and Humanities Research Council and Birmingham, University of Birmingham.

Staeheli, L., & Nagel, R. (2009). Rethinking security: Perspectives from Arab-American and British Arab Activists. *Antipode.* pp. 780–801. Available from: http://search.ebscohost.com.ezproxy.aus.edu/login.aspx?direct=true&db=aph&AN=34805477&site=ehost-live. [Accessed: 12th September 2015].

Taylor, C. (2009). *A good school for every child: How to improve our schools.* London: Routledge.

Thomas, P. (2011). *Youth, multiculturalism and community cohesion.* Basingstoke: Palgrave Macmillan.

Toynbee, P. (2005, June 10). My right to offend a fool. *The Guardian.*

Tyrer, D. (2008). The unbearable whiteness of seeing: moderated Muslims, (in)/visibilities and Islamophobia. Thinking Thru' Islamophobia Symposium Papers. *Centre for Ethnicity & Racism Studies* (CERS). Available from: http://www.sociology.leeds.ac.uk/assets/files/research/cers/Islamophobia%20Symposium%20Papers%20e-working%20paper%20%283%29.pdf. [Accessed: 12th November 2015].

Khawlah Ahmed has a PhD in English with a minor in TESOL, a Masters in English Education and a BA in English Literature with a minor in Sociology. Her research interests include examining new approaches/theories of teaching that facilitate teaching and learning, curriculum development, intercultural communication, and culturally relevant pedagogy. She has worked in the USA and MENA region in capacities ranging from education specialist, computer management instructor, to Administrator (as Dean and Associate Dean), Director, Coordinator, faculty member in undergraduate and graduate levels, associate editor of an international journal, member of numerous editorial/review boards for research grants, scholarly journals, and international associations.

CHAPTER 9

The Prevent Policy and the Values Discourse: Muslims and Racial Governmentality

Shamim Miah

INTRODUCTION

The Counter-Terrorism and Securities Act (2015) has raised a number of important questions relating to the government's counter-terrorism strategy and schooling. Section 26 of the Act places statutory duties for all schools (including nursery schools) to exercise 'due regard to the need to prevent people from being drawn into terrorism'. The government's revised Prevent policy (HM Government 2011) published as part of the Contest 2 (HM Government 2011) strategy defines extremism as 'vocal or active opposition to fundamental British values (FBV)', and these non-negotiable British values include 'democracy, the rule of law, individual liberty and mutual respect and tolerance of different faiths and beliefs'. In fact, the new guidance (Department of Education 2015) issued to schools in July 2015 urges schools to play an active role in promoting British values through the school curriculum. It also advises school teachers to 'identify pupils who may be at risk to radicalization' and also demands schools to build pupil resilience to radicalisation by promoting 'FBV'.

S. Miah (✉)
School of Education, University of Huddersfield, Huddersfield, UK
e-mail: s.miah@hud.ac.uk

© The Author(s) 2017
M. Mac an Ghaill, C. Haywood (eds.), *Muslim Students, Education and Neoliberalism*, DOI 10.1057/978-1-137-56921-9_9

131

The Prevent strategy has generated considerable attention within academic (Husband and Alam 2011; Thomas 2009) and public discourse (Birt 2009; Dodd 2009). This chapter will highlight how the Prevent policy within educational discourse not only responds to radicalisation through racialised biopolitics, but more critically it does this through blurring the boundaries between education, securitisation and counter-terrorism. Paradoxically, these policies have been developed and implemented at a time when neo-liberal discourse has signalled the notion of the 'post-racism' within political discourse (Kapoor et al. 2013).

PREVENT AS RACIAL GOVERNMENTALITY

The relationship between Muslims, securitisation and racial governmentality has a long and complicated history principally linked with colonialism and the 'politics of the Empire' (Said 1978; Kumar 2012). Whilst the idea of 'race' has long been a contested term (Rex 1986), nevertheless, it is clear that Muslims have long been marked not only as a religious group but also as a *'racial'* group (Meer 2014; Soyer 2014). The premise of racial governmentality is linked to the *racial state*, whereby the politics of race is very much 'integral to the emergence, development, transformations of the modern nation-states' (Goldberg 2002: 4). The defining, overseeing, regulating, governing and managing of racial matters through disciplinary practices are at the core of racial governmentality (Goldberg 2002). In short, racial states 'define populations into racially identified groups, and they do so more or less through census taking, law and policy in and through bureaucratic forms, and administrative practices' (Goldberg 2002: 110).

The sociology of race and schooling in the UK has long been associated with a number of diverse themes, including racism (MacDonald 1989; Gillborn 1995, 2008), racial inequality (Tronya 1987; Swann 1985), identity (Mirza 1992; Shain 2003, 2011), masculinities (Sewall 1996; Mac an Ghaill 1994), citizenship and integration (Mullard 1982; Diwan 2008; Miah 2015b). In recent years there has been a marked shift in educational policy to an over securitised model of schooling in matters of race; these have largely been shaped by local and international events (Miah 2014; Bhattacharyya 2013; Kalra and Mehmood 2014).

The local events are shaped by the Trojan Horse saga associated with the state schools in Birmingham and the 'concerns' relating to the strategy of Muslim 'entryism' predicated upon radicalisation and Islamist politics. The process of 'entryism', according to the latest counter-extremism strategy occurs 'when extremist individuals, groups and organisations consciously seek to gain positions of influence to better enable them to promote their own extremist agendas' (HM Government 2015: 19). For the government and other political actors, the 'entryism' linked to the 'Trojan Horse' saga associated with the Birmingham schools represents a worrying trend of creeping 'Islamification' of publicly funded schools (Clarke 2014; Kershaw 2014; Cameron 2015; Gove 2014). For others, the story signifies the racial patholigisation of Britain's Muslim communities (Miah 2015b), especially given the fact that the Education Select Committee, having considered evidence from a range of experts including the Chief Executive of Birmingham City Council, Sir Michael Wilshaw (Ofsted), Secretary of State for Education, Nicky Morgan MP, Ian Kershaw, Birmingham City Council's Independent Adviser, Peter Clarke, Education Commissioner for Birmingham, Lee Donaghy, Assistant Principle of the Park View Academy and others made the following conclusion:

> The Trojan Horse affair epitomises many of the questions and concerns expressed elsewhere about the changing school landscape and the overlapping roles of the organisations responsible for oversight of schools. No evidence of extremism or radicalisation, apart from a single isolated incident, was found by any of the inquiries and there was no evidence of a sustained plot nor of a similar situation pertaining elsewhere in the country. (House of Commons, 2015: 3)

These national concerns were raised following the events of the Arab Spring, the civil war in Syria and the subsequent rise of Islamic State in Iraq and Syria (ISIS) and the politics of the Islamic State (Cockburn 2015; Weiss and Hasan 2015; McCants 2015; Atwan 2015). It is estimated by the International Centre for the Study of Radicalisation (ICSR) that during the period of late 2011 to 10 December 2013, between 3,300 and 11,000 individuals have travelled to Syria to fight against the Assad government. The ICSR also indicates that between 396 and 1,937 recruits came from Europe; representing 18 per cent of the foreign fighters in Syria with significant fighters from France (63–412), Britain (43–366) and Germany (934–240) (cited in House of Commons, Home Affair Select Committee 2014: 17). Furthermore, some of them travelling to ISIS territory have been school-aged children travelling with families, such as the nine children taken by their mothers in the Bradford case (Halliday et al. 2015), and also the events involving four teenage school friends, between the ages of 15 and 16 years old, leaving to join the Islamic State (Benhold 2015) have made the question of radicalisation a key government priority. Whilst the interest of Muslims and ISIS has often been seen through a linear connection between Islamist ideology, the connection between the two is slightly more complex than what is often projected (Kundnani 2014).

These events signified a radical shift away from the politics of racial inequality/multi-culturalism to racialised politics of racial governmentality. A clear example of how minority communities are racialised and also criminalised can be seen through the politics associated with *Prevent* as an educational policy discourse. The debate around *Prevent* within schooling demonstrates the inter-connected nature between the state and its racialised subjects that has a long and complicated history (Hall et al. 1978).

The key questions arising from the above debates have ultimately been the government's response that has taken an institutional and disciplinary nature. One of the answers to this question of governing Muslims has ultimately been through the power of discourse (Ball 2013); in this particular case it has been revolved around the discourses associated with loyalty, citizenship and patriotism. Whilst this values discourse has been at the centre of the government's counter-terrorism and de-radicalisation strategy and an apparent theme of Prime Minister's David Cameron's most recent speech at the GLOBSEC 2015 – Global Security Conference, held in Bratislava (Cameron 2015). In fact, the values discourse takes on the form of racial governmentality, as it aims to govern Muslim subjects through the rhetorical features of discourse and policy. These discourses have a long history within UK racial politics and they draw upon the same logic of *spatial segregation*, as noticed in 2001 race riots debate, leading to urban disorder, with the view that cultural self-segregation contributed towards the London bombing (Miah 2015b).

In response to the terrorism and extremism agenda, the government published one of its central programmes in tackling *violent* extremism, in which it recognised in light of the taskforce report that not all forms of extremism should be the target of policy – only violent forms of extremism. *Preventing Violent Extremism: Winning Hearts and Minds* was published by the Department of Communities and Local Government (DCLG) in April 2007. The Prevent approach was part of CONTEST Strategy an overarching government approach to counter-terrorism, initially developed in 2003, and later revised in 2006, 2009 and more recently in 2011.

As the title of the above Prevent programme demonstrates, the government was interested in winning 'hearts and minds' of British Muslims away from the violent extremist narrative of the al-Qaeda. One of the central features of the government *'hearts and minds'* is its discourses on integration, which is articulated through the prism of British values debate which draws upon the ideas of Britishness and neo-liberalism.

The *Prevent* strategy is seen by many as one of the key features of government counter-terrorism policies; it has come to reflect government's *soft* approach to counter-terrorism which aims at tackling self-segregation through education and community development. It is hoped that this approach will complement the government's *hard* approach, which involves responding to acts of criminal violence by the Police, Counter-terrorism officials and most crucially a raft of anti-terror legislations, including the Crime and Security Act 2001 (connected with the internment of foreign national terror suspects), the Prevention of Terrorism Act 2005 (placing terror suspects under control orders), the Terrorism Act 2006 (clamping down on extremist influences with the introduction of acceptable and unacceptable behaviours), the Counter-Terrorism and Securities Act 2015 (that places a public duty on schools etc. to prevent extremism) and the pending Extremism Bill which was mentioned in the recent Queen's Speech that aims to extend further powers to the Home Secretary to ban extremist groups.

The CONTEST strategy was revised in 2009 (often referred to as Contest 2), which further intensified the grip on Muslim communities by extending surveillance and governance to target any verbal expression of dissent associated with or questioning or even undermining secular liberal values. The emphasis on non-violent extremism linked to notions of Britishness or 'FBV' marked a significant shift away from the discourses of violent extremism as enshrined in the Contest 1 logic. This is clearly demonstrated below:

> We will also continue to challenge views which fall short of supporting violence and are within the law, but which reject and undermine our shared values and jeopardise community cohesion – the strong and positive relationships between people of different ethnic, faith and cultural backgrounds in this country. Some of these views can create a climate in which people may be drawn into violent activity. (HM Government 2011: 88)

The focus on Muslim communities shifted significantly from a legalistic approach to counter-terrorism, as identified with the Contest 1 (HM Government 2006), whereby the emphasis was placed upon tackling violent extremism, either through actively promoting, propagating or participating in *violent* extremism. Contest 2, however, viewed challenges to FBV as deeply problematic. Indeed, the idea of FBV as a guiding principle of counter-terrorism strategy reflects wider political debates and a broader integration agenda within public discourse. Thus it wasn't surprising to note that the revised Prevent strategy published under the Tory-led coalition government in June 2011 drawing upon similar sentiments of FBV, further advocated the notion that the al-Qaeda ideology can be challenged and undermined by the British ideology of shared values. Moreover, it argued that 'Prevent depends upon a successful integration policy' (HM Government 2011: 6).

PREVENT AS VALUES DISCOURSE

In the last decade there has been a consensus amongst both New Labour and the coalition-led Tory government to frame the Prevent discourse through the lens of British values. Violent extremism in general and extremism in particular are seen as arising largely due to the weakening of collective identity and poor sense of attachment to the neo-liberal state. These political actors draw mainly on the communitarian approach which argues that a decline in moral standards and an increase in social ills are largely due to the expansion of citizens' rights. According to the communitarian logic, civil rights need to be balanced with responsibilities; it's only through a collective political project that the social problems in society can be addressed.

The recent debates on FBV of democracy, the rule of law, individual liberty and mutual respect and tolerance as a way of tackling extremism in schools are part of ongoing debates that can be traced back to Tony Blair's seminal speech after the London bombings in 2006 to Runneymede Trust; this was followed by Gordon Brown's speech at the Fabian Society's New Year's conference also in 2006, and David Cameron, in his Munich speech (2011). More recently, promoting British values is part of a legal duty (HM Government 2015), constitutes part of the revised Ofsted Inspection Handbook (Ofsted 2015) and also part of the Teachers Standards (DoE 2011). In fact, the legislative framing of Prevent makes it difficult, if not impossible, for public sector organisations to mount any challenges. For example, in cases where schools are reluctant to comply with the duty then the Prevent Oversight Board has the 'power of direction' through the Secretary of State (see Section 30 of the Act) to ensure schools *do* comply with this section of the legislation. Recent cases have begun to highlight the impact of the Securities Act (2015) on racial profiling of Muslim pupils, especially in primary schools (Belaon 2015). More crucially, in the last three years a total of 918 children – 84 under the age of 12 and one as young as three – have been referred to the Government's de-radicalisation programme called Channel (Weatstone 2015).

There are a number of problems associated with the British values debates within the Prevent agenda. First, the context to the British values discourse is critical, especially given that it derives from the Prevent strategy (HM Government 2011), and in doing so, it helps imbed secur-itisation and de-radicalisation at the core of teaching and schooling. For example, one of the key strands of the Teaching Standards makes it difficult if not impossible to contest British Values especially given the following clause: Teachers uphold public trust in the profession and maintain high standards of ethics and behaviour, within and outside school, by not undermining FBV, including democracy, the rule of law, individual liberty and mutual respect, and tolerance of those with different faiths and beliefs [Department of Education (DoE) 2011: 14].

Second, the idea of Britishness is associated with an oppositional posi-tioning for the Muslim problematic. In fact, there seems to be a consensus on British values by most political actors; indeed, a certain moral panic can nevertheless be seen to have been generated through the 'suspect' Muslim presence. This suspect 'presence' is seen to present an ontological threat to the West in general and secular liberal values in particular. Third, there are also a number of fundamental flaws in the way in which shared values are conceptualised, especially given the starting premise of the debate, it is difficult to see how the values discussed by the above political actors are 'shared values'; rather, it is clear from the style and content of the debate that these are essentially values enforced by a politically dominant class onto a powerless minority group. More crucially, the Britishness debate views Islam through an Orientalist lens – Islam is essentially different from Western secular mores and it's only through adopting an enlightened Western secular world view that Muslims can have a future in the West.

PREVENT AND THE DEFAULT MUSLIM

Prevent, since its inception, has had a tendency to play into the idea of a Good Muslim and Bad Muslim (Mamdani 2004) debate – thus further demonising the idea of a 'suspect community'. Indeed, the definition of 'Good Muslim' has often been fluid and loosely defined and has often been subject to change. For example, as part of the government's wider national framework of 'winning hearts and minds' (DCLG 2007), a number of national Muslim representative organisations were considered to be 'Good Muslims' only to find themselves outside the government's sphere of influence – a number of organisations have gone through this process throughout the duration of Prevent, ranging from the Muslim Council of Britain, British Muslim Forum, Sufi Muslim Council, to others. In many respects the ideas underpinning the government's desire to promote 'Good Muslims' was based upon a wider global strategy as seen in the much cited RAND Report aptly titled, *Building Moderate Muslim Networks* (2007), which actively aimed to promote alternative moderate voices as a way of countering the 'radical' or 'extremist' voices within Muslim communities.

Since the publication of Contest 2 (July 2011), there was a significant shift away from the RAND Report logic, that is to say there are 'moderate' or 'liberal' Muslims that governments can work with or indeed promote. The shift in this logic has translated into the idea that 'all Muslims are essentially' 'bad' unless or until they have proved they are 'good' – in other words, Muslims are 'bad' by default. A recent example in support of this view is the letter written, in the wake of the *Charlie Hebdo* shootings in France (2015) by the former Communities Secretary, Eric Pickles (2015) to over 1,000 mosques and community organisations in the UK asking them to do more to root out violent extremism and thereby proving 'good' Muslimness. Similar sentiments were also echoed by David Cameron's recent speech which asked Muslims to assume that Muslims were 'quietly condoning' violent extremism associated with Islamic State of Iraq and the Levant. The ontological threat of Muslims also takes the form of racialised sexual politics. Racialised sexual politics has a long complex history through colonialism (Young 1994; Masad 2007), the War on Terror (Bhattacharyya 2008; Miah 2014), racial politics (Delphy 2008) and more recently with media discourses surrounding Muslim men and sexual grooming (Miah 2015a). Racialised sexual politics also takes a recurring theme within policy discourse revolving around the notion that Muslims are essentially homophobic and sexist. For example, in a recent interview to the BBC's Today programme, the Education Secretary Ms Morgan described how intolerance towards homosexuality could be seen as an example of extremism which should be challenged by teachers as part of the Prevent duty. Ms Morgan suggested that some views on homosexuality, which might be potentially expressed by a child should be seen as a form of extremism. When pushed by the interviewer to give an example of behaviour that might be a cause for concern, she said: 'sadly, ISIS are extremely intolerant of homosexuality', and when asked whether a student should be reported to police if they said homosexuality was 'evil', she replied it would 'depend very much on the context of the discussion' (BBC 2015).

There are a number of problems associated with such an approach. The charge of homophobia is a priori conclusion against Muslims assuming that Muslims have a sole monopoly over homophobia. This is particularly clear from the way Ms. Morgan attempted to draw connections between the Prevent agenda and the question of homophobia. More significantly, this discussion does raise an interesting question of the 0power of whiteness (Brader et al. 2001). An example of this can be found in the same BBC interview, whereby the interviewer failed to challenge the irony of conflating homophobia with extremism, especially given Ms Morgan, a devote Christian voted against the legislation for same-sex marriage in England and Wales (Mason 2014).

CONCLUSION

'There is strong evidence that a significant part of the Prevent programme involves the embedding of counter-terrorism police officers within the delivery of local services, the purpose of which seems to be to gather intelligence on Muslim communities, to identify areas, groups and individuals that are "at risk" and to then facilitate interventions, such as the Channel programme' (Kundnani 2009: 6)

The above sentiments expressed by Arun Kundnani as early as 2009 in his detailed report, titled *Spooks: How Not to Prevent Extremism* made a lasting impression in the way the Prevent initiative is perceived. Indeed, Prevent in some sections has long been associated with 'spying' on Muslim communities. Similar claims are also made especially in light of Prevent being a public duty for schools, colleges and universities. The recent Counter-Terrorism and Securities Act (2015) has raised a number of important questions relating to the government's counter-terrorism strategy. The *Prevent* strategy has generated considerable attention within academic and public policy discourse. This has led some to argue that *Prevent* not only responds to radicalisation through racialised assumptions but also through securitisation, grounded upon 'intelligence gathering', 'spying' and 'surveillance'. It is further argued that the role of securitisation within education has further blurred the boundaries between education, securitisation and counter-terrorism. Paradoxically, these policies have been developed and implemented at a time when neo-liberal discourse has signalled the notion of post-racism and de-racialisation within the sphere of education.

Ever since the inception of Prevent it has further intensified the framing of the Muslim community through the lens of the 'problematic'. Conventional debates around educational underachievement, discourses around racial inequality or anti-Muslim racism are all disregarded for broader security concerns. As a result, Muslims are no longer established communities of faith with vibrant and complex histories but rather problems that need to be addressed. The Prevent discourse views Muslims only through their 'Muslimness' which is often defined by political actors and the security services and not through Muslim agency. It also establishes the view of 'Muslim' as the only subject position that Muslims can hold. Thus public policy debates are no longer about social inequality, anti-Muslim racism or even spiralling levels of poverty but rather questions of governing the Muslim problematic. Such policies are not grounded upon well informed policy analysis but rather political construction of Muslims as the 'Other'. The racialised politics of securitisation incorporates the idea of post-race; that is to say that race is no longer the salient excluding marker that it once was and the continuing racial practices of the state which impact upon racial experiences of minority groups. This logic permeates the current hysteria around Muslims as the existential security threat that follows a particular thought pattern; that is, there is a ubiquitous security threat and something exceptional has to be done about this threat. In the spirit of a moral panic, parameters for these debates around security are so narrowly defined to limit any critical discourse – so that criticism of FBV leads to one being defined as an extremist. Thus, policy formation is no longer based upon evidence or rational thought but rather, as the following statement by Paul Flynn (member of the Public Administration Select Committee), suggests that: 'much of our policy making is evidence free, prejudice driven and hysteria driven (particularly hysteria generated by the press)' (cited in Gillborn 2014: 26).

Muslim pupils are no longer individuals with their own autonomy; they are *problems* that need addressing. Thus conventional debates around educational underachievement, discourses around racial inequality or anti-Muslim racism are all disregarded for broader security concerns.

Such debates around Prevent in schools 'marks' Muslims in class as the racialised 'Other', a group that is de-humanised and stigmatised; ironically whose de-humanisation and stigmatisation is silenced.

REFERENCES

Atwan, A. A. (2015). *Islamic state: The digital caliphate.* London: Saqi.

Ball, S. J. (2013). *Foucault, power and education.* London: Routledge.

BBC. (2015, June 30). Nicky Morgan says homophobia may be sign of extremism. *BBC.* Available at: http://www.bbc.co.uk/news/education-33325654 [Accessed on 9 December, 2015].

Belaon, A. (2015). *Building distrust: Ethnic profiling in primary schools.* London: Claystone.

Benhold, K. (2015, August 17). Jihad and girl power: How ISIS lured 3 London girls. *New York Times.* Available at: http://www.nytimes.com/2015/08/18/world/europe/jihad-and-girl-power-how-isis-lured-3-london-teenagers.html?_r=0 [Accessed on 8 November, 2015]

Bhattacharyya, G. (2008). *Dangerous brown men: Exploiting sex, violence and feminism in the 'war on terror'.* London: Zed Books.

Bhattacharyya, G. (2013). Racial neo-liberal Britain. In N. Kapoor, V. Kalra, & J. Rhodes (Eds.), *The state of race.* Basingstoke: Palgrave.

Birt, Y. (2009). Promoting virulent envy? Reconsidering the UK's terrorist prevention strategy. *RUSI, 154*(4), 52–58.

Brader, B. B., Klinenberg, E., Nexica, I., & Wray, M. (Eds.). (2001). *The making and unmaking of whiteness.* Durham: Duke University Press.

Cameron, D. (2015). *PM at 2015 Global Security Forum.* Available at: https://www.gov.uk/government/speeches/pm-at-2015-global-security-forum. [Accessed November, 2015].

Clarke, P. (2014). Report into allegations concerning Birmingham schools arising from the 'Trojan Horse' letter: Available at: https://www.gov.uk/government/uploads/system/uploads/attachment_data/file/340526/HC_576_accessible_-.pdf [Accessed 18 October, 2015].

Cockbourn, P. (2015). *The rise of Islamic State: ISIS and the New Sunni Revolution.* London: Verso.

Delphy, C. (2008). *Separate and dominant.* London: Verso.

Department for Communities and Local Government (DCLG). (2007). *Preventing violent extremism – Winning hearts and minds.* London: DCLG.

Department of Education (DoE). (2011). *Teachers standards.*

Department of Education. (2015). The prevent duty: Departmental advice for schools and childcare providers. Available at: https://www.gov.uk/government/uploads/system/uploads/attachment_data/file/439598/prevent-duty-departmentaladvice-v6.pdf [Accessed June, 2016].

Diwan, K. (2008). *Education for inclusive citizenship.* London: Routledge.

Dodd, V. (2009). Government anti-terrorism strategy 'Spies' on Innocent. *The Guardian,* 17 October.

Gillborn, D. (1995). *Racism and anti-racism in real schools.* Buckingham: Open University Press.

Gillborn, D. (2008). *Racism and education: Coincidence or conspiracy.* London: Routledge.

Gillborn, D. (2014). Racism as policy: A critical race analysis of education reforms in the United States and England. *The Educational Forum, 78*(1), 26–41.

Goldberg, D. T. (2002). *The racial state.* London: Wiley-Blackwell.

Gove, M. (2014). *Celsius 7/7.* London: Weidenfield and Nicolson.

Hall, S., Critcher, C., Jefferson,T., Clarke, J., and Roberts, B. (1978). *Policing the crisis: Mugging, the state and law and order.* London: Palgrave.

Halliday, J., Pidd, H., and Elgot, J. (2015, June 16). Police 'knew of risk Bradford women would follow brother'. *The Guardian.* Available at: http://www.the guardian.com/uk-news/2015/jun/16/bradford-missing-womenchildren-syria-police-risk-brother-islamic-state [Accessed on June, 2015].

HM Government. (2006). *Countering international terrorism: The United Kingdom's strategy,* Cm 6888. London: The Stationary Office.

HM Government. (2011). *Prevent strategy,* Cm 8092. London: The Stationary Office.

HM Government. (2015). *Counter extremism strategy,* Cm 9145. London: The Stationary Office.

House of Commons (Home Affairs Select Committee). (2014). *Counter-Terrorism.* Seventeenth Report of Session 2013–14. Available at: http://www.publications.parliament.uk/pa/cm201314/cmselect/cmhaff/231/231.pdf [Accessed on 14 December, 2015].

House of Commons, Education Select Committee. (2015). *Extremism in schools: the Trojan Horse affair.* Seventh Report of Session 2014–15. Available at: http://www.publications.parliament.uk/pa/cm201415/cmselect/cmeduc/473/473.pdf [Accessed on 19 December, 2015].

Husband, C., & Alam, Y. (2011). *Social cohesion and counter-terrorism: A policy contradiction?* Bristol: The Policy Press.

Kalra, V., & Mehmood, T. (2014). Resisting technologies of surveillance and suspicion. In N. Kapoor, V. Kalra, & J. Rhodes (Eds.), *The state of race.* Basingstoke: Palgrave.

Kapoor, N., Kalra, V., & Rhodes, J. (Eds.) (2013). *The State of Race.* Basingstoke: Palgrave.

Kershaw, I. (2014). Investigation report: Trojan Horse letter. Available at: http://www.nga.org.uk/getattachment/News/NGA-News/May-Sept-14/Trojan-Horse-Review/Ian-Kershaw-s-report.pdf.aspx [Accessed on 13 December, 2015].

Kumar, D. (2012). *Islamophobia and the politics of empire*. Chicago: Haymarket Books.

Kundnani, A. (2009). *Spooked: How not to prevent violent extremism*. London: Institute for Race Relations.

Kundnani, A. (2014). *The Muslims are coming: Islamophobia, extremism and the domestic war on terror*. London: Verso.

Mac an Ghaill, M. (1994). *The making of men: Schooling, masculinities and sexualities*. Buckingham: Open University Press.

MacDonald, I. (1989). *Murder in the playground*. London: Longsight Press.

Mamdani, M. (2004). *Good Muslim, bad Muslim: America, the cold war and the roots of terror*. New York: Doubleday.

Masad, J. (2007). *Desiring Arab*. Chicago: Chicago University Press.

Mason, R. (2014, July 15). Nicky Morgan's gay-marriage stance causes equalities role confusion again. Available at: http://www.theguardian.com/society/2014/jul/15/equalities-minister-voted-against-gay-marriage-nicky-morgan [Accessed on January, 2015].

McCants, W. (2015). *The ISIS Apocalypse: The history, strategy, and doomsday vision of the Islamic state*. New York: St Martin's Press.

Meer, N. (Ed.). (2014). *Racialization and religion: Race, culture and difference in the study of antisemitism and Islamophobia*. London: Routledge.

Miah, S. (2014). Trojan Horse, Ofsted and the 'prevent'ing of education. *Discover Society*. Available at: http://www.discoversociety.org/2014/07/01/trojan-horse-ofsted-and-the-preventing-of-education/ [Accessed on September 2015].

Miah, S. (2015a). The groomers and the question of race. Identity Papers. *Journal of British and Irish Studies*, *1*(1), 54–66.

Miah, S. (2015b). *Muslims, schooling and the question of self-segregation*. London: Palgrave.

Mirza, H. (1992). *Young, female and black*. London: Routledge.

Mullard, C. (1982). Multiracial education in Britain: From assimilation to cultural pluralism. In J. Tierney (Eds.), *Race, migration and schooling*. Norfolk: Holt Education.

Ofsted. (2015). *School inspection handbook from September 2015*. Available at: https://www.gov.uk/government/publications/school-inspection-handbook-from-september-2015 [Accessed on June, 2016].

Pickles, E. (2015). Letter to Muslim leader. Available at: http://www.independent.co.uk/news/uk/eric-pickles-letter-to-muslim-leaders-the-text-in-full-9987249.html [Accessed on 19 October, 2015].

Rex. J. (1986). *Race and Ethnicity*. London: Routlege.

Said, E. (1978). *Orientalism*. London: Routledge.

Sewell, T. (1996). *Black masculinities and schooling: How Black boys survive modern schooling*. Stoke on Trent: Trentham Books Ltd.

Shain, F. (2003). *The schooling and identity of Asian girls.* Stoke on Trent: Trentham Books.

Shain, F. (2011). *New Muslim folk devils: Muslim boys and education.* London: Trentham.

Soyer, F. (2014). *Faith, culture and fear: Comparing Islamophobia in early modern Spain.* In N. Meer (Ed.), *Racialization and religion: Race, culture and difference in the study of antisemitism and Islamophobia* (pp. 2014). London: Routledge.

Swann Report. (1985). *Education for all.* London: Her Majesty's Stationery Office.

Thomas, P. (2009). Between two stools? The government's preventing violent extremism agenda. *The Political Quarterly, 80* (2), 21–43.

Troyna, B. (Ed.). (1987). *Racial inequality and education.* London: Tavistok.

Weatstone, R. (2015). More than 900 British children identified as potential extremists at risk of radicalisation from ISIS and terror groups. Available at: http://www.mirror.co.uk/news/uk-news/more-900-british-children-identified-6080066 [Accessed on 18 November, 2015].

Weiss, M., & Hasan, H. (2015). *ISIS: Inside the army of terror.* London: Regan Arts Books.

Young, M. (1994). *Colonial desire: Hybridity in theory, culture and race.* London: Routledge.

Shamim Miah is a senior lecturer at the School of Education, University of Huddersfield. He is the author of '*Muslims, Schooling and the Question of Self-Segregation'* (Palgrave, 2015). Shamim's research is concerned with the framing of race and religion in public policy. His research interests draw upon both empirical and theoretical approaches to the study of public policy. Shamim is also the co-convenor (Race and Ethnicity) for BERA (British Educational Research Association).

CHAPTER 10

Islamophobia in Quebec Secondary Schools: Inquiries into the Experiences of Muslim Male Youth Post-9/11

Naved Bakali

INTRODUCTION

In the decade since 9/11, there has been a significant increase in mistrust and prejudice towards Muslims in Canada (CAIR-CAN 2008). Recent polls indicate that 69 per cent of Quebecois(es) have biases towards Islam, while 54 per cent of Canadians as a whole have a negative opinion of the faith (Angus Reid 2013). In the Quebec context, identity politics combined with feminist and French secularist discourses have framed Muslims as a threatening 'Other' outside the 'nationalist space' (Bilge 2013; Leroux 2010; Wong 2011). These negative perceptions of the threatening Muslim 'Other' have also appeared in textbooks across Quebec secondary schools (McAndrew et al. 2007). In this chapter, I explore the themes of race and racism and the complexity of prejudices that exist in Quebec secondary schools resulting from identity, nationalism and culture in the experiences of Muslim male youth. Additionally, this chapter will discuss how notions surrounding the state policy of secularism have facilitated the 'Othering' of Muslims in the context under study. *Laicité*, or the Quebec state policy of secularism as I will be using the term, can be understood as a

N. Bakali (✉)
McGill University, Montréal, QC, Canada
e-mail: naved.bakali@gmail.com

© The Author(s) 2017
M. Mac an Ghaill, C. Haywood (eds.), *Muslim Students, Education and Neoliberalism*, DOI 10.1057/978-1-137-56921-9_10

normative political culture in which there is a strict separation between church and state on matters of public policy (Baubérot 2012). It differs from the term 'secularism', which some have described as the co-existence of multiple religious and non-religious perspectives in a given social context (Taylor 2007). *Laicité* has traditionally been rooted in separating Catholicism from the state. In more contemporary times it has been geared towards dichotomizing Muslims as 'Other' in French society. As Selby (2011) notes, '[i]f during the first half of the twentieth century the separation of church and state was intended to displace Catholicism, in recent decades Islam has been increasingly depicted as the new challenge for French secularism' (p. 442). Additionally, this chapter examines the emergence of identity conflicts as an overriding force in daily life and in interactions with others in school and society.

The questions guiding my inquiry were: (1) how did Muslim men attending Quebec secondary schools feel they were perceived in their schools?; and (2) if the participants perceived that anti-Muslim racism existed in their Quebec secondary schools, what were its causes and how did it manifest? The findings of this study suggested that anti-Muslim racism experienced by participants was influenced by the domestic state policy of secularism and media discourses in Quebec, as well as the clichéd archetypes and tropes of Muslims that have emerged in the context of the War on Terror.

THEORIZING ANTI-MUSLIM RACISM

The theoretical framework which undergirded this study was informed by a Critical Race perspective (Bilge 2013; Razack 2008; Thobani 2007). Critical Race theory is a theoretical approach in which race and racism are central to its analysis and often articulated through narrative (Bell 2009). From this perspective, 'racism is defined as a structure embedded in society that systematically advantages Whites and disadvantages people of color' (Marx 2008, p. 163). A number of Critical Race theorists have examined anti-Muslim racism within North American, Canadian, and the Quebec contexts (Bilge 2013; Razack 2008; Thobani 2007). A common theme in the works of these scholars is the social construction of the Muslim 'Other'. 'Otherness' is 'the condition or quality of being different or "other," particularly if the differences in question are [deemed] strange, bizarre, or exotic' (Miller 2008, p. 587). Often the concept of 'Other' is represented as a diametrically opposed 'self'. Hence, designating a group or individuals as 'Other' not only defines that group or individuals but also defines the 'self' as its anti-thesis. The 'Othering' of Muslims in the aftermath of 9/11 has been inextricably linked to the War on Terror. As Razack (2008) observes, 'three allegorical figures have come to dominate the social landscape of the "war on terror" and its ideological underpinning of a clash of civilizations: the dangerous Muslim man, the imperiled Muslim woman, and the civilized European' (p. 5). The 'imperiled Muslim woman' is the figure of the oppressed Muslim woman in need of rescue from her backwards culture and religion. The 'dangerous Muslim man' is possessed of rage and inflicts violence through terrorism and abuse towards women. The 'civilized European' represents the anti-thesis of the archaic Muslim. His/her interventions in Muslim majority nations are legitimized and sanitized through the aforementioned figures.

In the Canadian context, Thobani (2007) has described how the 'Othering' of Muslims has been enacted through the concept of 'exaltation'. Exaltation is a power-inscribed way of attributing certain qualities that characterize the nationality of a people. Those who do not embody these qualities are considered strangers to the national community. As Thobani (2007) notes, 'national subjects who fail to live up to the exalted qualities are treated as aberrations... The failings of outsiders, however, are seen as reflective of the inadequacies of their community, of their culture, and, indeed, of their entire race' (p. 6). In other words, there are certain imagined qualities inherent within English/French white Canadians. Those qualities exalt them over others and in essence define who gets to be a 'real' Canadian. Exaltation has been operational in the Canadian and Quebec contexts through the notion of race thinking.

According to Razack (2008), race thinking is 'a structure of thought that divides up the world between the deserving and undeserving according to descent' (p. 8). Hannah Arendt (1944) discussed in great detail how race thinking was an ideology that laid the ground work for imperialistic actions. Arendt (1944) views race thinking as an ideology which 'interprets history as a natural fight of races' (p. 39). Hence, it is a perspective that constructs privilege through race. In the context of the War on Terror, race thinking has obfuscated and vilified Muslims to garner support for laws that have suspended due process and violated their fundamental rights (Kumar 2012; Razack 2008; Sheehi 2011; Thobani 2007). The operationalization of race thinking in media and political discourses has been the subject of many studies, which argue that Muslims have been perceived and presented as a 'race' of people fomenting the deterioration of Canadian and

Quebecois culture (Bilge 2012; Mahrouse 2010; Zine 2009). Hence, experiences of race and racism have been central to narratives of Muslim discrimination in the Canadian context.

Grounding my analysis of anti-Muslim racism through the archetype of the 'dangerous Muslim man', in conjunction with the notion of exaltation, and race thinking, will help explicate comments discussed by the participants. I turn now to elaborate on the methodological processes utilized in this study.

METHODOLOGY

This chapter examines the lived experiences of six Muslim men who attended secondary schools in Quebec after the 11 September 2001 attacks (9/11) between 2006 and 2013. I employed a critical ethnographic approach in this inquiry, which drew from the tradition of institutional ethnography (IE) (Campbell and Gregor 2008; Smith 2005, 2006). According to Smith (2005), IE is a process which, 'explores the social relations organizing institutions as people participate in them and from their perspectives. People are the expert practitioners of their own lives, and the ethnographer's work is to learn from them' (p. 225). Therefore, this inquiry viewed participants as the subjects and not the objects of the study. As I am a Muslim man working in the Quebec educational system, I engaged in a self-reflexive process throughout this inquiry. Reflexivity can be understood as a 'process of self-examination that is informed primarily by the thoughts and actions of the researcher' (Russell and Kelly 2002). I engaged in a self-reflexive process through writing journal entries, re-examining audio-recordings of interviews and transcripts, as well as consulting friends and colleagues about my analysis. This process was important in my study because my subjectivities were inevitably entangled in my interpretations, as I have personally experienced and observed instances of anti-Muslim racism within Quebec secondary schools. Through engaging in a self-reflexive process I wanted to avoid overstating participants' comments, as well as avoid an over-deterministic analysis.

The participants for this study were drawn from the Greater Montreal Region in Quebec, Canada. They were drawn from contacts that I had within mosques and Muslim community organizations. My interviews with these participants were part of a larger study relating to my doctoral research, which involved interviews with 18 former and current Muslim students and Muslim and non-Muslim teachers in Quebec secondary schools in the post-9/11 context. In examining the experiences of former secondary school students, I relied on retrospective narratives while conducting my interviews. An issue with relying on memories when doing ethnographic research is that responses might be subject to one's present perspective, therefore they might be malleable and susceptible to inaccuracy or loss (Davis and Starn 1989). However, as Pignatelli (1998) observed, memory has the potential to enrich a critical ethnography, '[m]emory binds the rich potential of the narrative to fascinate, seduce, and draw us closer to the practical, activist intentions of a critical ethnography' (p. 407). In other words, relying on memory or the use of telling stories is in line with some of the foundational principles of critical ethnography, which is to give voice to socially marginalized members of society. Interviews were audio recorded and transcribed verbatim over a span of six months from May 2013 to October 2013 and were semi-structured, posing open-ended questions relating to: (1) how Muslims were perceived in society; (2) if perceptions of Muslims were shaped by media representations; (3) if they had encountered racism against Muslims within educational contexts.

THE PARTICIPANTS

There were a total of six Muslim male participants in this study, only one of which was a high school student at the time of the interview. The five other participants were all recent high school graduates, having completed their high school diploma within three years of the interview. All of the participants attended high school in the Greater Montreal Region and came from middle-class socio-economic backgrounds. Two of the participants attended English public schools, three attended public French schools, while one of the participants attended a private French school. All of the participants identified themselves as practicing Muslim men while they were in high school. The names of the participants were as follows: Yusuf, Ismail, Ahmad, Adam, Zaid, and Ali.[1] Yusuf and Ismail were interviewed individually, while the other four participants were interviewed together in a single focus group discussion. This was done to accommodate the participants as these four men felt more comfortable doing the interviews in a group setting. Yusuf was in his second year at a university preparatory college, referred to as Collège d'enseignement général et professionnel (CEGEP) in Quebec, during the time of the interview. He was the sole participant that had attended a private school throughout his secondary education, which had only a few Muslim students. Ismail was a first year CEGEP student during the time of his interview. He also attended a school where there were very few Muslims; as such he felt he was clearly identifiable as a Muslim in his school. Ahmad was completing his final year of high school during the time of the focus group discussion and he attended a school that had many different minority groups, including a number of Arabs and Muslims. Adam and Ali were both completing their final year of CEGEP and Zaid was an undergraduate student during the time of the focus group discussion. All three of them attended high schools that had a number of Muslim students.

SOCIETAL PERCEPTIONS OF ISLAM

I began the interviews by asking the participants how they felt Muslims and Islam were perceived by society before delving into their high school experiences. In the focus group discussion, Ahmad indicated that he strongly felt there were biases against Muslims in Quebec society. He believed that Islam was viewed as a 'bacteria' in Quebec, implying his faith was perceived as a contaminant that infected society. Consequently, being Muslim or adhering to Islam was likened to a sickness which was 'untreatable' and therefore 'need(ed) to be expelled'. Ahmad's responses also suggested that he felt there were certain assumptions surrounding Muslims in Quebec, which predisposed them to violent behaviour. He argued that when Muslims committed acts of violence, whether politically motivated or not, there was no analysis in the media seeking to understand why these acts were committed. Rather, they were understood to be manifestations of inherent tendencies towards violence which would be labelled as terrorism. However, according to Ahmad, similar types of violent actions were constructed as aberrations and exceptions when committed by members of the dominant culture. Hence, such behaviour would be explained away through mental illness because actions of violence and abuse were not essential to the make-up of the white majority and did not reflect the true qualities of their race. Ahmad's comments related to the notion of exaltation (Thobani 2007), as he alluded to a certain set of imagined qualities present in the nationalist subject. Because Muslims were perceived as 'Other' and outside the nationalist imaginary, when Muslims engaged in violence it could not be understood to arise from mental illness. Such acts were believed to be a natural consequence of *their* culture, excluding them as nationalist subjects.

Of all the members in the focus group discussion, Ahmad most strongly felt that Islam was negatively perceived in Quebec society. However, Adam felt that he was making generalizing statements. This, according to Adam was unfair because it engaged in a similar type of essentializing discourse which was often done to Muslims. However, despite Adam's views that Ahmad was generalizing, he did not voice disagreement over what was being said. There was a type of implicit acknowledgement from Adam that what Ahmad was saying was true, as Adam himself mentioned how 'they [i.e. the white majority] generalize on us'. In other words, Adam did acknowledge that there were generalizing stereotypes of Muslims in Quebec society; however, he felt that Ahmad's statements implicated all Quebecers, which he believed was an over-exaggeration. Ismail, who was interviewed individually, also felt that there were a number of reductive stereotypes in Quebec society that associated Muslims and Islam to violence. He suggested that the dominant conceptualization of Muslims in Quebec was that of the 'dangerous Muslim man' (Razack 2008), who was out to harm the Westerner. Ismail believed Muslims were perceived as people who just wanted to engage in indiscriminate violence and murder through acts of terrorism.

Participants' comments when discussing how they felt Islam and Muslims were perceived in Quebec society suggested that they had encountered varying forms of bias and prejudicial treatment which racialized their faith. This involved encountering perceptions relating to inherent deviant tendencies relating to their 'Muslimness', which excluded them as nationalist subjects. The perceptions that participants encountered in Quebec society resonated with a number of their high school experiences.

Experiences in Secondary School

Most of the participants generally felt that their overall experience in high school was positive. However, all the participants felt that there were some levels of racism against Muslims in their secondary schools. Yusuf described how being a high school student was a time of self-exploration. This was difficult for Yusuf because of certain assumptions associated with Muslims and the Islamic faith in his secondary school. Yusuf was cognisant of his 'Otherness' in his high school setting as well as the types of understandings people had of Muslims and Islam. Hence, he would feel the need to try and 'fit in', suggesting that being an accepted member of the student body was not a taken-for-granted situation for Yusuf. Rather, he needed to make efforts to be perceived as 'normal' even if this meant telling students 'what they want[ed] to hear' at the expense of misrepresenting his faith. Some studies have shown that within educational institutions, students have been able to assert their Muslim identity through participation with Muslim student groups formed within the school, as these groups help ease tensions relating to peer pressure and prevent marginalization (Khan 2009; Zine 2001). Unfortunately in Yusuf's school such an organization did not exist.

The challenges of being a Muslim minority in school were compounded with further difficulties when teachers would show materials casting Muslims in a negative light. Yusuf's comments suggested that he would be at odds with the types of media portrayals of Muslims presented by his teacher as he described a video that was shown to his classmates that gave a 'general image of how women [were] inferior to men in Islam', which was something that Yusuf did not agree with. Such imagery of Muslim women in the Canadian context have been documented in depth by Jiwani (2010) as she observers, '[t]he tendency within the news media and current affairs programming has been to project representations of the veiled woman as essentially an abject and victimized Muslim figure' (p. 65). Yusuf felt that in his classroom setting he had no 'choice but to accept' the types of portrayals of Islam that were disseminated to the students despite the fact that he felt such information was casting his faith in a negative light. Instead of the classroom being a space where Yusuf felt comfortable to express himself, his identity and his beliefs, he described feelings of alienation, 'Otherness' and was forced to accept prejudicial discourses of his faith. Yusuf described how the archetype of the 'imperiled Muslim woman' was perpetuated in his experiences in secondary school through media presented to his class. Despite disagreeing with these portrayals, Yusuf felt the need to regulate his views and beliefs about the issue. Perhaps Yusuf did not want to engage in a confrontation with his teacher, as doing so would potentially draw more attention to his Islamic faith and further create feelings of alienation with his peers. Abo-Zena et al. (2009) observe that children in educational settings often have fears and anxieties over being disliked because of their religious affiliations. Such a situation not only inhibits social adjustment and causes marginalization, but can also affect school performance. Yusuf's experiences of being exposed to prejudicial forms of media in his classes were similar to those of other participants.

Participants from the focus group discussion felt that school curricula in Quebec, as well as teachers, in some instances, facilitated anti-Muslim biases. Zaid discussed how his Ethics and Religious Culture class would be a source of tension in his high school, particularly when religions were discussed. These tensions involved debates within the classroom and at times even escalated to violent confrontations outside of the class. Zaid did not specifically mention that his teacher was responsible for the confrontations; however, other participants in the focus group discussion felt that teachers facilitated tensions towards Muslims and Islam in their classes.

Ali discussed how teachers wanted students to regurgitate dominant media and political discourses relating to the state policy of secularism in classroom discussions even if these contradicted his beliefs. Ali asserted that teachers only wanted to hear 'politically correct' views, which he believed stemmed from what was being said in the media. Adam added to these comments and stated, 'the most secular response' to which Ali agreed. These comments demonstrated how a state-funded institution, like a secondary school, reproduced Quebec media discourses and state policies relating to secularism, as teachers seemingly wanted students to mimic these views to receive 'full marks'. Not conforming to state policies and media discourses carried the penalty of not getting 'full marks' in their class discussions and assignments. These comments suggested that some of the participants perceived their classrooms as apparatuses of state indoctrination, as they felt obliged to give 'the most secular response' even if this was at odds with their views. As was the case with Yusuf, other participants felt the need to regulate their speech with regards to their beliefs in their classes. A similar pattern has been noted by Maira (2014) in her study of Arab, South Asian and Afghan communities in the USA. In this study it was found that Muslim youth felt their right to free speech was restricted in the context of the War on Terror because they believed they were under constant surveillance. It would appear that in the post-9/11 context Muslim youth in this study as well as in other contexts fear reprisals by state institutions for their beliefs and thus regulate their speech.

In Ahmad's experiences some teachers not only expected students to accept state and media discourses but also engaged in the process of miseducating their students about Islam and Muslims. Ahmad described how one of his teachers singled him out as an object of ridicule because he was an observant Muslim who prayed the afternoon prayer in school. He went on to describe that he felt a sense of conflict and tension towards his teachers when he would speak about his religion in a way that contradicted state and media discourses. Ahmad felt a strong bias from his Ethics and Religious Culture teacher when discussing Islam. He felt that his teacher would pick and choose what to present about Islam creating a distorted picture of his faith. Ahmad described how his Ethics and Religious Culture teacher facilitated constructing his Islamic faith as 'Other', a process that frequently occurs in Quebec political and media discourses (Bilge 2013; Wong 2011; Mahrouse 2010; Mookerjea 2009). He felt that his faith was being unfairly presented and if he wanted to get 'full grades' he would have to be 'with the teacher'. In other words, Ahmad was indirectly being forced to accept media and state discourses surrounding Muslims within his Ethics class. If he did not do so he would be penalized.

An important recurring theme that came up with participants when recounting their high school experiences was the stereotype of 'dangerous Muslim men' (Razack 2008), which would regularly manifest in different forms within their secondary school settings. As mentioned previously, the participants would sometimes have taunts thrown at them relating to violence and terrorism. Some of these stereotypical views towards Muslim men manifested within the school culture during dress-up days like on Halloween. Zaid discussed how the topic of Muslims and Islam came up in his Contemporary World class and his Ethics and Religious Culture course. Though Zaid did not directly indicate that these courses negatively depicted Muslims, his comments did suggest that through these courses students in his school received a lot of exposure to Muslims and the Islamic faith. Hence 'the topic of Islam was pretty popular' in these courses. As such, when it came time for Halloween a group of students thought it would be a good idea to come to school dressed up as Muslims. Zaid's comments linked the instruction in his Contemporary World and Ethics and Religious Culture classes with this incident. One can infer from this that the information that students obtained about Muslims and Islam in these courses reproduced the image of the 'dangerous Muslim man'. This archetype employs a number of visual signifiers including the beard and clothing items such as the turban (Gottschalk and Greenberg 2008), which is what students wore to embody this archetype. Zaid mentioned how in his Ethics class other faiths were also discussed, specifically mentioning Christianity, Judaism and Buddhism. However, of the faiths discussed, only Islam and Muslims were identified as threatening figures worthy of imitating on Halloween.

The presence of the 'dangerous Muslim man' archetype was further confirmed when Zaid discussed why he thought non-Muslim students would think that dressing up as Muslims on Halloween would be an appropriate costume, as he stated, 'the purpose of Halloween costumes is to look scary'. Zaid's description of this episode was very telling. He stated that a group of students came dressed up as the so-called Muslim. Zaid did not state that the students came dressed as violent terrorists, as this was implied by their appearance. The students came dressed as the 'Muslim', at least how the figure of the 'Muslim' has come to be known in Western discourse (Mamdani 2005; Salaita 2006; Sheehi 2011). This incident demonstrated the students' understanding of what it meant to be 'Muslim'. Their understanding of 'being Muslim' on Halloween embodied the tropes of violence and intimidation, as the purpose of the attire was to 'look scary' by posing as terrorists.

There were a number of common themes and issues that emerged from the discussion of secondary school experiences. The most obvious of these trends was that most participants experienced, directly or indirectly, some form of anti-Muslim racism and prejudice in their secondary schools. However, there was a wide range in how participants interpreted the racism that they experienced. For example, Ahmad adamantly suggested that there was anti-Muslim racism in his secondary school through his experiences. Zaid and Ismail were not as troubled by their experiences and did not articulate very strong sentiments of racism. They held these views despite the fact that they encountered a number of instances which demonstrated that anti-Muslim racism clearly existed in their secondary school experiences. Zaid and Ismail both described racist incidents in which their classmates associated them with terrorism, as not being a very serious issue. Zaid and Ismail interpreted these incidents as 'funny' or as 'jokes'. It is my contention that this attitude was emblematic of how racism was seemingly normalized in the day-to-day experiences of these participants. They were not attuned to how they were experiencing racism, as they were not offended and seriously concerned over these issues. In a way, it would seem that they had unconsciously accepted this type of treatment and categorizations, possibly because they were prevalent in state policies and practices, as well as political and media discourses in Quebec.

Most participants described how they regularly encountered the archetype of 'dangerous Muslim man' in their secondary schools. Some of the participants discussed how they faced taunts and racial slurs associating them with terrorism and violence in their schools. They also described how at times they felt the need to regulate their speech in conformity to Quebec values and norms associated with the state policy of secularism in

their classrooms. Participants discussed how they feared reprisals or punishment for having beliefs that contradicted these policies or were not in
line with their teachers' beliefs. Hence, the participants did not describe
racism in the form of physical violence and abuse, but rather in how they
were perceived, stereotyped and treated by classmates and teachers.

CONCLUSION

This article examined the lived experiences of six Muslim men who
attended secondary schools in Quebec in the aftermath of the 9/11 terror
attacks. Though most of the participants had generally positive experiences
in secondary school, they clearly felt that anti-Muslim racism was present in
Quebec society, which also manifested in their secondary school experiences. Participants described how they encountered tropes relating to
Muslim men being inherently violent through the archetype of the 'dangerous Muslim man', which have become endemic in the context of the
War on Terror. Participants also discussed how their perceived 'Otherness'
created feelings of exclusion and alienation excluding them as exalted
nationalist subjects. This inquiry drew from the experiences of six participants to provide rich and contextualized data, which may have been
unattainable in a larger scale inquiry. While one can situate the participants'
experiences within the broader context of the post-9/11 and War on
Terror era, quite importantly, their experiences resonated particularly
with racism and discrimination prevalent in Quebec state policies and
media discourses. Participants' comments in this study provided valuable
and important insights shedding light on how many Muslim youth may
have experienced racism in Quebec secondary schools in the post-9/11
context. Additionally, participants' comments demonstrate some of the
complexities of prejudices that people might harbour, not conveniently
defined in a single form but rather existing in a web of sentiments encap-
sulating ideas about race, racism, ethnicity, nationalism, religion, gender
and culture.

The experiences of racism by these former and current Muslim students
suggest the opportunity for future researchers to explore what, if anything,
is being done to challenge racist attitudes and perceptions in Quebec
secondary schools. The findings of this study indicate a need to further
explore the issue of anti-Muslim racism in Quebec schools. Such an
examination could employ a gendered approach comparing experiences
of Muslim women and men, as well as involve Muslim teacher and student

experiences in public/private and English/French educational settings in Quebec to further shed light on issues raised by this study.

NOTE

1. All names are pseudonyms.

REFERENCES

Abo-Zena, M., Sahli, B., & Tobias-Nahi, C. (2009). Testing the courage of their convictions: Muslim youth respond to stereotyping, hostility, and discrimination. In O. Sensoy & C. Stonebanks (Eds.), *Muslim voices in school: Narratives of identity and pluralism* (pp. 3–26). Rotterdam: Sense Publishers.
Arendt, H. (1944). Race-thinking before racism. *The Review of Politics*, 6(1), 36–73.
Baubérot, J. (2012). *La Laïcité falsifiée*. Paris: La Découverte.
Bell, D. (2009). Who's afraid of critical race theory. In E. Taylor, D. Gillborn, & G. Ladson-Billings (Eds.), *Foundations of critical race theory in education* (pp. 37–50). New York: Routledge.
Bilge, S. (2012). Mapping Quebecois sexual nationalism in times of 'crisis of reasonable accommodations'. *Journal of Intercultural Studies*, 33(3), 303–318.
Bilge, S. (2013). Reading the racial subtext of the Quebecois accommodation controversy: An analytics of racialized governmentality. *Politikon: South African Journal of Political Studies*, 40(1), 157–181.
CairCan. (2008, May 23). *CairCan: News release*. Retrieved March 25, 2014, from CairCan website: http://www.caircan.ca/itn_more.php?id=A2984_0_2_0_M
Campbell, M., & Gregor, F. (2008). *Mapping social relations: A primer in doing institutional ethnography*. Toronto: University of Toronto Press.
Davis, N., & Starn, R. (1989). Introduction. *Representations*, 26(2), 1–6.
Gottschalk, P., & Greenberg, G. (2008). *Islamophobia: Making muslims the enemy*. Lanham: Rowman & Littlefield Publishing Group.
Jiwani, Y. (2010). Doubling discourses and the veiled other: Mediations of race and gender in Canadian media. In S. Razack, M. Smith, & S. Thobani (Eds.), *States of race: Critical race feminism for the 21st century* (pp. 59–86). Toronto: Between the Lines.
Khan, S. (2009). Integrating identities: Muslim American youth confronting challenges and creating change. In O. Sensoy & C. Stonebanks (Eds.), *Muslim voices in school: Narratives of identity and pluralism* (pp. 27–40). Rotterdam: Sense Publishers.
Kumar, D. (2012). *Islamophobia and the politics of empire*. Chicago: Haymarket Books.

Leroux, D. (2010). Québec nationalism and the production of difference: The Bouchard-Taylor commission, Québec Identity Act, and Québec's immigrant integration Policy. *Quebec Studies, 49*, 107–126.

Mahrouse, G. (2010). Reasonable accommodation' debates in Quebec: The limits of participation and dialogue. *Race and Class, 52*(1), 85–96.

Maira, S. (2014). Surveillance effects: South Asian, Arab, and Afghan American youth in the War on Terror. In S. Perera & S. Razack (Eds.), *At the limits of justice: Women of colour on terror* (pp. 86–106). Toronto: University of Toronto Press.

Mamdani, M. (2005). *Good Muslim bad Muslim: America, the cold war, and the roots of terror*. New York: Three Leaves Press.

Marx, S. (2008). Critical race theory. In L. Given (Ed.), *The Sage encyclopedia of qualitative research methods* (Vol. 1, pp. 163–167). Thousand Oaks: Sage.

McAndrew, M., Oueslati, B., & Helly, D. (2007). L'évolution du traitement de l'islam et des cultures musulmanes dans les manuels scolaires québécois de langue française du secondaire. *Canadian Ethnic Studies, 39*(3), 173–188.

Miller, M. (2008). Otherness. In L. Given (Ed.), *The Sage encyclopedia of qualitative research methods* (Vol. 2, pp. 587–589). Thousand Oaks: Sage Publications.

Mookerjea, S. (2009). Hérouxville's Afghanistan, or, accumulated violence. *Review of Education, Pedagogy, and Cultural Studies, 31*(2), 177–200.

Pignatelli, F. (1998). Critical ethnography/poststructuralist concerns: Foucault and the play of memory. *Interchange, 294*, 403–423.

Razack, S. (2008). *Casting out: The eviction of Muslims from Western law and politics*. Toronto: University of Toronto Press.

Reid, A. (2013). *Canadians view non-Christian religions with uncertainty, dislike*. Vancouver: Angus Reid Global.

Russell, G., & Kelly, N. (2002). Research as interacting dialogic processes: Implications for reflexivity. *Forum: Qualitative Social Research, 3*(3), 18.

Salaita, S. (2006). *Anti-Arab racism in the USA: Where it comes from and what it means for politics today*. Ann Arbor: Pluto Press.

Selby, J. (2011). French secularism as a 'guarantor' of women's rights? Muslim women and gender politics in a Parisan banlieue. *Culture and Religion, 12*(4), 441–462.

Sheehi, S. (2011). *Islamophobia: The ideological campaign against Muslims*. Atlanta: Clarity Press.

Smith, D. (2005). *Institutional ethnography: A sociology for people*. Lanham: AltaMira Press.

Smith, D. (2006). *Institutional ethnography as practice*. Lanham: AltaMira Press.

Taylor, C. (2007). *The age of Secularism*. Cambridge: Harvard University Press.

Thobani, S. (2007). *Exalted subjects: Studies in the making of race and nation in Canada*. Toronto: University of Toronto Press.

Wong, A. (2011). The disquieting revolution: A genealogy of reason and racism in the Québec press. *Global Media, 4*(1), 145–162.

Zine, J. (2001). Muslim youth in Canadian schools: Education and the politics of religious identity. *Anthropology & Education Quarterly, 32*(4), 399–423.

Zine, J. (2009). Unsettling the nation: Gender, race and Muslim cultural politics in Canada. *Studies in Ethnicity and Nationalism, 9*(1), 146–163.

Naved Bakali is an educator, researcher and social activist. He completed his PhD from McGill University, Montreal, in Cultural and International Studies in Education, where he also serves as a sessional lecturer. Drawing from critical race theory, cultural and media studies, and post-colonial theory, his research focuses on the study of anti-Muslim racism in Canada and the USA. Naved's research provides a fresh and innovative perspective on Islamophobia within institutional settings, thus demonstrating the institutionalization of anti-Muslim racism in Western contexts. He is an innovative and dynamic scholar who believes in socially oriented action-research that challenges prejudice and inequality by combining his research with grassroots activism.

CHAPTER 11

At the Intersection of Neo-liberalism and Islam: Being a Muslim Woman in Turkish Universities

Pınar Enneli and Çağlar Enneli

INTRODUCTION

This chapter will focus on the interaction between political Islam and neo-liberalism in Turkey on the basis of female university students who openly express their religious identities by wearing a headscarf. After the 9/11 attack and various similar incidents, policy-makers, academicians and politicians tended to approach Muslim communities living in the West as a suspect community (Mac an Ghaill and Haywood 2014). The integration and inclusion of Muslim communities were connected to issues of security (Ajala 2014; Sunier 2014). Though the way to approach the issue might vary from country to country (Hofhansel 2010), there are many reported incidents of racist and xenophobic behaviour against members of the Muslim community (Bangstad 2013). In this context, young Muslims in general and young Muslim women in particular received special attention. Discrimination and

P. Enneli (✉)
Sociology Department, Abant Izzet Baysal University, Bolu, Turkey
e-mail: ennelip@gmail.com

Ç. Enneli
Department of Anthropology, Ankara University, Ankara, Turkey
e-mail: cenneli@ankara.edu.tr

© The Author(s) 2017   161
M. Mac an Ghaill, C. Haywood (eds.), *Muslim Students, Education and Neoliberalism*, DOI 10.1057/978-1-137-56921-9_11

exclusion of the Muslim young women with headscarves has become an important subject of studies (Allen 2015). Existing studies usually discuss the problem of the exclusion and discrimination of Muslim communities as a citizenship identity issue (Anisa 2016) or as a policy issue of religious governance in religiously diverse societies (Peucker and Akbarzadeh 2012). Moreover, existing multi-culturalist policies have been evaluated in relation to secularism and Muslim demands (Modood 2015).

The discussion on Muslim communities in the West seems to embrace largely cultural and political perspectives. A similar comprehension could be observed in the discussion of Islam and Islamic movements in Turkey, a secular country with a majority Muslim population. More specifically, it has been a matter of political rights and cultural representations of the various ethnic and religious communities including Sunni ones. In these discussions, women's struggle to enter universities with their headscarves has become especially important and a central issue for years (Kadıoğlu 2006). At the beginning of the Republic, the headscarf ban in the public sphere was not a de jure enforcement since the veiling was ideologically associated with uneducated rural women, and educated urban women had nothing to do with religious symbols. However, as a part of mass migration from rural areas to cities throughout the 1960s and 1970s, millions of rural women came to take their part in urban settings, and veiling become an issue for rightist and Islamist parties like Milli Görüş (National View) of 1970s. Besides, as Peres (2012) suggests, the Iranian Revolution in 1979 added to the fears of the Turkish military, who historically viewed itself as the guardian of secularism (Peres 2012). Especially after the 'military intervention' in 1980, the headscarf became a subject to ongoing formal restrictions. The political and social struggle against the headscarf ban in the universities and very discussion related to it, however, came to an end with AKP (Justice and Development Party) governance. At that point, the AKP with its Islamic expressions and representations gave these women a chance to express their own identities more freely.

The AKP government, with its Islamic agenda at social and political levels, followed a strict neo-liberal agenda at an economic level. These neo-liberal policies create a severe inequality in the country (Atasoy 2009; Gürcan and Peker 2015). In this period, a group of people used their Islamic or Muslim identity at the social and political level as a social cleavage in order to gain economic advantage (Hoşgör 2015; Yılmaz 2014). In this respect, the Turkish case might add an extra dimension to existing studies based on cultural representation and political rights of Muslim communities in the West. Indeed, Muslim identity understood as a source of disadvantage and exclusion in Western circumstances might become an advantage in the Turkish case through building a social network for economic purposes.

In this regard, based on qualitative research conducted among 22 female students wearing headscarves in two universities in Ankara (one private and one public university) between July and November 2015, this chapter will argue that the headscarf issue is not only a matter of cultural and political rights but also a class marker for a newly emerging Muslim middle class in a sense that the women with headscarves might actively be involved in producing and reproducing their class boundaries, especially through their interpretative patterns of the headscarf itself.

Muslim Students' Struggle Against Headscarf Ban in the Universities

It is very conventional to read the recent history of the Turkish Republic from the very beginning since 1923 as a kind of confrontation between republican elites with their top-down developmentalist reforms ascribing modes of appropriateness to almost all aspects of daily life, including codes of dress, belief etc., and those who were subject to their actions. With the exception of some Western scholars (Lindisfarne 2002; Stokes 1993) studying in Turkey, who underline the similarities between these so-called opposite poles in their everyday modes of practice, this history has been portrayed and accepted as a conflict between centre and periphery by most well-known native intellectuals (Mardin 1989; Berkes 1964). By the military coup of 12 September 1980, the politics based on the long-standing division between centre and periphery or the Left and Right were initially challenged and then replaced by political movements and claims based on religious, ethnic, racial and gender identities (Kadıoğlu 2006). In this context, by means of initiating debates on who were allowed to participate in the public sphere, the visibility of headscarf wearing in universities has provided probably the most salient illustration of change in recent Turkish politics.

At the end of 1980s, a group of Turkish female university students with headscarves started a movement against the headscarf ban on campuses.

Having come to power in 2002, AKP (Justice and Development Party) had several inconclusive attempts to lift the ban until 2008. In 2008, they overturned the ban through a constitutional amendment. The Constitutional Court, however, annulled the proposed amendment on the ground that it is against the founding principles of the constitution. This final attempt even became one of the main arguments of the General Prosecutor of the Supreme Court of Appeal's failed closure case against the AKP in the same year. The fact that the decision taken by the Constitutional Court could not be appealed led the government to a solution through the Higher Education Council, which sent a circular directing universities not to enforce dress code in prohibiting the wearing of headscarves. The circular also stated that it would take legal action against non-compliant institutions and lecturers. Since then, a de facto lifting of the headscarf ban has been observed in universities (Peres 2012).

Nevertheless, the headscarf ban started a fierce debate on the ground of political rights and representations, citizenship, discrimination and women's rights (Göle 1991; İlyasoğlu 2013; Kadıoğlu 2006; Seggie 2015). Göle (1991) conducted one of the earliest studies on women wearing headscarves and she concluded that these women had modern claims on the public realm, such as freedom to choose what they wear, equal access to education, etc., rather than demand an Islamic system which imposes certain rules on women. Similarly, İlyasoğlu (2013) argued that the Islamic women choose to cover their heads in order to neutralise and make invisible their feminine identity in the male-dominated public space. By doing this, the women believed that they can be more equal with the men in the public and never gave up their education and employment demands.

On the other hand, there is also some emphasis that these demands might give way to construction of a Muslim-gendered public space that restricts freedom of expression for non-practicing Muslims (Onar and Baç 2011). Similarly, Arat (2010) argued that unless given viable alternatives to religious moral grounding, women might be liable to accept the secondary roles prescribed by religion and adapt their preferences to the religious choices and that the orthodox religious choices seem to be promoted against secular ones in Turkey. Kaya (2014) even goes further by claiming that Islamic demands, including the headscarf issue, is nothing to do with modernity, rather it is losing modern ideals such as women's equality to Islamic conservatism.

Indeed, the AKP government from the beginning also discussed the headscarf issue on the merit of liberal citizenship, human rights for education and choice of wearing style freely. The party programme has been written with a consistent usage of a Western-originating liberal democratic vocabulary in order to carve out a wider space for the lifestyles and preferences of its conservative and religiously oriented core constituency (Alaranta 2014). Coşar and Yeğenoğlu (2011) called AKP's approach as a neo-liberal–conservative version of patriarchy that perceives women's education primarily to fulfil their domestic responsibilities, while rejecting and being hostile towards feminist activities. On the other hand, it is a fact that the women are a very important part of AKP's political success. They are very active in reaching potential voters through home visits, participating in weddings and circumcision ceremonies and providing social assistance to the poor, the elderly and handicapped.

On the other hand, a majority of the discussions have overlooked the different class belongings of veiled Muslim women. As Jelen (2011) mentioned in her study on professional Turkish middle to upper middle-class working women with headscarves, while mostly insensitive or at least silent to structural limitations (educational, material, social), these women complained about the discrimination and negative treatment in employment arising from their headscarves. The class issue, however, is not totally absent from the discussion of Islamic politics in Turkey. On the contrary, the potential of Islamic identity to create cleavage in an unequal opportunity structure due to neo-liberal economic policies is analysed thoroughly. What is absent in these discussions is the role and the position of Islamic women in producing and reproducing this cleavage. Before this issue, we will discuss neo-liberal economic policies and the creation of the Muslim middle class in Turkish society.

Neo-liberal Policies During the AKP Era: Creating a New Muslim Middle Class

The military coup in 1980 did not only bring cultural identities into political debates, but also introduced neo-liberal economic policies. The military regime endorsed export-oriented policies together with a privatising process of state-owned enterprises. All the previous governments had more or less followed this path and the 2001 economic crisis accelerated neo-liberal applications in order to ease the recession. In that crisis, the Turkish Lira was devalued by 40 per cent overnight, unemployment increased, the banking sector shrunk and widespread bankruptcies of small businesses were experienced. The rescue programme was introduced by Kemal Derviş, who was unilaterally appointed to the existing cabinet while he was vice president of the World Bank. Later, Derviş's economic programme was retained by the Justice and Development Party (AKP), which came to power in 2002 at the first election following the crisis (Öniş 2003).

The accelerated neo-liberal policies during the AKP period have resulted in huge inequality and poverty. Turkey ranks among the top third of Organization for Economic Cooperation and Development (hereinafter OECD) countries in terms of earnings inequality (OECD 2014). Women are the most severely affected. Only 28.7 per cent of women in the economically active age-group were employed, compared to 69.2 per cent of men (OECD 2014). According to the OECD's Better Life Index, Turkey is among the last three of 36 countries in the ratings for housing conditions and spending, household income and financial wealth, earnings, job security and employment, work–life balance, environment and education (OECD 2015). The unemployment rate has been 8.2 per cent, while the youth unemployment reached 15.7 per cent (OECD 2014). Employment for those with an education has been particularly problematic. The unemployment rate of higher school graduates in Turkey rose from 7 per cent in 2000 to 12.9 per cent in 2014 (TBMM Araştırma Merkezi 2015).

In this economic environment, the AKP government especially used the Islamic network in order to provide some support for its hegemony. The poor segment of the society without proper formal welfare support was offered social and economic assistance through Islam-based community work – charities, schools, clinics and cooperatives, while Muslim professionals were provided employment opportunities in municipal governments, state bureaucracies, companies, schools, dormitories, hospitals and law firms established by Islamic capital and other networks (Hosgör 2015). Islamically oriented professionals, who certainly existed before, were able to gain privileged positions and advantages during the time of the AKP government in comparison to secularly oriented ones.

A significant portion of the working class has become reliant on the AKP's Islamic patronage networks, which would be very risky and costly to abandon for poor people (Gürcan and Peker 2015). At the same time, the growing Muslim middle class reveals itself with distinct tastes and consumer choices represented in the establishment of mosques, schools, universities, training centres and student residences (Gürcan and Peker 2015). Lifestyle expressions are considered by some as a marker of a newly emerged Muslim middle class's power struggle with secular counterparts for economic and political opportunities and sources (Yılmaz 2014). Some others, however, suggest that although Islamic and secular-oriented middle classes might have different ideological and cultural pasts and orientations, both of them converged into a new status group characterised by social differentiation by spatial separation, the added value of appreciating real estate prices, their educational aspiration for their children, their obsession with consumption motivated by television programmes, slick magazines and billboards (Balkan and Öncü 2015).

In the process of keeping their boundaries from their secular counterparts, veiling might serve as a significant marker. Indeed, as Atasoy (2009) revealed in a study of the veiled students during the headscarf ban, the ban served as a protection for the privileged position of the traditional upper classes from the formation of an alternative upper class of modest Muslim families. Likewise we argue that the headscarf itself provides the means of keeping the privileged position of the newly emerged Muslim middle class. It might also serve as a symbol of social mobility for women from less fortunate class backgrounds. Indeed, Winter (2010) points out that for elite women, headscarf wearing has become both a fashion statement and a display of status, while for women in large working-class districts, the headscarf might be a symbol of upward mobility and conferred a 'city look'. The following section will analyse the role of the women wearing headscarves to keep the boundaries of the Islamic cleavages by referring to the research conducted in two universities.

METHODOLOGY AND RESEARCH SETTINGS

In accordance with the declaration of the Council of Higher Education (COHE 2014), there are two types of universities in Turkey: State and Non-profit Foundation Universities. Students are selected for both types through the results of the central exam. The fact that while the former requires nothing else from the enrolled students, the latter charges tuition and fees that vary by schools but start from 9,000TL and go up to 40,000TL in 2015 (one US dollar and one Euro in the same year accounted for 2.7 and 3 Turkish lira (TL), respectively, in average of 12 months), which is the main difference between them. Dissimilarity in this respect, however, cannot be taken lightly. Universities are apparently valuated and classified by their names at first in Turkey. Students and their parents follow widely recognised assessments in making a choice of university and department related to better employment opportunities in the future. Apart from this, however, private universities are beyond the options of many to the extent that having adequate income to pay for private school may mark class boundaries. It was the reason we chose to carry out research in both types of universities.

We have included 22 veiled students in total from Ankara University's Faculty of Letters (hereinafter AU-FL) and Bilkent University, both in Ankara, through personal contacts. Initially, the research began with 3 students in July 2015 and then by means of snowball sampling reached 11 from each university in November. As the first private university established in Turkey, Bilkent was without a doubt a significant choice. It has constructed a very prestigious position from its inception and maintained it amongst both public and private schools since then. Ankara University, on the other hand, was selected as a result of the fact that it is one of the first state universities established at the beginning of twentieth century that still makes the presence of the state felt. Our choice to narrow the research with students from social sciences, linguistics and administrative sciences made the selection feasible as well.

In order to collect data, we have conducted face-to-face interviews accompanied with the observations of the university settings. The research, thus, reached an ethnographic insight to some extent through the mixture of interviews and observations. All interviews which were about an hour in length were recorded on audiotape and several jottings produced from observations at first and then all were transcribed, coded and analysed using the qualitative analysis software, NVivo.

Religion and veiling are hot issues. People may easily find some 'hidden' intentions in the questions and tend to refuse to take part in research related to them. We experienced some difficulties concerning the vulnerability of the research theme as well. Though we had 3 interviewees beforehand and reached the rest with their directions and references, it was sometimes hard to convince students to participate in the research. For instance, one of the students continuously postponed and finally cancelled the interview appointment on the grounds that she was afraid of her name been seen in the research. On the contrary, we convinced another student with the same concern and conducted probably one of the most efficient interviews of the research with her. We have generally used places like cafeterias, dining halls, classrooms and outside benches for interviews. Students who had experienced the headscarf ban in the past by themselves or through their relatives or friends had considerably different attitude in participating in the research. They were thinking that the headscarf issue was full of historical earnings and any account related to it must refer to the experiences of those who were banned once from attending universities. Thus, they very openly wished to take part in the research.

Like most qualitative work, our research too is not based on claims related to broad representations of all veiled students in Turkey or in Ankara, on the one hand, and in Bilkent or Ankara universities on the other. Rather it seeks to reach some narratives by means of which women's own experience with the headscarf may lead to be comprehended better in their own terms. As Gubrium and Holstein (1999) state, '[n]arrative can be seen to constitute meaningful social experience, as well as produce distinction and nuance, but we must not shortchange the broader social organization of storytelling' (568).

The Muslim Young Women Negotiating Multiple Identities

Though familiar with the headscarf images outside the university setting beforehand, we did not know at the beginning of the research how veiling was strikingly signified and detailed in universities by headscarf preferences including fabrics, colours, brands, etc. Whether one covers her shoulders as well, allows her earrings to be seen, uses eye-catching colours and designs, wears trousers or puts on some makeup are just a few references on which one's identity is interpreted and positioned in accordance with the distance from the beholder, the other veiled student. Universities are historically significant fields for veiled students. Once they faced some legal obstacles and struggled to attend there. Today, however, after the headscarf ban came to an end, having a professional career through university graduation is much more a significant issue for veiled women. Twenty-two interviewed students, a majority of whom economically described themselves as having a middle-class background (with the exceptions of 4 from lower middle and 2 from upper middle classes) and with various parental employment, including academics, private sector executives, native or foreign workers, teachers and mostly housewife mothers (12 in total), almost never referred to the headscarf ban of very recent history in their accounts and, when asked, never expressed any fear or sense of threat related to veiling today. Instead, they chose to talk about their education, career expectations and employment.

Veiling was like something that seemingly began to lose its importance. Besides, employment was not only linked to university attendance but also to the argument of self-development and getting associated with some kind of network. However, while self-development was a kind of commonly perceived prerequisite for employment opportunities, veiled students from Bilkent and AU-FL universities varied in addressing the proper network for labour market inclusion. For interviewed students in Bilkent, attendance at highly developed student clubs of the university, a quantity of which, as some stated, reached 130, was like a first step to opportunities after graduation. Veiled students of AU-FL, however, found student organisations in the university very non-functional and even useless in providing employment opportunities and were following some fraternities outside it to reach some advantages after graduation.

Interpretation of religiosity produced narratives that linked religion, on the one hand, to an identity formation, lifestyle, and a kind of psychological inculcation related to serenity, order and happiness. On the other hand, religion is interpreted in terms of a blessing, avoidance of wrongdoing and pursuit of religious depth. An apparently significant difference here was about whether veiled students found both comfort for religious expression and opportunities for career building at the same time in their university settings. In Bilkent, the possibilities of getting education, organising career opportunities and expressing religiosity were thought to be provided at the same time in the same space. Attempting to build their career opportunities outside the university, whose education and validity in the labour market were criticised to a certain extent, veiled students of AU-FL, however, frame their religiosity much more like a pursuit between the divided settings of inside and outside the university. It was probably for this reason that they attributed much more Islamic significance to the organisations outside the university they followed in comparison to the Bilkent interviewees who strictly adhered to student clubs of the university. While interviewing with a veiled student from AU-FL, who was working on the Koran and trying to read it from the original Arabic to see what was lost or hidden in translation, we were very surprised to see that she could not produce a response to the meaning of Islam in her life. She chose to highlight the ownership of morality at first but immediately retracted her response with dissatisfaction. Then she continued by saying:

> Islam is the conceptualisation of my life and I always keep it in my mind throughout the day...When I see any behaviour or event, I interpret it in

terms of Islam. How appropriate this is for Islam on the one hand and how appropriate Islam is for the lives of people . . . I am continuously questioning it and by this way being a Muslim every moment in my life.

Another student from AU-FL, who had worked in part-time jobs since high school and continued to do so at the time of interview, underlined the significance of worshipping and blessing for everything given by God. She stated:

> No matter how hard grab onto doing something religious, I feel as if I have done nothing. I don't know how much is enough or not. For now, my God, I can do that much. I would like to give alms and help people within my possibilities. I have right now this amount of financial possibility but I may have more in the future and do much. I know he does not overburden anyone with the loading one cannot carry. This is how I live.

The pursuit of religious correctness together with questioning religion itself through theorisation of daily life, we remember, gave the former a gloomy tone. The latter expressed a kind of religious pursuit in daily life as well. Religiosity as a pursuit in daily life appeared significant in the AU-FL context, where almost all interviewees' after graduation career realisations oriented nominally towards public service and school teaching. However, the fact that Bilkent was thought to be providing better career expectations especially in the private sector seemed to be accompanied by the formulation of religiosity differently. An interviewee from Bilkent, one of those who positioned her family background as lower middle, clearly stated that though only one religious righteousness existed she could still use her own interpretations. She said:

> In my life, I am trying to do what religion necessitates but cannot allocate time too much. I am just doing what has to be done. There are lots of people who restrict becoming Muslim with such and such worshipping. For me it is more like a life perspective and guidance. . . . Indeed it is an interpretation. Religion specifies everything clearly but when I hesitate over something I can find the right and wrong in my mind. One interprets it in this way, I in that way. Practices, in fact, are evaluated by intentions.

It was surprising to hear this formulation of absolute religious truth and personal interpretations and almost a joyful transition from the one to the other without any hesitation. The revelation of the same attitude came from another Bilkent student in justification of her veiling and the meaning of religiosity. She stated:

> The way I am surely depends on the way the Muslim I am. I think it organises me. I cannot say that uncovered woman is disorganised in her life. This is her decision and that is no concern of mine. But I feel serene and happy in this way. I think I have to be like this, veiled.

Religion and veiling, in this context, were more like an identity or, as another Bilkent interviewee put it, character negotiated to signify one's very existence.

Pursuit of religiosity and religion as a marker of identity in terms of lifestyle were two dominant patterns that emerged in the research. Though the approach to religion as a pursuit itself might be an argument for identity as well, the tones of expression in these two patterns were significantly different. While the former much more emphasised one's inner religiosity and, as mentioned, produced some heavy tone in interviews, the latter generated expressions of verification and relief based on possibilities of interpreting religion.

Apparently, these distinct patterns approached veiling itself differently as well. The degree of veiled women's visibility was a highly discussed issue and whether Islam required women to be invisible was often problematised. Indeed, even women's observable preferences of veiling contributed to the discussion. While some of them were deliberately avoiding drawing attention to themselves and dressed in modest clothes and headscarves, others did not intend to abstain from visibility. Instead, they were wearing trousers, putting on some makeup and choosing colourful headscarves. For the former, they clearly crossed the line in appearance. At the level of discourse, interestingly, almost all of the interviewed students found the former much more devoted, ideal and filled with religiosity. However, it did not lead the latter to feel disquiet with themselves. The preference of visibility could be easily justified in explanations by pointing to human nature and how hard it is to control it under the circumstances of daily life. Besides, in practice the mode of inclination to express religiosity in polished mode produced in its entirety its own argument of visibility of religious women and the very proper way of representation of being veiled.

While a majority of the interviewed students approached veiling fashion negatively (13 in total in comparison to 6 positive and 4 neutral), they much more positively discussed veiling style in terms of personal freedom and taste. Fashion apparently was a discursive context not easily challengeable under the negative connotations it had, as a kind of capitalistic expression of consumption. Style, however, seemed to open a social field for one's evaluations and classifications on who was like them and who was not and on class-based claims related to being an educated woman and pursuing a professional career. According to Bourdieu, any social field involves social actors with their own intentions, claims and benefits based on economic, social and cultural capitals, all of which are embedded in the habitus they own and are subject to. Universities, shopping malls, public offices or any other social space in which actors meet are social fields and have their own rules working to regulate the interactions. People in social fields are, however, not just the simple followers of the rules but actively engaged with their own practices of distinction based on differentiated claims on taste. For Bourdieu, class divisions are more like phenomena of flow of daily life or practice and almost everything including the rules of the field are subject to ongoing structuring (Bourdieu and Wacquant 1992). Veiling style in itself is central in providing class-based claims at the intersection of being religious and educated in pursuit of having a part in the labour market.

One of the Bilkent interviewees, when asked whether she came to any opinion from the appearance of another veiled student, responded:

> Sure, I do. From the shape of headscarf, style of dressing, and whether she uses single-colour headscarf which gives the impression of being economically better. The quality of the fabric is also recognised by sight. You just say these are economically better.... They even choose friends from their own circle. Both are Muslim but they choose their friends from different circles in accordance with their economical levels. I have a friend who is economically very good but we are good friends. There is no difference between us. But amongst some, I observe it. There are lots of veiled people and groups segregated economically.

Associated sometimes with economic considerations and sometimes with lifestyle and taste, veiling preferences provided means of reaching quick conclusions and classifications amongst veiled students. Observed differences, however, were not only read in respect of whom the others were but also whom the spectator herself was. Her future expectations were joined to reading the veiling setting as well. The first narrated Bilkent student told her experience of meeting with an executive of a firm. She said:

> For instance, yesterday we were talking to the executive of.... I asked several questions and he dealt with me personally. When he was finally

alone, I approached him and said whether I could ask something personal. He directly said 'Just apply to the job later.' . . . These firms appear like they only have employees who have no relation with the religion. I mean I have never seen any veiled employee there. That's why I was shocked to hear such a thing from him. If an unveiled woman was there instead of me, she would very probably not get his attention. He told me to apply for the job because I attracted his attention as a veiled woman. I even think that if I apply there he can positively discriminate for me.

When considering the fact that 8 out of 11 interviewed students in Bilkent clearly associated their universities with private sector opportunities, her point was significant. When asked about her career expectations, another interviewee from Bilkent first emphasised how religious men could hide themselves and become invisible in the employment setting in comparison to veiled women's open religiosity, and then interpreted this distinctively in favour of women. She stated:

In any firm, you can recognise a veiled woman and say that she is Muslim. Our identities are always evident. You cannot do the same for a religious man. Today this is not a problem. But in the past when expression of religiosity and veiling in particular were taken a back seat, men were advantaged by their invisibility . . . But I am advantaged today because my identity is apparent. I can reveal who I am to others. I am Muslim and people can see it from outside. This is completely the same for the work environment. I would be very happy to express and highlight my religious identity there.

This approach was clearly different from expressing headscarf with religiosity and questioning whether it signified religion properly. It underlined a different representation of veiling in a professional career and employment. Reflected as a distinct tone clearly observable in interviews, owners of this representation were well aware of the ongoing negotiation on how appropriate their veiling was and hence how their religiosity was intense. They, however, did not take a step back from the way they veiled. On the contrary, they seem to embrace the 'violation' and even liked and were proud of the narrative of success in a professional career. Veiling, then, apparently produced a social field in which possessing a university education, seeking an employment career and having a religion were negotiated at the same time with the exhibition of different modes and tones of representing something religious, veiling.

CONCLUSION

In this chapter, we tried to analyse the headscarf issue in the universities beyond political and cultural scopes by referring to Muslim female university students' narratives that produced and reproduced an Islamic cleavage in the settings of neo-liberal economic policies. It was argued that in Turkey the headscarf was a direct marker of a new Islamic middle class by the interpretations and arguments on its religiosity and representation. It appears then that Muslim identity as a source of disadvantage and exclusion in the West may provide a privileged position in Turkey

As discussed, we observed two patterns of affiliation with veiling amongst the interviewed students. It was an issue, on the one hand, in respect of whether one avoided drawing attention or attributed sufficient religious significance to it. On the other hand, it was interpreted as an identity, character or the way one was. We argued that these patterns were embedded with the possibilities of the attended university in building career opportunities. Positively approached and actively used student clubs in the private university provided the means of negotiation of education, professional career and veiling within the same social space. On the other hand, in the absence of such opportunities, the veiled women in the state university tended to make contacts with Islamic institutions outside the university and heavily relied on access to public sector jobs, such as teaching or clerical positions. Through the means of negotiation, the latter mainly underlined the proper representation of religion in respect of veiling preferences and the former strongly underlined the significance of the representation of veiling in economic life and highlighted the success in a professional career. Veiling itself, in conclusion, was a negotiated and contested social field comprising of something not necessarily religious or economical, but the coalescence of both.

REFERENCES

Ajala, I. (2014). Muslims in France and Great Britain: Issues of securitization, identities and loyalties post 9/11. *Journal of Muslim Minority Affairs, 34*(2), 123–133.

Alaranta, T. A. (2014). Political parties and the production of an Islamist – secularist cleavage in Turkey. *Approaching Religion, 4*(2), 113–124.

Allen, C. (2015). 'People hate you because of the way you dress': Understanding the invisible experiences of veiled British Muslim women victims of Islamophobia. *International Review of Victimology, 21*(3), 287–301.

Anisa, M. (2016). Active citizenship, dissent and civic consciousness: Young Muslims redefining citizenship on their own terms. *Identities: Global Studies in Culture and Power, 23*(4), 454–469.

Arat, Y. (2010). Religion, politics and gender equality in Turkey: Implications of a democratic paradox? *Third World Quarterly, 31*(6), 869–884.

Atasoy, Y. (2009). *Islam's marriage with neoliberalism: State transformation in Turkey.* Houndmills: Palgrave Macmillan.

Balkan, E., & Öncü, A. (2015). Reproduction of the Islamic middle class in Turkey. In N. Balkan, E. Balkan, & A. Öncü (Eds.), *The neoliberal landscape and the rise of Islamist capital in Turkey* (pp. 166–200). New York: Berghahn Books.

Bangstad, S. (2013, 27–28 September). On xenophobia and nativism. *Recycling fatred: Racism(s) in Europe today.* Brussels, Belgium. Brussels: European Network Against Racism aisbl (ENAR), pp. 87–94.

Berkes, N. (1964). *The development of secularism in Turkey.* Montreal: McGill University Press.

Bourdieu, P., & Wacquant, L. J. D. (1992). *An invitation to reflexive sociology.* Chicago: The University of Chicago Press.

COHE. (2014). *Higher education system in Turkey.* Available at: https://www.yok.gov.tr/documents/10348274/10733291/TR'de+Y%C3%BCksek%C3%B6%C4%9Fretim+Sistemi2.pdf/9027552a-962f-4b03-8450-3d1ff8d56ccc (Accessed 15 December 2015).

Coşar, S., & Yeğenoğlu, M. (2011). New grounds for patriarchy in Turkey? Gender policy in the age of AKP. *South European Society and Politics, 16*(4), 555–573.

Göle, N. (1991). *Modern mahrem: Medeniyet ve örtünme.* İstanbul: Metis.

Gubrium, J. F., & Holstein, J. A. (1999). At the border of narrative and ethnography. *Journal of Contemporary Ethnography, 28*(5), 561–573.

Gürcan, E. C., & Peker, E. (2015). A class analytic approach to the Gezi Park events: Challenging the 'middle class' myth. *Capital & Class, 39*(2), 321–343.

Hofhansel, C. (2010). Accommodating Islam and the utility of national models: The German case. *West European Politics, 33*(2), 191–207.

Hosgör, E. (2015). The question of AKP hegemony: Consent without consensus. In N. Balkan, E. Balkan, & A. Öncü (Eds.), *The neoliberal landscape and the rise of Islamist capital in Turkey* (pp. 201–234). New York: Berghahn Books.

İlyasoğlu, A. (2013). *Örtülü kimlik: İslamcı kadın kimliğinin oluşum öğeleri.* İstanbul: Metis.

Jelen, B. (2011). Educated, independent, and covered: The professional aspirations and experiences of university-educated hijabi in contemporary Turkey. *Women's Studies International Forum, 34*(4), 308–319.

Kadıoğlu, A. (2006). Muslim feminist debates on the question of headscarf in contemporary Turkey. In I. Abu-Rabi' (Ed.), *The Blackwell companion to contemporary Islamic thought.* (pp. 609–623). Oxford: Blackwell Publishing.

Kaya, I. (2014). Contemporary Turkey: An Islamic-capitalist variety of modernity? *Social Science Information, 53*(2), 197–212.

Lindisfarne, N. (2002). *Elhamdülillah laikiz: cinsiyet, İslam ve Türk milliyetçiliği.* İstanbul: İletişim Yayınları.

Mac an Ghaill, M. M., & Haywood, C. (2014). Pakistani and Bangladeshi young men: Re-racialization, class and masculinity within the neo-liberal school. *British Journal of Sociology of Education, 35*(5), 753–776.

Mardin, Ş. (1989). *Religion and social change in modern Turkey: The case of Bediüzzaman Said Nursi.* New York: SUNY Press.

Modood, T. (2015) *Multiculturalism and moderate secularism (EUI Working Paper).* Italy: European University Institute.

OECD. (2014). *OECD economic surveys: Turkey 2014.* Available at: http://www.oecd-ilibrary.org/economics/oecd-economic-surveys-turkey-2014_eco_sur veys-tur-2014-en, (Accessed 15 December 2015).

OECD. (2015). *OECD Better Life Index-Turkey.* Available at http://www.oecd betterlifeindex.org/countries/turkey/. (Accessed 15 December 2015).

Onar, N. F., & Baç, M. M. (2011). The adultery and headscarf debates in Turkey: Fusing "EU-niversal" and "alternative" modernities? *Women's Studies International Forum, 34*(5), 378–389.

Öniş, Z. (2003). Domestic politics versus global dynamics: Towards a political economy of the 2000 and 2001 financial crises in Turkey. *Turkish Studies, 4*(2), 1–30.

Peres, R. (2012). A history of the headscarf ban in Turkey. *Turkish Review, 2*(5), 34–46.

Peucker, M., & Akbarzadeh, S. (2012). The vicious cycle of stereotyping: Muslims in Europe and Australia. In F. M. Mansouri & V. M. Marotta (Eds.), *Muslims in the West and the challenges of belonging* (pp. 171–197). Melbourne: Melbourne University Press.

Seggie, F. N. (2015). Academic and cultural experiences of covered women in Turkish higher education. *Comparative Education, 51*(4), 575–591.

Stokes, M. (1993). *The Arabesk Debate: Music and musicians in modern Turkey.* Oxford: Oxford University Press.

Sunier, T. (2014). Domesticating Islam: Exploring academic knowledge production on Islam and Muslims in European societies. *Ethnic and Racial Studies, 37*(6), 1138–1155.

TBMM Araştırma Merkezi (2015) *Türkiye'de üniversite mezunu nüfusun işgücü durumu.* Available at: http://spm.ku.edu.tr/wp-content/uploads/2015/01/Turkiye_de_Universite_Mezunu_Nufusun_Isgucu_Durumu-1.pdf (Accessed 15 December 2015).

Winter, B. (2010). Women and the 'Turkish paradox': What the headscarf is covering up. *Modern Greek Studies (Australia & New Zealand), 14*, 216–238.

Yılmaz, S. (2014). Social mobility and its discontents: The center-periphery cleavage of Turkey. *Tarih Kültür ve Sanat Araştırmaları Dergisi, 3*(2), 28–44.

Pınar Enneli is an associate professor in Sociology Department at Abant Izzet Baysal University, Bolu, Turkey. After graduating from Sociology Department of Middle East Technical University, she received her MPhil and PhD in Sociology from Bristol University. Her research interests are young people, poverty, women, ethnic and religious identities and their relations with class identities. Apart from her academic publications and reports, she was the co-editor of the books *Societal Peace and Ideal Citizenship for Turkey* (Lexington Books, USA, 2011) and *Crossing and Conflicting Religious and Ethnic Identities in Turkey* (Say Yayınları, Turkey, 2010).

Çağlar Enneli is an assistant professor in Social Anthropology. After graduating from Sociology Department at Hacettepe University in Turkey, he received his MSc in Social Anthropology from Anthropology Department of University College London (UCL) in 2001 and PhD in Social Anthropology from Anthropology Department of Ankara University in 2007. Since then he has been working in Ankara University as a social anthropologist. His major research themes and areas are anthropology of kinship and kinship-based organisations and networks; daily religious rituals, discourses, practices and organisations; contemporary art and anthropology.

CHAPTER 12

Being Uyghur or Being Muslim? – Identity Construction of Tertiary-Level Uyghur Students in China

Mingyue Gu and Xiaoyan Guo

INTRODUCTION

Muslim minority youths' subjectivity has drawn wide research attention in the education field in recent years, as they are reported to be negatively perceived on the whole, and discriminated against in host communities (Gu 2014; Mac an Ghaill and Haywood 2014; Shain 2011). These studies found that ethnicity and racial identities can be reconfigured under neo-liberalism, the currently dominant economic and political logic informing globalization and socio-economic policies, which champions the idea that 'individuals can best be advanced by liberating individual entrepreneurial freedoms and skills within an institutional framework characterised by strong private property rights, free markets, and free trade' (Harvey 2005: 2). Education was found to play a critical role in reproducing neo-liberal ideology, thus reinforcing imbalanced power relations (e.g. Shain 2011). In the field of language, education specifically, ethnicity has long been researched. Whilst ethnicity

M. Gu (✉)
Chinese University of Hong Kong, Sha Tin, Hong Kong
e-mail: mygu@cuhk.edu.hk

X. Guo
Chinese University of Hong Kong, Hong Kong, China
e-mail: gracexyguo@gmail.com

© The Author(s) 2017   179
M. Mac an Ghaill, C. Haywood (eds.), *Muslim Students, Education and Neoliberalism*, DOI 10.1057/978-1-137-56921-9_12

used to be taken as an entry point for analysis, and language as its essential marker (Giles and Johnson 1987), recent studies have increasingly problematized the essentialized understanding of ethnic identity and its essential link with language, as language per se has been commodified (Heller 2011). Moreover, researchers have established the linkage between ethnicity and language, on the one hand, and globalized economic and political orders and ideologies on the other (Giroux 2008; Piller and Cho 2013; Price 2014; Shin and Park 2016). These studies have focused mainly on transnational Muslim minorities, whereas scant research attention has been paid to Muslim students' identity construction as a result of intra-national migration.

China is a multi-cultural and multi-ethnic country, and more than 22 million of its total population of nearly 1.3 billion are Muslims, according to the 2010 census (National Bureau of Statistics of the PRC 2010). There are ten Muslim minority groups officially recognized by the People's Republic of China (PRC); Uyghur is one of the largest Muslim minorities, with a 2010 population of 10 million (National Bureau of Statistics of the People's Republic of China 2010). It is the dominant ethnic group in the Xinjiang Uyghur Autonomous Region (Xinjiang hereafter), accounting for around 41 % of its total population, slightly larger than its Han population (National Bureau of Statistics of the People's Republic of China 2010). Whilst other Muslim minority groups appear to be generally placid, the Uyghur possessed a strong cultural and religious identity, and have thus been viewed as a problematic group by the government (Chen and Postiglione 2009). Throughout history, the government has used education as an important means of building nationalism and promoting ethnic integration (Chen and Postiglione 2009; Clothey 2005). However, the influence of 'neoliberalism with Chinese characteristics' (Harvey 2005: 120) over the past three decades (Mok and Lo 2007) has led to the deregulation of higher education and its imbalanced development between both regions and ethnic groups; as such, affirmative action programmes, in terms of both score lines and quotas, have been implemented to ensure certain numbers of Uyghur students are enrolled in tertiary-level institutions, particularly in top universities in China's eastern cities. Unlike the Muslim Hui, whose mother language is Chinese, the Uyghur have their own language, which is mainly used within the Uyghur community and in some public spheres (e.g. education and media) within Xinjiang (Tsung 2014). Although Chinese has been promoted as the PRC's national language (simplified Chinese characters as its written form; Putonghua as its spoken form), Uyghurs (like Tibetans and many other minorities) learn Chinese as a second language, one that contrasts with their mother tongue in terms of pronunciation, vocabulary, syntax, written form, and literature (Adamson et al. 2013). In addition, the teaching of English, which has been a part of China's education agenda since 1980, has progressed slowly in minority regions, due to policy issues and resource scarcity (Adamson et al. 2013). Consequently, ethnic minority students tend to have relatively lower proficiency than Han students and this may place the minority students at an educational disadvantage when they study or live in such economic centres as Shanghai and Beijing. Given these complex linguistic issues, it is worthwhile exploring how Muslim Uyghur students are positioned in relation to multilingual practice as they move from their hometown to other areas of China, how they respond to that positioning and the ways in which their language behaviours and identity negotiation is connected with the socio-economic order.

ETHNICITY AND LANGUAGE

From a post-modernist perspective, identity can be understood as 'positioning'; that is, the ways in which subjects position themselves and are positioned by others (Davies and Harré 1990). In the investigation of minority students' identity and linguistic practice, it is tempting to see ethnicity as a necessary feature in identity positioning (e.g. Giles and Johnson 1987), or to take it for granted as a salient feature comprised of essentialized 'things' (Martín Rojo 2010). It might thus be used as a subtle tool to divide and rule subordinate populations (Heller 2011). Researchers have increasingly criticized essentializing ethnicity as constructing relations of difference between a dominant majority and a subordinate minority (Hall 1992; Heller 2011; Hobsbawm 1990). Hall (1992) formulated a new ethnicities perspective, challenging the dominant idioms of classification and arguing that ethnicity is 'essentially a politically and culturally constructed category, which cannot be grounded in a set of fixed transcultural or transcendental racial categories and which therefore has no guarantees in nature' (p. 443). Ethnicization is, in essence, a process of essentialization, in which negative features are attributed to certain groups based on their culture, ethnicity or place of origin, and a hierarchizing effect is produced (Martín Rojo 2010). Giroux (2008) further pointed out that, in the age of neo-liberalism, which governs individuals through inciting various virtues among individuals to guide them to govern themselves, ethnicity can take on different forms. As morality is assessed in terms of one's capacity for 'self-care' and the ability to meet one's own needs (Brown 2005: 43), the process of ethnicization shifts from rabid and overt forms, towards more insidious forms (Giroux 2008). This understanding of ethnicity will enable the present study to investigate how Uyghur students are ethnicized in the host education context, and in what ways their ethnicized differences and categories can be understood within the context of 'neo-liberalism with Chinese characteristics' (Harvey 2005: 120).

Language can be understood as linguistic capital in the market, where different values are attributed and unevenly distributed among social participants (Bourdieu 1986; Heller 2011). It can thus be viewed as a form of symbolic capital social participants use to construct or contest social categories, according to the logic of production, distribution, and valuation of contexts (Bourdieu 1991; Heller 2011). Language is also a socio-political construct that is traversed by the socio-economic processes of regional, national, and international activity (Pérez-Milans and Patiño-Santos 2014). As such, language constitutes of and is constituted by unequal power relations, whereby social inequalities are played out and ethnic differences are constructed. Meanwhile, language, as a resource, provides an arena in which agency can be exercised to contest or perform identities (Pennycook 2007). Underpinned by neo-liberal ideology and practice, language has, by turns, been conceived of as a private commodity and reduced to sets of skills and functions as an important field of competition, through a set of planning and assessment mechanisms (Heller 2011; Shin and Park 2016). For example, various forms of English tests initiated at national and international levels, such as the Test of English as a Foreign Language (TOEFL), play a central role in confirming and reproducing the neo-liberal order and in marginalizing unprivileged groups (Block and Gray 2015; Shin and Park 2016). This study will explore how neo-liberal conceptions of languages (e.g. English and Chinese) and linguistic practice reproduce social differences and impinge upon the ethnicization of Uyghur minority students.

RESEARCH METHODOLOGY

Research Context and Participants

From its founding in 1949, the PRC implemented a Soviet-influenced 'identification of nationalities' project, in which language was a fundamental index, with the result that 56 ethnic groups (including the majority

Han) were eventually recognized (Ma 2010). Whilst Chinese has been promoted as the national language throughout China, linguistic minority groups have been granted the right to use their native languages in diverse social fields, including education (Adamson et al. 2013).

China has witnessed dramatic transitions in its economic, social, and educational spheres over the past three decades due to its 'socialism with Chinese characteristics' development strategy (Dong 2010: 155). Neo-liberal ideas and policies of promoting the market economy and prioritizing regional development have led to huge regional divisions, both between rural and urban centres, and between China's western areas (inhabited largely by minority groups) and its Han-dominated eastern coastal provinces (Harvey 2005). This, together with the decentralization of education and devolution of education finance responsibilities, has caused gaps in the provision of education. In order to integrate minorities through education, a series of measures have been taken. For instance, Inland Xinjiang Boarding Schools (*Neidi Xinjiang gaozhong Ban*, abbreviated as *Neigao ban*) have been established in different cities (such as Beijing and Shanghai), mainly to service Uyghur students (Chen and Postiglione 2009).

China's need to integrate itself into the world economy and the impact of globalization have increased the importance of the English language in education and other spheres of social life. Since 2003, English has been taught from the 3rd year at primary school in economically developed cities and regions; in minority regions, such as Xinjiang, in contrast, bilingual education has focused on Chinese and ethnic languages, with English being taught in a rather piecemeal fashion. Even though trilingual education (in Chinese, heritage language, and English) has been planned in recent years, it has been hard to implement due to a lack of resources (Adamson et al. 2013); as a result, many Uyghur students have limited exposure to English prior to attending university. In terms of Chinese and minority language education, whilst minority students have the right to attend either a minority language primary school (民校, *Minxiao*), Chinese language school (汉校, *Hanxiao*), or Bilingual Class (双语班, *Shuangyu ban*),[1] in recent years, *Minxiao* schools have gradually been merged into *Hanxiao*, resulting in the dominance of Chinese and the marginalization of minority languages (Tsung 2009).

The present study was conducted, against this backdrop, in a top multilingual university (anonymized as Zhendan University) in Shanghai, the economic and financial centre of China. Multiple languages are used at the

Table 12.1   Participants' profile

Participants	Gender	Major
P1	M	Information Security
P2	M	Information Security
P3	M	Cultural Heritage and Museology
P4	M	Public Service and Administration
P5	M	Public Service and Administration
P6 ·	M	Pharmacy
P7	M	Clinical Medicine
P8	F	Clinical Medicine
P9	F	Public Service and Administration
P10	F	International Trade
P11	F	Clinical Medicine
P12	F	Nursing
P13	F	Information Security
P14	F	Economics

university, although Putonghua is both the medium of instruction and the dominant language for general communication; English is of paramount importance for both academic studies and socialization, whereas other ethnic languages are de facto limited to intragroup use. In terms of the university's demographics, at the time of the study, Han students accounted for 79 % of its 32,000 students, while 16 % were international students, and the remaining 5 % (including around 200 Uyghur undergraduate and graduate students) were ethnic minorities from across China.

The present study considers a cohort of Uyghur students studying at Zhendan University, with whom the second author became acquainted in 2012, when she was a student teacher. These students had a complicated language education background, as they had attended different types of schools prior to university. All participants indicated their willingness to participate by signing an informed consent form. Their brief background information, with pseudonyms, is set out in Table 12.1.

Data Collection and Analysis

The primary data drawn on to answer this study's research questions were collected through three rounds of fieldwork during 2013 and 2016, and include recorded interviews with 14 participants and observational notes taken during the fieldwork. All of the interviews were carried out in

Putonghua, which is the mainstream language and lingua franca for communication between the ethnic minorities and the majority Han. Three to five rounds of formal interviews were conducted with participants, each one lasting between one and three hours. During the interviews, participants were encouraged to talk about their experiences, both within and beyond the campus, and to recall critical events or moments to which they attached particular significance. Furthermore, field notes were taken, both during the researcher's interactions with the participants at different sites (e.g. restaurants) and during non-participant observations, for instance in classrooms.

Data analysis began during the fieldwork, when the researcher took notes and reflected on the interviews, and was an inductive process in which relevant categories and themes were allowed to emerge from the data, rather than predetermined (Merriam 2009). Frequently recurring words, phrases, and statements (e.g. regarding the importance of English at Zhendan, difficulties with English and Chinese, the advantages of knowing and using one's mother language, etc.) were examined to reveal their subjectivities. Key emergent categories were synthesized to generate provisional hypotheses, which were then tested against other participants. Cross-case analysis of a series of hypotheses eventually produced two theoretical categories: 'multilingual practice and multiple marginalization' and 'transformation of linguistic and cultural practice and refashion of a Uyghur elite identity'.

FINDINGS

Multilingual Practice and Multiple Marginalization

Data analysis showed that participants experienced multiple marginalizations in the host context due to their insufficient command of market-valuable linguistic capital. Specifically, they found themselves unfavourably positioned in academic studies within the institution, constrained from socialization within the host society, and excluded from the job market. In the study, English was found to play a critical role in relegating the students to a lower status through such stratification mechanisms as English-medium courses, high-stakes university-based English tests, and various assessment mechanisms at different junctures. During the first fieldwork, when asked about their challenges in learning English, a majority of the participants mentioned that they were in the lower Band of the English course, and shared their feelings about such categorizations:

> *Researcher:* How do you feel about being put in Band 1 English course?
> *P2:* I felt very disappointed and frustrated. It's like I suddenly became the worst student. We did not learn much English in senior high school. The textbook contained too much new vocabulary and was so difficult (Interview with P2, 1st fieldwork)

Undergraduates at the university were stratified into three bands (Bands 1, 2, and 3) at the outset, with Band 1 being the lowest competency level and Band 3 the highest. Uyghur students had had rather limited English language immersion prior to attending university, particularly compared with local students and other Han peers from the eastern regions of China, and were immediately categorized as low performers. It can be seen that the institution's English language policy and practice, together with its student management, resemble private sector market principles, in that they are based on competition and driven by the pursuit of greater efficiency (Block and Gray 2015). Moreover, market commodities are tailored to ideal consumers, as interviewees observed when speaking about English textbooks; although Uyghur minority students' basic language learning was covered, their deeper language learning needs and challenges were ignored by the market-oriented approach to language education.

Participants were constantly alienated and excluded by a series of English-medium courses, as shown by field notes taken during the observation of a Finance course:

> Of the roughly 50 students in the class, eight 'international students' and some Chinese students sat in the front, while P4 together with several other students sat at the very back of the classroom. I noticed that although he borrowed a book in Chinese to assist him in understanding the contents, it took him a long time to turn to the pages that corresponded to what the teacher was talking about. We had a very brief conversation during the break.

> *Researcher:* Can you follow the teacher?
> *P4:* Almost not, I have to spend a lot of time on it after class.
> *Researcher:* Why not sit near the front? It is easier to communicate with the teacher.

P4: It is always those international students and some top students who sit in the front and ask questions. My English is not good so, if I have questions, I search answers on the Internet after going back to my dorm.
(Observational notes, 3rd fieldwork, 12 Dec., 2015)

There are four indices related to English to measure a university's degree of 'internationalization' (which, in turn, influences its ranking), including the proportion of English-medium lectures and the number of international students. To enhance its level of 'internationalization' and global competitiveness, around 10 % of the courses offered at Zhendan University are designed to be delivered in English. As the field notes show, the English-medium course, whilst affording the international students and those with high English proficiency distinct academic performance advantages, silenced the Uyghur participant and excluded him from classroom participation. As English has been naturalized as a neutral instrument for judging academic excellence, Uyghur students might be easily perceived as 'inactive learners' or 'incompetent academic performers,' exacerbating the pre-existing disadvantageous position in which their weak English language education placed them.

In addition, English has been institutionalized as an important criterion for becoming a qualified Zhendanese, and all undergraduates must pass a university-based English test (which simulates such international English tests as TOEFL) before graduating and being awarded a bachelor's degree, creating further difficulties for Uyghur students. No training is provided for the test and students are responsible for their own results. In conversation with the researcher, student counsellors described Uyghur participants who had difficulty with the test as 'non-motivated' English learners.

Although participants were subsumed to an unfavourable academic status by their lack of linguistic capital, almost all of them regarded the school as a 'safe', 'tolerant', and 'free space' that provided them with equal opportunities. For example, many participants mentioned that they could work part-time in the school supermarket or magazine stand to ease the financial burden on their family; however, a majority of participants were stuck within the school and had limited interactions and socialization with the host society. This was in stark contrast to their Han counterparts, who, in casual talks with the researcher, said that Shanghai, as an international city, offered them ample opportunities to 'broaden their horizons' by participating in diverse social activities, such as interning at an international corporation. As one participant explained when asked about her experiences in Shanghai:

> P9:   I wanted to be a tutor for local students to learn the local culture, on the one hand, and to earn money to relieve my family's burden on the other. Parents expect you to speak perfect Putonghua, [but] my physical appearance may tell them that I am a Uyghur. . . .
>
> (Interview with P9, 3rd fieldwork)

While neo-liberalism wears the benevolent masks of 'freedom', 'choice', and 'rights', it in fact reconstructs imbalanced power relations between ethnic (racial) groups through market means, in part based on language (Giroux 2008; Harvey 2005; Shin and Park 2016). The data show that standard Putonghua and a Han physical appearance were valued symbolic capital in the market, and the insufficient possession thereof could lead to exclusion and social marginalization. However, the extra difficulties encountered by P10 and P14, the only two participants who had intern experiences, further prove that language constitutes part of the inequalities and is, in turn, constituted by the socio-economic order. For instance, P14 was competent in both Putonghua and English, but struggled because her name identified her Uyghur minority status on her curriculum vitae. It seemed more difficult for Uyghur minorities to translate the symbolic resources they had gained into economic advantages, compared to their Han counterparts. Language and culture functioned as gatekeepers to the employment market, further positioning the Uyghur participants as incapable market participants, as shown below:

> Researcher: Have you started hunting for jobs?
>
> P5:   I am planning to open a halal pilaf (手抓饭, a popular cuisine item among Uyghurs and other Islamic groups) restaurant in Shanghai. Now the major problem is the rental fee is too high. Fortunately, I can apply for funding from an association that aims to support graduate entrepreneurs. It is much easier to start a business here than in Xinjiang regarding its social and political situations.
>
> Researcher: It's a good idea. But have you thought about finding a job?
>
> P5:   My major is economics, and many jobs related to my major involve charging interest, and according to Islam is wrong to charge interest. But my parents were against me . . . they

thought as a graduate of a top university, I should find a decent job. However, they have no idea of the situation here in Shanghai and they also do not understand Islam well.

. . .

Researcher: What do you plan to do next?

P5: Maybe I will continue to find a job, but my English is not that good and I do not want to embarrass myself in the interview...

(Observational notes on P5, 20th November, 2015)

The participant faced daunting challenges and a trilemma during his job hunting. P5 had long told the researcher that he would stay in Shanghai due to its more-developed socio-economic status and less authoritarian nature, compared with Xinjiang. The first part of the conversation seemed to suggest that the participant planned to start his own business, but as the talk went on, we found that P5 in fact desired a proper job, and opening a halal restaurant was only a last resort. He was marginalized in the job market due to his low English proficiency, which has become an important instrument for workforce selection in Shanghai.

The conversation also indicated that P5's religious and cultural beliefs were critical to his ability to resist the unfavourable situations he faced. First, his religion was related to the halal food business, which is popular among Chinese Muslims, and helped to counteract his disadvantageous position in the fiercely competitive Shanghai job market. Moreover, he consciously drew upon his Islamic heritage to contest being labelled an incompetent job seeker and to build a powerful identity as an entrepreneur. Finally, he used his religion to set up a counter-discourse that subverted the low status imposed on restaurant management by traditional culture, and replaced it with that of a pious Muslim businessman. While participants were subjected to multiple marginalizations in the host society, they also embraced its free and mature market and learned to exploit available resources (e.g. funding for new graduates) to negotiate a desirable identity.

Transformation of Linguistic and Cultural Practice and Refashioning of a Uyghur Elite Identity

Data analysis shows that a majority of the participants experienced a transformation from a 'Uyghur only' or 'pure use of Uyghur' language ideology to one more inclusive of languages and the flexible use thereof.

Moreover, they negotiated alternative and desirable identities by marking boundaries, in terms of linguistic attitudes and cultural practices, with other Uyghur students in less prestigious institutions, and by drawing upon multiple linguistic capital and symbolic resources. Such distinctive linguistic practice also built their identity as Uyghur elites. During the first two fieldwork periods, a majority of participants regarded code-switching between Uyghur and Putonghua within a Uyghur group as unacceptable:

> For a Han like you, it might make you feel fashionable (高大上) to code switch between English and Putonghua. Switching between Uyghur and Putonghua among us, however, meant betrayal and sinicization (忘本). Well, you know, um um, regardless of history, this is about the deteriorating situations now in our hometown, where wearing a headscarf or worshiping in the mosque are even restricted or monitored by local government and wherever we go we are required to undergo security checks... Many students attending Chinese schools (汉校)) cannot speak our mother language (Interview with P11, 1st field work)

The above conversation indicates that participants' attitude towards Putonghua was connected with the socio-economic and political environment back in Xinjiang, heavily shaped by their experiences while growing up in their hometown, and deeply entrenched in the linguistic ideology fostered among the Uyghur community. Compared with Shanghai, where the full-fledged implementation of neo-liberal economic policy and fierce market competition has, despite placing people under a huge amount of pressure, fostered a respectful environment for individual freedom (Connell and Dados 2014); in Xinjiang, however, local officials placed strict restrictions on religious practices and exerted rigid and sweeping surveillance of people's public life. According to P11, using Uyghur language and rejecting Putonghua seemed a symbolic instrument for combating the highly regimented governance environment in Xinjiang.

However, both interview and observational data showed that participants' views towards code-switching and Putonghua changed across time. Code-switching between Uyghur and Putonghua during conversations became a common practice during daily conversation, particularly in digital spaces in which Chinese was the major medium for communication:

> Last time, a student from a university in Nanjing posted an essay on Wechat saying that we should reject Putonghua and speak only our mother

language. I cannot agree with her. To be honest, I was not used to the way *minkaohan* (民考汉) in our university spoke [Putonghua]. But now I can understand them. Of course, we should maintain our mother language, but we need to speak Putonghua well in the meantime. We can use it to communicate with Han students and transmit our mother culture. In a word, we should not be narrow-minded.... I do not know exactly how, but Zhendan University has gradually shaped how I look at things over the past years. (Interview with P6, 3rd fieldwork)

P6 illustrated a case in which discussions regarding Uyghur and Putonghua were made between Uyghur students from different universities and cities. In this excerpt, he differentiated himself (and other Zhendan Uyghurs), not only from a Uyghur student at another university, but also from his previous views on Putonghua. P6 shifted from an exclusive view of language to a more eclectic and inclusive linguistic practice, and now viewed Putonghua as a tool for communicating with the host society and maintaining his mother culture. He deemed this change a consequence of his education at Zhendan University and in the host city, and in so doing, constructed a prestigious institutional identity. Participants were also shown to strategically capitalize on heritage resources to construct themselves as qualified Zhendanese:

> *Researcher:* I remember that you told me you had a small vocabulary when you were in my class last year. Did you encounter any other difficulties in learning English?
>
> *P1:* It is the major challenge I have. We did not start learning English until high school, you know. However, Han students, they.... Yeah, Zhendan students are renowned for their English proficiency. But I do think we learn English fast and our pronunciation is better than our Han counterparts'. It is because our mother language has a sophisticated phonology and many Uyghur words are almost the same as English in pronunciation and meaning. There are many successful Uyghurs whose English is very good, like Aili (艾力), a famous English teacher at the New Oriental School. (Interview with P1, 2nd field work)

In view of the general gap in English proficiency between Uyghur participants and their Han counterparts, as well as the high value placed on

English by the institution, P1 drew upon a key figure in their ethnic group and mother language to contest his unfavourable position as a Uyghur language learner. Furthermore, he emphasized the particular English language skills advantages that Uyghur students had compared with their Han peers to negotiate a more desirable identity as a 'qualified Zhendanese, and to construct a positive image of Uyghurs being talented language learners. It should be noted that the participant seemed to have internalized the idea that individuals' morality could be judged by their English performance.

Many Uyghur students also reported that to distinguish themselves from students at other institutions, they performed individualized religious views and practices:

> *Researcher:* I notice that you friend wears a hijab, but you do not. Do you think such differences influence your friendship?
>
> *P9:* No, not at all. In our university, we all respect each other no matter you wear a hijab or not. It is individual freedom. I heard that, in many other universities, if you do not wear it, the senior male student (学长) will come to have a talk with you. Uyghurs in our university are all open-minded, it's like we have been well nurtured by the motto our university advocates: pursuing the freedom of soul and spirit of the non-utilitarian (自由而无用的灵魂). (Interview with P9, 3rd fieldwork)

My field observations revealed that Uyghur students performed rather diverse religious practices and expressed their religious identity in diverse ways; for example, very few students wore a hijab, a small number wore a headscarf, and the majority did not wear either. It seemed that students could get along peacefully while following different religious practices, in contrast (according to P9) to 'other universities', where religious constraints were enforced by senior male fellows. Furthermore, P9 emphasized that the ethos of freedom and tolerance permeating the institution cultivated their willingness to be respectful of individuals' religious rights. An analysis of the above two excerpts suggests that Uyghur students in the study negotiated an educated elite identity by associating it with valuable qualities, and refashioned themselves as 'educational citizens that are rational, responsible and of high esteem' (Wright 2012, p. 291). Yet, the constant inner group contrast and otherization of Uyghur fellows at other institutions may lead to in-group divisions and the projection of negative images.

DISCUSSION AND CONCLUSIONS

This study has explored how a cohort of tertiary-level Uyghur students were positioned in relation to multilingual practice, and the ways in which they responded to that positioning and negotiated their identities in the receiving community. Findings show that participants were (re)ethnicized in the host context, whereby they experienced multiple marginalizations constituted by linguistic practices that were underpinned by the infiltration of neo-liberal values and practices into the spheres of education and of social reality. Participants struggled over the (re)ethnicization process and contested their disadvantageous social positions by capitalizing on a repertoire of linguistic and cultural resources they possessed. Moreover, they tried to negotiate a powerful educated Uyghur elite identity by marking boundaries between themselves and Uyghur counterparts in less prestigious institutions in terms of linguistic attitude and usage. Despite the powerful social positions that they negotiated and imagined, the minority elites faced potential challenges when translating symbolic resources into economic capital in the neo-liberal economy.

Echoing previous studies on transnational migrant minorities in the host context of multilingual settings (e.g. Gu 2014; Martín Rojo 2010; Pérez-Milans and Patiño-Santos 2014), this study finds that, as a social category institutionalized through political force, ethnic identity is easily subjected to socio-economic and political agendas, and can be conveniently drawn upon by the majority as a label to which immoral attributes and negative behaviours are attached. In this study, Uyghur students were unfavourably positioned in academic studies, in integration with the host society, and in entering the workforce market, regardless of their language learning background and the language education division between China's western and eastern provinces. They were categorized as incompetent English language learners, and perceived as passive or ineffective academic performers and fragile market players. The negative features and stereotypical images projected onto the minority participants can be readily linked to ethnic and cultural differences in the host community, and thus ethnicized.

It has been argued by Giroux (2008) that ethnicity (race) can take on different forms across time and space, whilst previous studies on transnational migrant minorities have attributed ethnicization to the historical processes of colonialization and neo-colonialization (e.g. Martín Rojo 2010). Findings from this study, conducted in a Chinese context, seem to indicate that Muslim Uyghur minority students were (re)ethnicized in the host context by the corporization of education, the capitalization of language, and the market-dominated economy. This is in line with a rising body of research on the forms of (re) ethnicity (re-racialization) in neo-liberalized education (e.g. Giroux 2008; Heller 2011; Mac an Ghaill and Haywood 2014; Shain 2011) and recent studies on the relationship between language and identity in the neo-liberal globalized economy, particularly in economically peripheral regions (Piller and Cho 2013; Price 2014; Shin and Park 2016).

In the present study, the planning, delivery, and evaluation of higher education and language education in the subject institution have been framed in terms of the principles of 'competition' and 'free market' applying to the private sector (Price 2014). The stratification of students according to certain standards may enhance efficiency, but may also confer upon minority students a lower status in the hierarchy; English-medium lectures and the high-stakes English test, as institutionalized instruments for globalized competition, may benefit the institution and help to open its doors to English-haves, but will entrench existing socio-economic orders for minority students, who possess less symbolic capital. Moreover, the 'free market' and 'equal competition' in fact have a tacit set of strict rules that favour particular forms of symbolic capital (e.g. ethnicity, language) (Block et al. 2012); the competition is pre-mised on pre-existing inequalities and penalizes those who do not con-form to these rules and standards. For instance, in this study, English and standard Putonghua were normalized as legitimate capital and served a gatekeeping function for entry into the market; as a result, the Uyghur students, being short of privileging capital due to their hometowns' primary and secondary school language education policies and practices and less-developed socio-economic situations, were sanctioned in the host context. Commensurate with Giroux (2008), who argued that marketization and capitalism hide racial inequalities by relocating iden-tity-based stereotypes to market rules, the present study seems to suggest that China's neo-liberalized language education and economy has shifted overt forms of ethnicity to more insidious and covert forms of ethnicity; in other words, minority students have been (re)ethnicized.

Language is a critical area in which unequal social relations are orga-nized, and social and economic inequalities played out (Blommaert 2010; Heller 2011). It is also a place for 'working out struggles that are fundamentally about other things' (Heller 2011: 49) and for contesting categorizations and negative attributes imposed by others. Driven by the new globalized economy and the neo-liberalization of education, language, particularly the English language, has been privileged as an important terrain in which testing, assessment and ranking mechanisms are played out, and individual and institutional worth are demonstrated (Piller and Cho 2013). In this study, participants were marginalized by their insufficient command of legitimate capital in multiple spheres; the fact that they were multilingual subjects was ignored, as was the value of their mother language. Deeper exploration showed that the socio-economic orders that placed the Uyghur minorities in a disadvantageous position prevented the participants from translating the symbolic capital they brought with them or gained in the host community into economic capital in the market. Hence, to understand how minority students were (re)ethnicized through multilingual practices in the host society, we need to 'look outside language and link language explicitly to the socioeconomic order' (Piller and Cho 2013: 24); that is, the neo-liberal globalized economy at both the local and international levels.

As a bottom-up and covert manner of governance that emphasizes freedom and individual responsibility, neo-liberalized institutions seem to offer space for minority participants to negotiate powerful identities through exercising agency. The Muslim Uyghur students in this study conceived a Uyghur educated elite identity by drawing upon the distinctive linguistic and cultural practices they developed in the host institution, and by differentiating themselves from other Uyghur in less prestigious institutions. Added value was even attached to the Uyghur language by relating it to their English language learning experiences, so as to construct a positive heritage identity and negotiate a desirable institutional identity. However, the negotiated identities were self-referent and transient, and thus vulnerable to and easily subverted by the market, as shown by the study's finding that symbolic capital can be devalued.

Affirmative action, as part of a national project intended to integrate minorities into mainstream Chinese society (Clothey 2005; Chen and Postiglione 2009), seems to have been impeded by the neo-liberal socioeconomic order and market-oriented education. In view of the study's findings, the following suggestions are offered for consideration when implementing educational and language policies for minorities.

First, policy-makers should consider implementing, in minority regions, proper trilingual education and flexible social policies that give due attention to both heritage and highly valued languages, and that respect ethnic cultural practices. Policies other than affirmative action and market regulation need to be considered if minority students are to translate the symbolic resources they gain through higher education into economic and social capital.

Host institutions should reflect on their language educational policies as they apply to globalization, including analysing both the benefits and costs of joining the competition; it is suggested that language accommodations be made to facilitate minority students' academic study and socializations within the community, and that minority students' multilingual and multi-cultural resources be validated to create a real multi-cultural community.

Finally, minority students are urged to be open-minded, to exploit local and community resources, and to release themselves from entrenched essentialist views of ethnic identity, language, and territory, so as to facilitate their integration and upward mobility within the host society.

This study is limited, in that it has focused on only a small number of Uyghur students in only one institution. As such, further study involving a larger population and more institutions should be carried out to improve our understanding of the underlying issues; in addition, longitudinal studies could be conducted to track how minority students negotiate subjectivity in the workplace.

Note

1. Uyghur students who attended these types of primary schools refer to themselves as *minkaomin (民考民), minkaohan (民考汉)*, and *shuangyu ban (双语班)* students respectively.

References

Adamson, B., Feng, A., Liu, Q., & Li, Q. (2013). Ethnic minorities and trilingual education policies. In D. Besharove & K. Baehler (Eds.), *Chinese social policy in a time of transition* (pp. 180–195). Oxford: Oxford University Press.

Block, D., & Gray, J. (2015). Just go away and do it and you get marks': The degradation of language teaching in neoliberal times. *Journal of Multilingual and Multicultural Development*, doi: 10.1080/01434632.2015.1071826.

Block, D., Gray, J., & Holborow, M. (2012). *Neoliberalism and applied linguistics.* London: Routledge.

Blommaert, J. (2010). *The sociolinguistics of globalization.* Cambridge: Cambridge University Press.

Bourdieu, P. (1986). The forms of capital. In J. Richardson (Ed.), *Handbook of theory and research for the sociology of education* (pp. 241–258). New York: Greenwood Press.

Bourdieu, P. (1991). *Language and symbolic power*. New York: Harvard University Press.

Brown, W. (2005). *Edgework: Critical essays on knowledge and politics*. Princeton, NJ: Princeton University Press.

Chen, Y. B., & Postiglione, G. A. (2009). Muslim Uyghur students in a dislocated Chinese boarding school: Bonding social capital as a response to ethnic integration. *Race/Ethnicity: Multidisciplinary Global Contexts, 2,* 287–309.

Clothey, R. (2005). China's policies for ethnic minority studies: Negotiating national values and ethnic identities. *Comparative Education Review, 49,* 389–409.

Connell, R., & Dados, N. (2014). Where in the world does neoliberalism come from? *Theory and Society, 43,* 117–138.

Davies, B., & Harré, R. (1990). Positioning: The discursive production of selves. *Journal for the Theory of Social Behaviour, 20,* 43–63.

Dong, J. (2010). Neo-liberalism and the evolvement of China's education policies on migrant children's schooling. *The Journal for Critical Education Policy Studies, 8,* 137–160.

Giles, J., & Johnson, P. (1987). Ethnolinguistic identity theory: A social psychological approach to language maintenance. *International Journal of the Sociology of Language, 68,* 69–99.

Giroux, H. (2008). *Against the terror of neoliberalism: Politics beyond the age of greed*. London: Paradigm Publishers.

Gu, M. (2014). A complex interplay between religion, gender and marginalization: Pakistani schoolgirls in Hong Kong. *Ethnic and Racial Studies, 38,* 1934–1951.

Hall, S. (1992). New ethnicities. In J. Donald & A. Rattansi (Eds.), *'Race', culture & difference* (pp. 441–449). London: Sage.

Harvey, D. (2005). *A brief history of neoliberalism*. Oxford: Oxford University Press.

Heller, M. (2011). *Paths to post-nationalism: A critical ethnography of language and identity*. Oxford: Oxford University Press.

Hobsbawm, E. (1990). *Nations and nationalism since 1780: Programme, myth, reality*. Cambridge: Cambridge University Press.

Ma, R. (2010). 'Culturalism' and 'nationalism' in modern China. In M. Guibernau. & J. Rex (Eds.), *The ethnicity reader: Nationalism, multiculturalism, & migration* (2nd ed., pp. 299–307). Cambridge: Polity Press.

Mac an Ghaill, M., & Haywood, C. (2014). Pakistani and Bangladeshi young men: re-racialization, class and masculinity within the neo-liberal school. *British Journal of Sociology of Education, 35,* 753–776.

Martín Rojo, L. (Ed.). (2010). *Constructing inequality in multilingual classrooms*. Berlin: Walter de Gruyter.

Merriam, S. B. (2009). *Qualitative research: A guide to design and implementation*. San Francisco, CA: Jossey-Bass.

Mok, K. H., & Lo, Y. W. (2007). The impacts of neo-liberalism on China's higher education. *Journal for Critical Education Policy Studies, 5*, 293–312.

National Bureau of Statistics of the People's Republic of China. (2010). *Tabulation on the 2010 population census of the People' Republic of China*. http://www.stats.gov.cn/tjsj/pcsj/rkpc/6rp/indexch.htm

Pennycook, A. (2007). *Global Englishes and transcultural flows*. London: Routledge.

Pérez-Milans, M., & Patiño-Santos, A. (2014). Language education and institutional change in a Madrid multilingual school. *International Journal of Multilingualism, 11*, 449–470.

Piller, I., & Cho, J. (2013). Neoliberalism as language policy. *Language in Society, 42*, 23–44.

Price, G. (2014). English for all? Neoliberalism, globalization, and language policy in Taiwan. *Language in Society, 43*, 567–589.

Shain, F. (2011). *The New Folk Devils: Muslim boys and education in England*. Stoke on Trent: Trentham Books.

Shin, H., & Park, J. S. Y. (2016). Researching language and neoliberalism. *Journal of Multilingual and Multicultural Development, 37*(5), 443–522.

Tsung, L. (2009). *Minority languages, education and communities in China*. Basingstoke; New York: Palgrave Macmillan.

Tsung, L. (2014). *Language power and hierarchy: Multilingual education in China*. London: Bloomsbury Academic.

Wright, A. (2012). Fantasies of empowerment: Mapping neo-liberal discourse in the coalition government's schools policy. *Journal of Education Policy, 27*, 279–294.

Mingyue Gu is an assistant professor in the Faculty of Education at the Chinese University of Hong Kong. She is the editor of Book Review section of *Journal of Asia TEFL*. Her research interests include language and identity, language and ideology, discourse theory and analysis, multilingualism and mobility, and teacher education. She has published in over 20 international referred journals such as *Journal of Pragmatics, Multilingua, Journal of Multilingual and Multicultural Development, System, Language Teaching Research, Journal of Education for Teaching, Ethnic and Racial Studies, Language and Education, Linguistics and Education, International Journal of Bilingual Education and Bilingualism,* and *Computer Assisted Language Learning*.

Xiaoyan Guo's research interests include identity, multilingualism, critical theory, language education and neo-liberalism. Her PhD thesis explores the processes of identity construction in relation to multilingual practices for a cohort of Uyghur students in tertiary education in China

Educating Muslim Students: Late Modernity, Masculinity, Inclusion/Exclusion and the Neo-liberal School

Máirtín Mac an Ghaill and Chris Haywood

INTRODUCTION

This chapter explores the experiences of schooling among Muslim young men (third-generation Pakistani and Bangladeshi background) to examine what inclusion/exclusion means to them. They are currently experiencing intensified forms of monitoring and surveillance, as part of a 'suspect community', recently made most visible through the legislation on the prevention of violent extremism (Kundnani 2009; UK Government 2009; see Miah, this collection). Qualitative research was undertaken with 48 young men living in areas of the West Midlands, England. The young men highlighted three key areas: the emergence of a schooling regime operating through neo-liberal principles, the recognition of class difference between themselves and teachers and their awareness of how racialization operated through codes of masculinity. It is argued that research on issues of

M. Mac an Ghaill (✉)
Graduate School, Newman University, Birmingham, UK
e-mail: m.macanghaill@newman.ac.uk

C. Haywood
Newcastle University, Newcastle upon Tyne, UK
e-mail: chris.haywood@newcastle.ac.uk

© The Author(s) 2017
M. Mac an Ghaill, C. Haywood (eds.), *Muslim Students, Education and Neoliberalism*, DOI 10.1057/978-1-137-56921-9_13

inclusion/exclusion should be cautious when interpreting new forms of class identity through conventional categories of ethnicity.

An important aim of the chapter, in understanding how inclusion and exclusion manifests itself in this context, is to explore Pakistani and Bangladeshi young men through an alternative representational space; a space that enables the research participants to reflect on a range of generationally specific social and cultural exclusions that are significantly mediated through and by the education system. More specifically, it focuses on young Pakistani and Bangladeshi men's experiences of neo-liberal discourses to examine how inclusion/exclusion is being experienced in light of the movement of schools away from a *local* shared community sensibility towards an institution positioned as a *global* performative academy. The second aim of this chapter is to examine how these young men's identities are intersected through class and how class difference operates as a method of ethnic coding. Finally, exclusion is examined in relation to the young men's experience of marginalization through gender, more specifically through the (dis)identifications with 'Muslim masculinities'. Underpinning these aims is an argument that a 'post-race' neo-liberal regulatory regime intersects with attempts by schools to contain and produce Pakistani and Bangladeshi young men by attempting to fix them into a reified singular category of religion. Therefore, as achievement and academic success become reframed through notions of individualized responsibility, the chapter examines the young men's experience of schools' exclusionary practice of reifying religion as an ethnic category.

In this chapter we argue that neo-liberalism and class and (re)racialization provide ways of reading and understanding Pakistani and Bangladeshi young men's experiences of exclusion/inclusion in educational contexts. At different moments within their narratives, a simplistic reductionism to one particular frame fails to capture the complexity of what it feels like to be growing up in England. This also has particular methodological implications that we now discuss.

PAKISTANI AND BANGLADESHI YOUNG MEN'S NARRATIVES: METHODS AND METHODOLOGICAL AUTONOMY

Our earlier work with a younger generation of Pakistani and Bangladeshi young men, in Newcastle, London and Birmingham, makes clear their geographically specific local experiences of growing up in a rapidly changing

Britain (Mac an Ghaill 1994; Mac an Ghaill and Haywood 2005). In other words, the young men in this Birmingham-based sample inhabit specific lifestyles within a spatial context of diverse social trajectories among a changing Muslim diaspora in Britain. This includes acknowledging young Muslim men's generationally specific reclamation of the concept Muslim as a self-referent, the re-articulation of class and gender-based being and belonging, the cultural politics of Islam and the media-projected visibility of their community as a 'home-produced' anti-British ethnicity. Within this context, such communities are highly diverse; and as a qualitative and explorative study, the chapter does not seek inductive validity by suggesting that the participants represent the experiences of the broader Muslim male population of the area or the general population. Instead, as Crouch and McKenzie (2006: 493) argue:

> Rather than being systematically selected instances of specific categories of attitudes and responses, here respondents embody and represent meaningful experience-structure links. Put differently, our respondents are 'cases', or instances of states, rather than (just) individuals who are bearers of certain designated properties (or 'variables').

Therefore, it is the exploration of the young men's meaningful experiences that was a key objective of the research design. During a three-year period (2008–11), we have recorded the experiences of 48 Pakistani ($n = 30$) and Bangladeshi ($n = 18$) self-identified Muslim young men living in areas experiencing high levels of poverty and unemployment. Aged 16–21, we use the young men's narratives of schooling to engage with issues of inclusion and exclusion. The majority of the young men ($n = 38$) attended local secondary schools, sixth-form colleges and further education colleges. Group and life-history interviews provided the framework through which to explore a range of critical incidents experienced by these young men. The group interviews were carried out at local community centres and the life-history interviews were carried out in various places, including at youth and community organizations and local cafes. These interviews lasted around 45–90 minutes and provided insight into growing up, family, schooling, social life and local community. The interview groups contained a mix of Bangladeshi and Pakistani young men, who shared not only intimate friendships but were part of a broader social community that included attending the same youth and community organizations and colleges, sharing the same employers and participating together in leisure activities. Furthermore, although they were diverse individuals, in terms of ethnicity, age, past experience and social status with different current experiences of being in education, work/training or unemployed, they held a shared critical reflexivity of their schooling experiences as Muslim students.

While carrying out empirical work with young people, we were introduced to two young men in the local area, who introduced us to other young people and this subsequently led to further snowballing of other friends, family and community representatives. The datasets from each of the methods was subject to thematic analysis (Braun and Clarke 2006) that enabled us to explore '...the underlying ideas, constructions and discourses that shape or inform the semantic content of the data' (Ussher et al. 2013: 3). All interviews throughout the study were anonymized and the research participants were given pseudonyms to protect their confidentiality (Popoviciu et al. 2006).

From the Local Community School to the Global Performative Culture of the Neo-liberal School

In this section, we explore Pakistani and Bangladeshi students' experiences of exclusion/inclusion through neo-liberal restructuring of education. The performative culture of the neo-liberal school can be understood as being subject to a series of state interventions that promote competition, entrepreneurialism and deregulation (Davies and Bansel 2007). Furthermore, schools are tasked with generating knowledge and skills that can be traded by students in the global marketplace. Becoming the 'right' kind of student enables and facilitates educational success. One of the important issues discussed by the students focused on how exclusion was articulated in relation to institutional performativity. This means that there is not a displacement of categories of racialization and their attendant exclusionary effects, but rather a re-racialization through performativity. Most interestingly, they suggested that schools through everyday curricular and pedagogical practices draw upon Muslim as a racialized category. Furthermore, they suggest that the specific teacher–student interactions that they experience are generated by constant government-led institutional changes. In developing their narratives of education around issues of inclusion and exclusion, they provided a comparative analysis based on their families' earlier experiences of local community schooling and a review of their own schooling biographies:

> *Imran*: Like the other day, when that group of kids were all talking, some saying that school is really Islamophobic cos the teachers really hate Muslims and the others were saying no that's not true.
>
> *M.M*: What do you mean?
>
> *Imran*: Other kids weren't sure if you could call the teachers Islamophobic or racist or something big like that. But what Ajaz says now seems more true. It's not like teachers thinking, you're a Muslim so I'm going to discriminate against you. It's nothing planned or anything. The way teachers treat pupils is just ordinary stuff, just like every day stuff, like they don't really care about kids. They'd probably treat all kids like this, maybe a bit worse cos they're Muslim. I agree with Ajaz.

For Imran, exclusion operates through racial/religious categories, and he highlights the complexities of identifying the subjectivities of young Muslims. The discussion on the appropriateness of classifying exclusion as Islamophobia or racism highlights the ambivalence within young people of how to make sense of their experiences. Part of the issue is to move away from the assumption that these young people have 'settled' understandings about their own identifications and their experiences of exclusionary practices. Crucially, these young men did not reduce exclusion to a singular notion of racism or Islamophobia but, rather, how that exclusion is articulated became linked to specific educational processes. In the context of this section, the framing of exclusion intersects with neo-liberal educational policies. To explore this in more detail, further questions were asked that highlighted a regulatory shift in how the school engaged with young people:

> *M.M*: Why do you think the teachers are like this?
>
> *Wasim*: When I started at secondary school and definitely at primary, going to school was like a community and the teachers were an important part of that community. But everything's changed, all the league tables, tests, all the time tests, tests, academies, everything. It's run just like a business.
>
> *M.M*: So, what was your school like?
>
> *Wasim*: You're a customer, but everyone knows business isn't about caring about people. And, Muslim customers would be at the bottom.

> Like in the past for our parents the racist stuff was about the 'Paki' corner shop, now the racist stuff is the Muslim school. Who'd wanna go there? Who'd wanna teach there, it's seen as the lowest. Like you go there, and no chance of getting a job. Employers, they'll look at what school you're from and say, no thanks.

The implication of the above discussion is that their inclusion/exclusion as Pakistani and Bangladeshi young men has become re-configured outside anti-racist theories that frame race through black/white dichotomies. Rather, performance and achievement become de-racialized in one moment, while in another the religious identity of Muslim has become a re-racialized source of exclusion. In this sense, exclusion becomes articulated across multiple discourses, which have been facilitated through a reconstitution of notions of the 'good' teacher, student and parent. We can see from the above extract that the notion of the 'good school' is being re-defined with a neo-liberal concept of the schooling self-aligned with the emergence of the entrepreneurial self, suggesting that individual subjects are responsible for their own academic 'under-achievement' (Walkerdine 2003). This new schooling regime differentially affects different social groups. So, for example, the disproportionate high levels of academic under-achievement among Pakistani and Bangladeshi students is primarily explained in terms of an assumed cultural deficit model of the (Muslim) students' learning identities that is directly connected to their home lives (Garner and Bhattacharyya 2011). The students below understand that, despite the rhetoric of all students being treated equally, social differentiation continues. The re-configuration of schools into academies, for example, serves to increase feelings of marginalization:

M.M: How does that affect students round here?
Sajid: Teachers aren't now rewarded for looking after kids in a general way, like supporting them, like encouraging them if the work is hard. I don't think they'd even know, if a pupil was doing bad work, if it was because they found the work hard or were just lazy.
Asif: I think they get paid for sorting kids out into difference levels. Like you're the clever ones, like we were told and you lot aren't the clever ones. But teachers, especially the younger teachers don't even know anything about us. Like out mates were just as clever as we were, even more ability, really clever, but they were slotted into the not clever, the failing group.
Azam: This is normal for loads of Muslim kids. You can't really blame the teachers. It's just the way it is.

These young men recognize that the schooling processes underpinned by an ideology of performativity continue to use cultural differences as a mechanism for segregation. It is suggested that the neo-liberal regulatory regime of the 'performative school' is of central constitutive significance in the conceptual manufacturing of British Muslim students. The fixing of this social group works through Muslim-specific discursive mechanisms of control imposed upon young Muslim men, alongside wider institutional processes that operate against the interests of working-class young people, experienced through the current fragmentation of state schooling. Therefore, the next section recognizes the ideological implication of neo-liberal discourses in the context of class differentiation as a constituent of these young men's experiences of inclusion/exclusion.

CLASS DIFFERENCE, NEO-LIBERALISM AND YOUNG MUSLIMS

The last decade has witnessed a fundamental shift in dominant British political and media discourses that have positioned the Muslim community, and more specifically young Muslim men and women, as a major social problem for the state (Bhattacharya 2008). They are projected as having broken the multi-cultural social contract that emerged during the 1970s around a notion of ethnic integration. Their projected refusal to integrate has manifested itself in pervasive images of a traditional religious community living a self-segregating, anti-modern existence that is alien to a British way of life. Importantly, it is not Muslims per se who are seen as a threat to social cohesion; rather, it is young (non-)working-class men (and women). Currently, at a time when commentators speak of a post-racial politics, there is much evidence of the historical continuity of racially inflected, class-based structural constraints on Pakistani and Bangladeshi working-class young men. Their collective profile includes the highest levels of unemployment and over-representation in low-skilled employment, over-representation in prisons, over-representation in poor housing, high levels of poor health and lowest levels of social mobility (Garner and Bhattacharyya 2011).

Recently, within the conditions of socio-economic austerity, increasing inequalities and regional socio-economic disparities, the success of UKIP, UK Independence Party, in local elections provides evidence of an emergence of an assertive English nationalism that serves to illustrate how different communities within Britain are impelled to live with different social realities. The increasing fear of an (imagined) all-pervasive Muslim

Fundamentalism articulated through English nationalism is captured by Majid, as he discusses social exclusion:

> *Majid*:   Can you imagine if white people had to live with a threat from racist groups, can you imagine it? It would be top of the news every day. But Muslim people in this country live with this every day. And you're not worried just for yourself but if your mother or sister or if the old people are going out. And the media love to stir it up every time there's something from Afghanistan, Iraq, just all the time talking about extremists and we don't even know any extremists. We're just trying to get on with our lives.

Class restructuring in Britain is being played out within the context of austerity and accompanying socio-economic divisions, which, as the students indicate above, differentially impact on racialized diasporian groups, such as Pakistani and Bangladeshi communities. More specifically, reading through the research literature, a main government and academic image of Pakistani and Bangladeshi students is that of under-achievement, with Pakistani and Bangladeshi male students, in terms of ethnicity, faith group, class and gender, placed at the bottom of league tables on academic school performance (Department for Education and Skills 2007; Office for National Statistics 2012; Birmingham Council 2013).

Shain (2011) provides one of the most sustained critical explanations of contemporary Muslim boys' experiences in England, arguing for a more theoretically sophisticated approach that includes the development of a socio-economic dimension. She adopts a Gramscian analysis emphasizing the articulation of multiple structures of race, gender and class with socio-economic and political relations of domination and subordination (Gramsci 1970). In our research, the young men's narratives serve to critique the dominant culturalist explanation that the state, including institutional sites, such as schooling and policing, ascribes to them. Rather, they are experiencing generationally specific material conditions, in which securing masculine subjectivities is a complex process that conceptually cannot be contained within the singular identity category of religion. Throughout the research there was evidence of a range of contemporary fragmented male subjectivities, social trajectories and cultural belonging. So, for example, for some of these working-class students there was an intense consciousness of how their divided lives from that of their teachers is materially structured, enacted and performed on each school day (Qureshi 2004). Thus, while in the previous section discourses of religion and ethnicity were articulated through neo-liberal regulations, in a similar way class difference was generated by teachers who actively distancing themselves from Pakistani and Bangladeshi working-class communities.

Imitiaz: I used to think it was all because we were Muslim that the teachers were really different to us, but becoming mates with some of the white kids here, I can see things differently. Teachers are just posh people. They don't live here in this area and our white mates are definitely closer to us than they are to them.

Tamim: Maybe the teachers have more problems with the white kids, because they're white, but the teachers know they're nothing like them.

In the above conversation, the students highlight the racialization of class difference. According to Jacobowitz (2004), this racialization refers to 'what we might call the displacement of class differences onto racial differences'. In this context, middle class becomes a code for whiteness, with young Bangladeshi and Pakistani men often developing friendships with young white working-class men living in the same neighbourhood. In effect, social inequality brought together young men from a range of ethnic backgrounds that was often articulated through a shared sense of difference from and enacted forms of resistance to middle-class teachers. Thus, normative whiteness and middle-classness become fused and projected onto the bodies of teachers. Importantly for these young men, whiteness and middle-classness become synonymous and are underpinned by an entrepreneurial self that is aligned to individualized choice. As Farooq points out:

Teachers wouldn't dare live in this area. Of course they would never send their kids to the same school as us. They live in posh areas, white areas, so really they're segregating not us?

This fusion of whiteness and class becomes emblematic of the exclusions that are a consequence of a shift in the meaning of social justice and citizenship. More specifically, this is a shift from an inclusive schooling premised on social justice and a recognition and acceptance of diversity, to one where diversity is not tolerated. Furthermore, as we illustrate in the next section, social justice is not only positioned as a threat to social equity but, in the context of contemporary England, it is being elided with the promotion of a terrorist threat (Khiabany and Williamson 2012).

In summary, we have argued that these young men are identifying the shift from community-based schools to that of Academies located within a globalized economy. They highlight how such ideologies of citizenship tended to hide the racialization of class differentiation. In the final section below, we explore how masculinity can be used to understand Pakistani and Bangladeshi young men's experience of inclusion/exclusion in the schooling context.

THE EMERGING FIGURE OF THE MUSLIM MALE STUDENT: FROM (THE LOCAL) FEMINIZATION TO (THE GLOBAL) MASCULINE CULTURAL WARRIOR

In an earlier period, policy, academic and teacher discourses operated with an oppositional logic that valorized the ascribed cultural unity of the Asian community, with Asian male students projected as 'pro-school' in contrast to 'anti-school' African-Caribbean students. At the same time, within the gendered politics of the playground, Asian young men were ascribed the lowest ethnic masculinity, with terms of abuse – for example, 'Paki' – carrying not simply a racial connotation but at the same moment connoting a gender meaning. Deriving from an imperial legacy of Orientalist discourses, this was part of a wider ascription of institutional processes of feminization that served to position them as 'non-proper' men (Said 1993; Haywood and Mac an Ghaill 2003).

Exploring the current conceptual manufacturing of the Muslim male student, for the Pakistani and Bangladeshi young men in this study, as suggested in the Introduction, a central feature of their lives are schools' attempted institutional containment of them within the singular category of religion. This has major effects in limiting the range of positions that can be occupied as a young Muslim man within schools, which is informed by a wider societal 're-categorisation of various ethnic (Mirpuri, Bangladeshi, Pakistani) groups into religious (Muslim) ones' (Shain 2011: 15). For the young men in our study, there is now an intensified global surveillance, local cultural pathologization and multiple forms of social and racial exclusion of their social lives that operate within this re-categorization. Here, they identify the specific ways in which its logic is played out within a schooling arena. More specifically, they were aware of the history of the racialized gendered positioning of earlier generations, outlined above, which contrasted with their current ascription as the '(global) bad boys' within schools.

Yasin: Teachers do it in their way. Like we say in a more hidden way, but it's like they're suspicious of us, all the time.

Tareq: It's true but they do it in their own way. I think they would mostly say they're not racist, not Islamophobic coz they probably don't think that we're bombers or terrorists. But they have their own ways of keeping you in a box.

Waqar: Basically, they see us as trouble. We're the bad boys. I remember in our school earlier on it was the black boys who the teachers picked on most but then it slowly changed and it was us.

M.M: So, what has changed?

Waqar: My cousins say that Asian pupils used to be seen as really weak, but now Muslims are seen as the strongest, like we're seen as like warriors.

Farooq: Yes, it's that but it's more than that. If you're a Muslim pupil, then they think of you always as a Muslim, whatever you're doing, P.E., walking in the playground, coming into the class, everything. They wouldn't think that about a Sikh or a black kid and never about a white kid. We're just marked out.

Ali: Yeah, as trouble makers.

Farooq: No. Not necessarily trouble makers. We're seen in a different way than any other group, any other group of pupils. But you're right that most Muslim kids know that if you scratch the surface then white people, teachers, even the good ones, the nice ones, see you in a certain sort of way. You can never escape.

Kashif: Do you understand? In the past the word 'Paki' was the stereotype. Now people say Muslims are called terrorists but the real stereotype now is to be called a Muslim. So how are you supposed to behave in school?

Javed: That is very true.

A key issue that emerges here is the question of how a socially constructed phenomenon, such as religion, becomes fixed as an apparently stable unitary category. Adopting a post-colonial analysis, we suggest that schools alongside other institutions currently attempt to administer, regulate and reify unstable social categories, such as religion, ethnicity, gender and sexuality (see Mirza 2009). Most particularly, the administration, regulation and reification of the boundaries of these categories are institutionalized through the inter-related social and discursive practices of staffroom, classroom and playground micro-cultures. In relation to young men, Muslim masculinity has been an alternative space where the State is attempting to reclaim a safe ethnic identity. Dwyer et al. (2008) highlight the different primary resources through which Pakistani men articulate their masculinities. They discuss 'religious masculinities', 'middle class masculinities', 'rebellious masculinities' and 'ambivalent masculinities' (often a combination of middle-class and rebellious masculinities) to capture the diversity of masculine styles taken up by men in their study. They use these characterizations of masculinity: 'because it allows us to highlight what we believe are significant insights; particularly the different ways in which class operates, how religious identities are mobilised in different ways and how young men with similar educational backgrounds may negotiate different choices' (Dwyer et al. 2008: 121 see; Hopkins 2009).

The accounts below suggest a fluid process of (dis)identification with young people taking up particular understandings of Muslim identities that facilitate different masculinities at different times. As indicated in the previous section, it is not self-evident how young people understand the notion of Muslim or indeed how this is a constituting feature of their 'masculinities'. In the context of schools and the young people in this research, a major theme that emerges from the students' narratives is the disjuncture between teachers and students on how they mobilize the concept of Muslim. From the students' perspective, this mobilization consists of students reclaiming the concept of Muslim as a collective self-referent and recognizing teachers' racialized ascription of the term Muslim that ultimately serves to contain and explain student subjectivities. Teachers were seen as operating with a highly reductive understanding of religion that assumed a homogeneous image of Muslims. In contrast, in the young men's self-representations, reclaiming the concept of Muslim did not necessarily mean an increase in religious identity or ethnic behaviour. Most importantly, the research participants illustrate throughout this article that the school's institutional attempt to contain young Muslim men by fixing them into a reified singular radicalized category of religious identity denies them the social power of self-authorization.

> *Shabbir:*   I think teachers see a Muslim and straight away think about religion. But most kids in our school are not really very religious. It's just the same like any other group, like the Sikhs. A few are very religious, but most are just ordinary, getting on with their lives.
>
> *Sajid:*   Teachers are probably confused by Muslims, cos the media show all these extremists, but Islam is not like other religions, like Christianity, there is no central system governing ordinary

	Muslims. So it's the opposite to what they think. We're not all brainwashed into acting the same.

Asif: Sometimes you'd like to explain to a teacher, there's no such thing as a Muslim. We're all individuals. But I don't think they'd understand, do you?

Abdul: Yes, definitely teachers are weird, especially with Muslim girls at school. If teachers saw a Muslim girl with traditional clothes as well as any modern fashion, you would hear them saying, look at her, wearing the fashionable clothes when she's supposed to be a Muslim. It's like they're the police and they're saying you're supposed to be a traditionalist Muslim girl, why don't you act like one. It's weird, it's like they're offended, so they feel they have to force her back into their stereotype of what a proper Muslim is.

Parvez: It's because teachers don't really know Muslims. So, they'll have these strange stereotypes of them been oppressed and forced to wear the veil and all that. It's like we've to act out what they think we are.

We need further research on the young men's (and women's) active involvement in the reconfiguration of the meaning of being Muslim by reclaiming the concept as a collective self-referent. For example, some of the Pakistani and Bangladeshi young men in our research emphasized the positive aspects of publicly identifying as Muslim in a society that exhibits high levels of faith-hate.

Shoaib: I sometimes think that for the teachers, the real issue is that they look at Muslims, and cos there's a lot at our school and we're strong and look after each other, they can't pick on us. Like you look at the white kids, there's not many of them and they get picked on more than us by some teachers. Even the black kids don't stick together like they used to and they get picked out as well.

M.M: So, Muslims get the best treatment?

Shoaib: No, nothing like that. We get a lot of bad stuff as well. But I'm saying there's a good side to being Muslim, like we won't get racist stuff cos we are seen to be strong. And our parents were seen to be weak, so they got attacked and beaten up, even at school. We are under more pressure from the racists now but they know Muslims can't now be messed with.

Broader dominant representations of young Asian/Muslim men projected across the state, media and popular culture are mediated within public institutions, alongside specific institutionally produced internal school representations. This has included a diverse range of cultural archetypes within the changing social formations of early and late modernity – the age of global migration. There is a long history of British schooling employing 'containing' categories that frame the possibilities of knowing and understanding Asian/Muslim male students. In turn, established educational research rationalities serve to rigidly catalogue the lives of these young men. Of particular significance in understanding the emergence of the figure of the Asian/Muslim male student has been the institutional deployment of key analytical categories, namely culture, community and religion, which are implicitly assumed to be ahistorical, unitary, universal and thus unchanging. As Westwood (1990: 59) notes: 'Discourses of registers of masculinity are worked out in a variety of spaces'. Therefore, the fear of Muslim young men does not simplistically operate outside the school; rather, these representations are produced and located within the school itself and most recently played out within the context of the war on terror. The formation of appropriate forms of Britishness resonates with a previous moment in British history, where English (masculinities) become recoded through ascendant registers of Britishness, in response to the catalyst of civil war and the Act of the Union (Kumar 2003). At present, the current initiatives explored above resonate a similar process of colonization and the designation of safe and dangerous young British men through school-based regimes of masculinity.

CONCLUSION

The historical reconfiguration of race/ethnicity in English schools through policy initiatives has resulted in a number of disparate intellectual interventions. The theoretical tensions and convergences between perspectives, such as anti-racism, multi-culturalism and post-colonialism facilitate a productive context systematically to engage with recent government strategy to address inclusion/exclusion in young Muslim men's lives. This engagement has enabled the recognition that Pakistani and Bangladeshi young men's experiences of schooling are being shaped by recent neo-liberal-based policy initiatives. Alongside this, their experience of inclusion/exclusion within the school context is also inflected by a broader cultural turn that involves the reconfiguration of Muslim as sign of religious membership to one of Muslim as an ethnic identity. One of the findings of the research highlighted how the shift to institutional performativity helped provide a context for ambivalence in young men about how inclusion/exclusion operated. They demonstrate that there is no settled understanding of why exclusion is taking place. They often oscillated between exclusion as Islamophobia or racialization. At the same time, they recognize that as an individualized entrepreneurial (neo-liberal) self is promoted, their academic failure becomes reducible to their (Muslim) family backgrounds. Alongside this, the research illustrated how the racialization of inclusion and exclusion operated through class dynamics. In the school context, teachers' embodied whiteness became a space wherein class difference could be displaced. Finally, the research identified how young Pakistani and Bangladeshi men are now being framed through particular notions of Muslim masculinity. The dominant inclusionary narratives about minority ethnic young men as victims are often juxtaposed with discourses that position these same young men as tough, aggressive and misogynistic. Thus, Pakistani and Bangladeshi young men highlight how schools use Muslim identity as a gendered construct that is indicative of a particular threatening masculinity. In conclusion, the increasing ambivalence surrounding race/ethnicity and the growing visibility of a neo-conservative nationalism that impels an absolute cultural (moral) difference means that categories of same and other are moving into sharper distinction. Theorizing how such distinctions operate and are deployed in schooling spaces is an increasingly necessary intervention in understanding contemporary racial/ethnic relations and the attendant practices of inclusion and exclusion.

References

Bhattacharya, G. (2008). *Dangerous brown men: Exploiting sex, violence and feminism in the war on terror*. London: Zed Books.

Birmingham City Council. (2013). Ethnic groups: Population and census. http://www.birmingham.gov.uk.

Braun, V., & Clarke, V. (2006). Using thematic analysis in psychology. *Qualitative Research in Psychology, 3*(2), 77–101.

Crouch, M., & McKenzie, H. (2006). The logic of small samples in interview-based qualitative research. *Social Science Information, 45*(4), 483–499.

Davies, B., & Bansel, P. (2007). Neoliberalism and education. *International Journal of Qualitative Studies in Education, 20*(3), 247–259.

Department for Education and Skills. (2007). *Gender and education: The evidence on pupils in England research information*. London: Department for Education and Skills.

Dwyer, C., Shah, B., & Sanghera, G. (2008). 'From cricket lover to terror suspect' – Challenging representations of young British Muslim men. *Gender, Place and Culture: A Journal of Feminist Geography, 15*(2), 117–136.

Garner, S., & Bhattacharyya, G. (2011). *Poverty, ethnicity and place.* York: Joseph Rowntree Foundation.

Gramsci, A. (1970). *Selections from the prison notebooks.* London: Lawrence and Wishart.

Haywood, C., & Mac an Ghaill, M. (2003). *Men and masculinities: Theory, research and social practice.* Buckingham: Open University Press.

Hopkins, P. E. (2009). Responding to the 'crisis of masculinity': The perspectives of young Muslim men from Glasgow and Edinburgh, Scotland. *Gender, Place and Culture, 16*(3), 299–312.

Jacobowitz, S. (2004). Hellenism, hebraism, and the eugenics of culture, in E. M. Forster's Howards end'. *CLCWeb: Comparative Literature and Culture, 6*(4), 1–10. http://dx.doi.org/10.7771/1481-4374.1250.

Khiabany, G., & Williamson, M. (2012). Terror, culture and anti-Muslim racism. In D. Thussu & D. Freedman (Eds.), *Media and terrorism: Global perspectives,* (pp. 134–151). London: Sage.

Kumar, K. (2003). *The making of English national identity.* Cambridge: Cambridge University Press.

Kundnani, A. (2009). *Spooked! How not to prevent violent extremism.* London: Institute of Race Relations.

Mac an Ghaill, M. (1994). *The making of men: Masculinities, sexualities and schooling.* Buckingham: Open University Press.

Mac an Ghaill, M., & Haywood, C. (2005). *Young Bangladeshi in the North East: A study of ethnic (in) visibility.* York: Joseph Rowntree Foundation.

Mirza, H. S. (2009). *Race, gender and educational desire: Why black women succeed and fail.* London: Routledge.

Office for National Statistics (2012) 2011 census: Religion (detailed), local authorities in England and Wales, Table QS210EW. http://www.ons.gov.uk.

Popoviciu, L., Haywood, C., & Mac an Ghaill, M. (2006). The promise of post-structuralist methodology: Ethnographic representation of education and masculinity. *Ethnography and Education, 1*(3), 393–412.

Qureshi, K. (2004). Respected and respectable: The centrality of "performance" and "audiences" in the (re)production and potential revision of gendered ethnicities. *Participat@Tions, 1*(2). http://www.participations.org/volume%201/issue%202/1_02_qureshi_article.htm.

Said, E. W. (1993). *Culture and imperialism.* London: Vintage.

Shain, F. (2011). *The new folk devils: Muslim boys and education in England.* Stoke on Trent: Trentham Books.

UK Government. (2009). *The United Kingdom's strategy for countering international terrorism.* Home Office. London: HMSO.

Ussher, J. M., Sandoval, M., Perz, J., Wong, W. K. T., & Butow, P. (2013). *The gendered construction and experience of difficulties and rewards in cancer care, qualitative health research.* http://qhr.sagepub.com/content/early/2013/04/03/1049732313484197.

Walkerdine, V. (2003). Reclassifying upward mobility: Femininity and the neo-liberal subject. *Gender and Education, 15*(3), 237–248.

Westwood, S. (1990). Racism, masculinity and the politics of space. In J. Hearn and D. H. (Eds.), *Masculinities and social theory,* (pp. 84–95). London: Unwin and Hyman.

Máirtín Mac an Ghaill is a professor and director of the Graduate School at Newman University. He is the author of *The Making of Men: Masculinities, Sexuality and Schooling.* He has published books and articles with Chris Haywood, including *Men and Masculinities; Education and Masculinities: Social, Cultural and Global Transformations.*

Chris Haywood is a senior lecturer at Newcastle University whose main interest and focus is on men and masculinities. He is currently exploring the emergence of new sexual cultures with a particular focus on anonymous sex with strangers. This is part of a broader study on men's dating practices with a particular focus on mobile dating, online dating and speed dating. Overall, he is interested in pushing the conceptual limits of masculinity models to consider ways of gendering that are not reducible to masculinity or femininity.

CHAPTER 14

Muslim Narratives of Schooling in Britain: From 'Paki' to the 'Would-Be Terrorist'

Tania Saeed

INTRODUCTION

My first ever experience of ever having any awareness that I was different in a way or my religion was suddenly something like a topic now people would talk about was after September 11th. I didn't really watch it on TV, didn't really know too much of what was going on, I knew that there was something. I remember I went to school and it was PE, you know we were in year 6 [...] and my friend asked me are you related to Osama Bin Laden? She asked me and I was like no, I don't think so. No, who is this person. That's like [...] the first time being Muslim ever touched my life in terms of like my friends. Before it was you go to school, you go home, you eat, you get ready, you go to madrassa, you come home, you eat again, you work and you go to sleep. That was it but this was like suddenly your religion is a thing and it hasn't changed since then.

Farzana, South West1, 20, Undergrad Medicine, British[1]

In the 14 years since 9/11 and the decade after the July 7 tragedies in London, Muslim students across educational institutions, including schools are continuously framed within a security discourse (HM Government, 2015a; Coppock and McGovern 2014; Miah 2012; Tindongan 2011;

T. Saeed (✉)
Lahore University of Management Sciences, Lahore, Pakistan
e-mail: tania.saeed@lums.edu.pk

© The Author(s) 2017
M. Mac an Ghaill, C. Haywood (eds.), *Muslim Students, Education and Neoliberalism*, DOI 10.1057/978-1-137-56921-9_14

217

Bonet 2011; El-Haj et al. 2011). While Farzana's friend's question may be regarded as an innocent inquiry of a child in Grade 6, the fear and suspicion it alludes to has become a stark reality for Muslim students of all ages. The nebulous nature of the existing terrorist threat has given birth to a security apparatus that permeates British society, with the average citizen now part of this apparatus. Institutions, such as schools, colleges and universities that were previously lauded as bastions of intellectual freedom and debate have also been drawn into this security discourse, bestowed a 'duty of care' under the Counter-Terrorism and Security Act 2015 to identify students 'at risk' of being radicalized (HM Government, 2015b). Given the biggest physical and ideological threat is posed by what are defined as radical 'Islamist' groups, Muslim students are considered prime suspects. Such an intervention is part of the government's 'Prevent' strategy that aims to disrupt what it believes is a 'process of radicalization' by strategically catching 'would be' terrorists at the beginning of this process, thereby rooting out extremism from its inception (HM Government 2015c; Kundnani 2012).

This chapter begins by exploring the counter-terrorism policy of the British government in schools across Britain, and its implications for Muslim children, especially adolescents studying in these schools. It highlights the cases of Muslim students who have been wrongly suspected of terrorism, as discussed in media reports. This is followed by an exploration of biographical narratives of young Muslim female students with a Pakistani heritage between the ages of 19–30, discussing their school experiences before the tragedies of 9/11 and 7/7, and in its immediate aftermath. The experiences of students vary depending on the demographic composition of their schools, but they nonetheless highlight instances of discrimination that existed before the tragedies of 9/11, at a time when their identity was associated with the troubled 'Paki', only to be replaced by the more dangerous 'would-be' terrorist. The narratives further reveal the important role of teachers in ensuring the well-being of all students irrespective of their religion or ethnicity, but also the biases and prejudices that may 'prevent' teachers from fulfilling their role as impartial educators. By being co-opted into the security discourse, teachers have become mere informants in an education system submerged in paranoia, and fear. The chapter therefore argues for the need to ensure that the welfare role of teachers is located outside the security discourse, where students, especially Muslim students, are not simply condemned as 'would-be' terrorists to be watched at all times.

SCHOOLS AND THE SECURITY APPARATUS

According to the Counter-Terrorism and Security Act 2015 under the 'Prevent duty guidance', schools

> are subject to the duty to have due regard to the need to prevent people from being drawn into terrorism. Being drawn into terrorism includes not just violent extremism but also non-violent extremism, which can create an atmosphere conducive to terrorism and can popularise views which terrorists exploit. Schools should be safe spaces in which children and young people can understand and discuss sensitive topics, including terrorism and the extremist ideas that are part of terrorist ideology, and learn how to challenge these ideas. The Prevent duty is not intended to limit discussion of these issues. Schools should, however, be mindful of their existing duties to forbid political indoctrination and secure a balanced presentation of political issues.
> (Her Majesty's Government (HM Government) 2015c: 10–11)

The British government's Prevent agenda that came into effect in 2007 under the mantra of winning 'hearts and minds', (also see HM Government 2009) first extended into schools through 'the Department of Children, Schools and Families' prevention of violent extremism toolkit, entitled *Learning Together to Be Safe'* (Miah 2012: 29). The 'toolkit' was 'launched in response to the conviction of sixteen-year-old Hamand Munshi, the youngest British person to be convicted under the UK Terrorism Act', for possessing information 'about bomb making' and 'notes about martyrdom' (*ibid*). The toolkit encouraged the role of schools in 'promoting community cohesion, and promoting equality and wellbeing'; 'schools using the "curriculum to challenge extremist narratives"'; and 'form good links with police and other partners to share information' (*ibid*). More recently, the link between schools and security has further been strengthened under the 'muscular liberalism' of the Conservative government that challenges both violent and 'non-violent' extremism (O'Toole et al. 2016: 162–169; Kuenssberg 2011). In combating 'non-violent' extremism and using a 'soft' approach to tackle terrorism, Prevent in educational institutions is directed towards the 'vulnerable', (predominantly Muslim students[2]), with an emphasis on reinforcing British values (O'Toole et al. 2016; Coppock and McGovern 2014).

The search for this 'would-be' terrorist is based on the idea that a 'process' of radicalization exists that can be interrupted, with a 'duty on local authorities and partners of local panels to provide support for people vulnerable to being drawn into terrorism' set out under the government's 'Channel programme'

(HM Government 2015a: 2). Channel 'uses a multi-agency approach to protect vulnerable people' by 'identifying' the individual 'at risk', 'assessing the nature of the vulnerability of that risk' and 'developing' a 'support plan' that is 'appropriate' for the concerned 'individual' (*ibid*, 5). Once the individual is identified 'detailed information about the individual's life and the social networks they are a part of is collected and a multi-agency panel led by the police recommends a course of action, such as a programme of mentoring or religious instruction designed to transform the person's ideology away from extremism' (Kundnani 2015: 34). However, as Kundnani (2012; 2015) and Githens-Mazer (2010; also see Githens-Mazer and Lambert 2010) have illustrated, there is no empirical evidence that suggests that such a process of radicalization exists. Given the diverse background of convicted terrorists, 'the micro-level question of what causes one person rather than another in the same political context to engage in violence is beyond analysis and best seen as unpredictable' (Kundnani 2012: 21). The best recourse for any government is to directly tackle groups that actively promote violence 'rather than wider belief systems that are wrongly assumed to be precursors to violence' (*ibid*; also see Kundnani 2015). By believing in a process that can be disrupted, the existing 'Prevent duty' as imposed on schools and other educational institutions has become more of a 'witch-hunt' (Allen 2014), that further normalizes a 'culture of surveillance' by turning educators into informants for security agencies. This is also evident in the measures being taken to ensure 'Internet safety', with schools installing Internet software to monitor student activity. Software, such as Impero Education Pro, flags students who use 'phrases specifically associated with online propaganda produced by the Islamic State of Iraq and the Levant (ISIL) such as YODO (You Only Die Once) and Message to America [...] as well as some associated with far-right doctrine' (Hooper 2015a). However, the danger of such policies is that far from ensuring that schools are 'safe spaces', it is encouraging an atmosphere of distrust and paranoia about Muslims, with teachers prioritizing their duty to inform in the name of security.

Vulnerability, Muslims and Adolescence

Schools as educational institutions play a crucial role in 'shaping citizenship and democratic participation for young people' (El Haj et al 2011: 48), with adolescence considered a time for political 'experimentation' and curiosity (Verkuyten and Slooter 2008). However, as Coppock and McGovern (2014: 242) illustrate in their exploration of 'vulnerability' within a counter-terrorism framework 'young British Muslims' are being treated as 'appropriate objects for state intervention and surveillance' removed from any 'meaningful social and political agency, divorced from the structural circumstances of their lived experiences, and problematized' as 'vulnerable' 'in terms of their mental well-being'. By placing what is akin to a social stigma of vulnerability on Muslim adolescents by virtue of their religious affiliation, the Prevent agenda in schools far from engaging with Muslim students have further isolated them as a potential threat. Tindongan (2011) in her discussion of Muslim youth in 'public schools' in the USA highlights how 'stereotypes' and 'misunderstandings' have an 'impact' on 'identity negotiations of Muslim adolescents as they navigate through their US school experiences' (2011: 80). Such negotiations are also evident for the youth in British schools, with the added pressure of being labelled 'at risk' because of their religious beliefs. By securitizing the Muslim identity of the student, any possibility of adolescent curiosity is placed within the rubric of 'vulnerability' that is reported rather than debated. Such 'vulnerability' may further be gendered, with Muslim girls viewed within the prism of 'culturally' or 'religiously' oppressed, while Muslim boys perceived as virulent, posing a more direct physical threat (see El Haj et al. 2011). However, with the emergence of 'jihadi brides', Muslim girls are also being implicated in the 'Prevent' strategy, especially against non-violent extremism. Far from providing the space for 'political' experimentation and debate for such young people, schools are instead imposing an artificial construct of 'safe' Muslim adolescents (read: apolitical) against 'at risk' adolescents.

This is clearly evident in the case of a 14-year-old at a North London school who mentioned the term 'L'ecoterrorisme' (eco-terrorism) in a French class discussion on 'violence and the environment', a term he had learnt in a 'school debating session' (Dodd 2015). 'A few days later he was pulled out of class and taken to an "inclusion centre" elsewhere in the school', on suspicion of radicalization. The child was questioned by two adults, a 'member of staff' and a 'child protection officer' about the use of the term 'terrorism' and the possibility of his 'affiliation with ISIS' (*ibid*). The case illustrates not just the paranoia that led the teacher and the school personnel to report him, but also the extent to which the Muslim identity, even that of an adolescent is securitized within the everyday context of a school classroom. It is fair to assume that if the child had been non-Muslim or white, the use of the term 'L'ecoterrorisme' would not have warranted a trip to the Orwellian 'inclusion centre'. It is further disconcerting that the incident took place in 'May 2015' before the introduction of the Prevent duty, highlighting the extent to which a statutory *duty to inform* will further reinforce such insecurities (*ibid*).

The 'Prevent duty', despite its emphasis on ensuring freedom of thought and discussion, has further led to censorship of ideas that may be deemed controversial by certain schools. For instance, a 15-year-old studying in a school in South England 'was accused of holding' terrorist-like 'views by a police officer who questioned him for taking leaflets into school promoting a boycott of Israel' (Hooper 2015b). A supporter of Palestine and the Boycott, Divestment and Sanctions (BDS) campaign, who explained his position on human rights and political activism to the police officer questioning him was also discouraged from discussing his views with other students (*ibid*). Not only was the child in question reprimanded, his 'teacher' also told his younger brother in the same school that his elder brother had 'radical ideas', and if he did not 'stop', would be reported 'to the intelligence agencies' (*ibid*). While the child eventually left the school, and continued his schooling elsewhere, a 'Prevent officer' and a 'case worker' from the government's 'Channel programme' 'visited' him at home. Questioned about Islamic State of Iran and Syria (ISIS), and 'the war in Syria' the 'Channel officer' once satisfied that he was not 'the ISIS type' told him that 'nothing further' would 'happen' unless he did 'something similar' (*ibid*). This case clearly illustrates how the 'Prevent duty' far from engaging with political ideals, can instead lead to censorship and isolation. The child in question left the school because he felt he was being singled out, considered 'at risk' because of his views on Palestine and Israel. If the aim of Prevent and the Counter-Terrorism and Security Act 2015 in schools is to promote British values, then the only lesson a child can learn from such behaviour is that censorship is the best policy. By asking the child to stay quiet, the school compromised its duty as an educational institution in the name of counter-terrorism, where what it termed 'radical' thought, far from being challenged, was brushed under the carpet.

While one cannot and should not overlook the dangers of radicalization as displayed in the case of British Muslim teenagers that joined terrorist organizations such as ISIS (Khan 2015), a policy that defines all Muslim students as 'potential terrorists', that turns trusted educators into informants will prove far more detrimental. The 'better-safe-than-sorry' (also see Thornton 2011) approach that essentially underlines the Prevent duty far from strengthening the role of educators, undercuts and weakens it.

It further overlooks the possibility of human error, and individual bias that may play a greater role in implicating Muslim students as potential terrorists, rather than any action or thought of the student by him or herself.

To understand the alienating effect of a policy that can isolate an entire group of children and teenagers, the next section offers insight of a group of Muslim female students at universities in England, reflecting on their experiences of discrimination and insecurity in schools. The narratives of 40 Muslim females were collected between 2010 and 2012, and were part of a larger study on Islamophobia and counter-terrorism in higher educational institutions in England.[3] The participants were contacted through student societies at different universities. Part of the biographical narratives are recollections of experiences in schools, for some before the events of 9/11 and 7/7, while for others in the aftermath of these tragedies. These experiences reveal the difficulties already confronted by Muslim teenagers in certain schools, regarded as outsiders, and in some cases labelled a 'Paki', with 9/11 turning them into 'potential terrorists'.

NARRATIVES OF SCHOOLING: REFLECTIONS OF MUSLIM FEMALE STUDENTS

You know [...] when Jack Straw made comments about the niqab, I was in secondary school, I must have been 13 or 14 and I remember a class where this had been brought up and it wasn't by a teacher who was qualified to address this, he was just a supply teacher [...] it was done in quite a let's discuss this issue. It is actually quite a volatile subject, it can get quite heated [...] I remember the class had 5 Muslim girls and one of them actually wore the niqab, one of my friends, and the rest were predominantly white people and not Muslim. I remember I was the only one speaking on the side of Islam because the others were too scared, and I remember some of the girls wanted to beat me up because of the things I was saying. [...]

Friends were just a bit scared, keep your head down kind of thing. Why would you want to draw attention to yourself.

Farzana, South West1, 20, Undergrad Medicine, British

Farzana's school experiences are located in the aftermath of 9/11, and highlight several issues that continue to be relevant for students and teachers especially in the context of 'Prevent' and the 'duty of care'. Farzana in her narrative clearly points to the fact that the teacher in question was a substitute, who started a discussion he was incapable of guiding. While the teacher may have been ill-equipped to discuss such a controversial topic, the reactions of both the Muslim girls in her class and the non-Muslim ones highlight the kind of tension that already exists in schools that are situated within a wider context, exposed to media and political narratives about Islam, Muslims and terrorism. This wider context already shapes the perception and responses of students, from the Muslim students' wanting to be invisible, and the non-Muslim students' offense at Farzana's comments. The reaction of students further point to the phenomenon of 'bullying' that students may experience in school, which take the form of Islamophobia against Muslim children viewed as outsiders, or alien. This was clearly witnessed and recorded by the organization 'TellMAMA' in the aftermath of the Charlie Hebdo attacks, with '22 reports of Islamophobic abuse against children' within a period of six months, with 'the youngest victim aged four' (Milmo 2015; TellMAMA 2015). 'Show Racism the Red Card, an educational charity' and 'NASUWT The Teacher's Union' have also highlighted this problem in schools, with NASUWT's *Tackling Islamophobia: Advice for Schools and Colleges* (Milmo 2015; NASUWT 2014) published as a resource for teachers to deal with Islamophobia.

The experiences of students in schools often vary depending on the school and geographical demographics (also see Stevens and Görgöz 2010; Verkuyten and Thijs 2002). Students in schools with a predominantly South Asian or Muslim student body are less likely to suffer such Islamophobic bullying than those with a minority of Muslim students. Faiza, who wears the niqab shares her encounter in secondary school with students of a neighbouring 'state school',

> Right next to our school was just a normal state school with majority white people and they would say nasty things about the girls, coz we wore hijabs, our uniform was hijab [. . .] then again they were young we were young and it was things like that. It wasn't so much discrimination but it was just something they saw different in their area. They felt it was strange.
> Faiza, West Yorkshire3, 22, Undergrad Humanities, British

Muslim students, especially young girls who wear the hijab or niqab[4] stand out because of their physical appearance. Being targeted because of one's religious beliefs can be traumatic, especially for a teenager already struggling with her adolescent identity. While Faiza dismisses the reaction of students from the neighbouring school as the actions of the 'young' who encountered something 'strange', Zubaida's experience of being bullied for being 'Paki' has left her traumatized.

> Had to do with maybe religion as well. Paki would be the main term you would be given 'paki paki bastards'. If you were wearing a headscarf they would pull it off, and play piggie in the middle. In 1991–1992. Quite early still. Then a lot more Asian girls started coming. Now I know school is full of Asian people, hardly any white people.
>
> Zubaida, London, 30, Graduate Sciences, British

Growing up in the late 1980s, early 1990s, Zubaida's experience of bullying took the form of racism against the 'Paki', a racial slur associated with criminality before 9/11. Zubaida also highlights the complicity of teachers who accused her of 'making up stories' despite her 'bruises'. Zubaida recalls an episode where she was also 'physically assaulted by a teacher in high school' with her parents unable to intervene, since the mother could not speak English and was generally dismissed by the school (also see Bhopal 2014), while the father was too busy earning to be around to intervene in such matters. Zubaida's account is important in highlighting the biases of teachers, and the kind of bullying that already existed in schools against 'South Asian' communities (also see Bhopal 2014; Stevens and Görgöz 2010; Shah 2008). Fatima, a student at a school in West Yorkshire recalls her memory of high school in the aftermath of 7/7 when her school walls were 'graffitied' with the term 'Paki'. She was planning to go on a school trip for which she 'had paid' but was not permitted:

> We went to school one day and on the walls it was graffitied Paki, not sure Islamophobia, but just Paki written all over it, swear words and all sorts. I told me mom and she said you are not going on the trip. They are going to attack your bus. At that point we were quite scared [...] So mom stopped wearing jilbabs and started wearing coats instead. We didn't want to stand out.
>
> Fatima, West Yorkshire2, 21, Undergrad Law, British

The Muslim community, from children to parents, become easy targets of anger and frustration in the aftermath of an attack by a terrorist group or individuals claiming to act in the name of Islam. In the aftermath of the Charlie Hebdo attacks for instance, a grade 10 student in a school in Oxfordshire was 'slapped' repeatedly and called 'Paki' and a 'terrorist' after a class discussion about Charlie Hebdo (Milmo 2015). In another case, a Muslim boy was labelled a terrorist by his teacher in a school in Rotherham (TellMAMA). With a Prevent policy in place that reinforces the potential guilt of a Muslim student because of his or her religion, this kind of Islamophobic bullying is likely to increase. Far from interrupting a 'process of radicalization' the existing 'securitized' focus on Muslim children will in effect make them 'vulnerable' to such incidents, rather than ensure their welfare. The danger of Islamophobia encountered from teachers is also an issue that cannot be overlooked. While such teachers may be in a minority, they nonetheless point to the kind of biases that may exist in reporting Muslim students under the Prevent strategy that may do more harm. Sabahat is a teacher who recalls her experience of discrimination in a college from her colleagues who were training to be teachers. 'Snide remarks', made to 'feel different' and 'left out', avoiding conversation or contact, were encounters that Sabahat had with her colleagues:

> We are going to talk about group opportunity, inclusion blah blah blah, does anybody feel segregated, does anybody feel left out or picked on and I felt a bit let down because three of my friends who were Asian were talking to me about this and they felt the same way and yet when the lecturer asked this in front of everybody they didn't feel confident enough to put their hands up and say yes it's true and I thought if it means me being alone [...] I'll be honest, so I put up my hand and said yes that is the case. It just kind of made things worse because I had people in the group come up to me and say oh we never did anything to make you feel like that, why are you feeling like that [...] The worse thing for me was that these people were training with me to be teachers. As teachers you have got to promote equal opportunities, inclusion for all regardless of migrant workers, refugees, people of different languages, it doesn't matter [...] but for these people to make Asians feel segregated [...] it got to a stage where we had no choice but to hang around each other.
>
> Sabahat, West Yorkshire3, 26, Alumnus, British

At the time of this incident, Sabahat did not wear a hijab. For her the attitude of her colleagues was more racist, one that would be repeated against Asian students in schools. This attitude further reinforced segregation within the college, one that has been reported in schools as well (see Miah 2012). The attitude of teachers, and the kind of racism they may exhibit towards religious or ethnic minorities is a topic that continues to be debated, with the implications of such racism linked to student under-achievement, insecurities, lowered ambitions, and in essence a reinforcement of the outsider status resulting in greater isolation (see Shah 2008; Abbas 2002).

While the attitude of the non-Asian, non-Muslim teachers is alarming, the response of Sabahat's Asian friends who are also training to be teachers is equally problematic. If the teachers lack the confidence to take a stand against discrimination with their colleagues, it is reasonable to assume that the same teachers would be hesitant in taking a similar stance for themselves or their Muslim/Asian students in schools. It also reflects similar sentiments exhibited by Farzana's friends, and Fatima's mom, the need to 'stay down' and remain invisible, in other words appear to be in the 'safe' zone, so one does not stand out as 'at risk' or 'vulnerable' to radicalization.

The 'Prevent duty' in schools is more likely to reinforce biases and further isolate students, who may become more distrustful of teachers, rather than looking towards them as educators and role models. If schools are to be implicated in this 'duty of care' against extremism, then teachers and educators need to move beyond their 'duty to inform', and carry forth their original role as unbiased educators.

CONCLUSION: BEYOND A DUTY TO INFORM

> When I started off, it was all new to me. Kids used to look at me in a weird way because I was the only brown coloured girl, OMG it was hard, it was really hard. There were so many issues that I faced, many days I'd come home crying because kids would laugh at me. The issue wasn't just me but they were having problem understanding me because they had never seen a brown girl [...] You can't really blame the kids. It was new for me so it was new for them as well.
>
> Bano, North West1, 22, Graduate Sciences, British

While schools and Muslim children are framed within the security discourse as 'soft targets' for terrorist recruiters, but also for a counter-terrorism strategy that can 'prevent' such recruitment, the strength of schools and teachers is in their fundamental role 'to educate'. Bano's recollection of her school experience, just like Faiza's, highlights the insecurities of all children, their inability to understand and the need to educate and spread awareness. Schools may be an asset precisely through their role as independent places of education and learning, clearly illustrated in the example of Isra Mohammad, a 15-year-old who was 'labelled a terrorist' but decided to speak up, and raise awareness at her 'school assembly' with the help of her teachers (O'Donoghue-Men 2015). Creating a space for young people to have such discussions is important in schools, one that the 'Prevent duty' claims to uphold in principle but as the cases discussed in this chapter have illustrated, is far from being implemented in schools. However, discussion on such topics by Muslim students also needs to be a voluntary exercise, without placing the onus of apologizing for terrorists who act in the name of Islam, or explaining what Islam is, solely on young people who may not want to 'stand out' (Freytas-Tamura 2014).

Furthermore, the role of teachers as impartial educators is at the core of creating such an environment of openness and debate. However, the narratives in the preceding section suggest that teachers far from being impartial may carry their own biases and prejudices against Muslim or Asian students that is reinforced within the classroom. Even in cases where teachers are unbiased, by placing Muslim students within the category of 'vulnerability' thereby separating them from their peers, teachers may fall victim to misunderstandings, reporting innocent Muslim students and thereby creating a trust deficit in their relationship with their students. Instead of placing teachers within the security discourse, schools and teachers need to invest more resources in building trust and enabling dialogue where students may talk about issues from ISIS to educational ambitions without being red flagged. However, as Farzana's narrative revealed, teachers need to have the requisite training to engage with such issues in a classroom of students who may have diverse political views or opinions that need to be discussed rather than judged or dismissed. Therefore, while the 'Prevent duty' focuses on giving training to educators to look out for 'at risk' students, schools and teachers may be far more successful in challenging 'mindsets' through their ability to create discussion on subjects that are controversial.

The way forward is therefore one where schools move beyond a *duty to inform*, reinforcing their *duty to educate*. The British government also needs to reassess its belief that a process of radicalization can be easily identified or disrupted, through what is akin to a form of 'thought policing' in schools. The way forward in countering an extremist threat is to reinforce a school environment where discussion and engagement with Muslim students fall outside the domain of security, where students and teachers are able to build and sustain a relationship of trust, where schools can engage with a student who uses the term 'L'ecoterrorisme' or has political views about the Middle East, instead of reporting him to the police, or relocating him to an 'inclusion centre' for interrogation, thereby reducing him to a 'would-be terrorist'.

NOTES

1. Interview Reference format: Name (Pseudonym), location of university, age, degree, nationality.
2. While 'Islamist' groups are a threat, the Prevent strategy also mentions 'terrorists associated with the extreme right' as a threat (HM Government 2015c: 3).
3. The author followed the ethics protocol of her university, ensuring that the participants were fully informed about the research, and their rights as participants. Pseudonyms have also been assigned to the participants to ensure their anonymity.
4. Hijab: head covering – a piece of cloth normally worn by Muslim women; Niqab: a piece of cloth that also covers the face showing just the eyes, normally worn with hijab and a jilbab, i.e. a long gown/coat.

REFERENCES

Abbas, T. (2002). The home and the school in the educational achievements of South Asians. *Race Ethnicity and Education, 5*(3), 291–316.

Allen, C. (2014). Operation Trojan Horse: Examining the 'Islamic takeover' of Birmingham schools. *The Conversation.* http://theconversation.com/opera tion-trojan-horse-examining-the-islamic-takeover-of-birmingham-schools-25764 [Accessed 10 November 2015].

Bhopal, K. (2014). Race, rurality and representation: Black and minority ethnic mothers' experiences of their children's education in rural primary schools in England, UK. *Gender and Education, 26*(5), 490–504.

Bonet, S. W. (2011). Educating Muslim American youth in a post-9/11 era: A critical review of policy and practice. *The High School Journal, 95*(1), 46–55.

Coppock, V., & McGovern, M. (2014). 'Dangerous minds'? Deconstructing coun ter-terrorism discourse, radicalisation and the 'psychological vulnerability' of Muslim children and young people in Britain. *Children & Society, 28,* 242–256.

Dodd, V. (2015, 22 September). School questioned Muslim pupil about ISIS after discussion on eco-activism. *The Guardian,* http://www.theguardian.com/edu cation/2015/sep/22/school-questioned-muslim-pupil-about-isis-after-discus sion-on-eco-activism [Accessed 13 November 2015].

El-Haj, T. R. A., Bonet, S. W., Demerath, P., & Schultz, K. (2011). Education, citizenship, and the politics of belonging: Youth from Muslim transnational com munities and the "war on terror". *Review of Research in Education, 35,* 29–59.

Freytas-Tamura, K. D. (2014, 27 September). For Muslims, social media debate on extremism is reflected in dueling hashtags. *The New York Times,* http://www. nytimes.com/2014/09/28/world/for-muslims-social-media-debate-on-extre mism-is-reflected-in-dueling-hashtags.html [Accessed 10 November 2015].

Githens-Mazer, J. (2010). *Rethinking the causal concept of Islamic radicalisation. Political Concepts: Committee on Concepts and Methods Working Paper Series.* Montreal: International Political Science Association.

Githens-Mazer, J., & Lambert, R. (2010). Why conventional wisdom on radicalization fails: The persistence of a failed discourse. *International Affairs, 86*(4), 889–901.

Her Majesty's Government (HM Government). (2009). *Pursue prevent protect prepare the United Kingdom's strategy for countering international terrorism.* UK: Crown.

Her Majesty's Government (HM Government). (2015a). *Channel duty guidance. Protecting vulnerable people from being drawn into terrorism. Statutory guidance for Channel panel members and partners of local panels.* UK: Crown.

Her Majesty's Government (HM Government). (2015b). Counter-Terrorism and Security Act 2015, http://www.legislation.gov.uk/ukpga/2015/6/notes/contents [Accessed 28 March 2015].

Her Majesty's Government (HM Government). (2015c). *Revised Prevent Duty guidance: For England and Wales.* UK: Crown.

Hooper, S. (2015a, 4 October 2010). UK: Keyword warning software in schools raises red flag. *Al Jazeera,* http://www.aljazeera.com/indepth/features/2015/10/uk-keyword-warning-software-schools-raises-red-flag-151004081940435.html;%20http://www.theguardian.com/uk-news/2015/jun/10/schools-trial-anti-radicalisation-software-pupils-internet [Accessed 20 November 2015].

Hooper, S. (2015b, 23 July). Stifling freedom of expression in UK schools. *Al Jazeera,* http://www.aljazeera.com/indepth/features/2015/07/stifling-freedom-expression-uk-schools-150721080612049.html [Accessed 15 November 2015].

Khan, D. (2015, 21 June). For ISIS women, it's not about 'jihadi brides': It's about escape. *The Guardian,* http://www.theguardian.com/world/2015/jun/21/isis-women-its-not-about-jihadi-brides-its-about-escape [Accessed 18 November 2015].

Kuenssberg, L. (2011, 05 February). State multiculturalism has failed, says David Cameron. *BBC News,* http://www.bbc.com/news/uk-politics-12371994 [Accessed 15 November 2015].

Kundnani, A. (2015). *A decade lost. Rethinking radicalisation and extremism.* UK: Claystone.

Kundnani, A. (2012). Radicalisation: The journey of a concept. *Race & Class, 54*(2), 3–25.

Miah, S. (2012). School desegregation and the politics of 'forced integration'. *Race & Class, 54*(2), 26–38.

Milmo, C. (2015, 23 January). British Muslim school children suffering a backlash of abuse following Paris attacks. *Independent,* http://www.independent.co.uk/news/education/education-news/british-muslim-school-children-suffering-a-backlash-of-abuse-following-paris-attacks-9999393.html [Accessed 15 November 2015].

NASUWT. (2014). Tackling Islamophobia: Advice for schools and colleges. *NASUWT The Teachers' Union*, http://www.nasuwt.org.uk/TrainingEventsandPublications/NASUWTPublications/Publications/TacklingIslamophobiaadviceforschoolsandcolleges/index.htm [Accessed 15 November 2015].

O'Donoghue-Men, D. (2015, 16 December). Newcastle teen branded a 'terrorist' after Paris attacks speaks out against Islamophobia. *Chronicle Live*, http://www.chroniclelive.co.uk/news/north-east-news/newcastle-teen-branded-terrorist-after-10610821#ICID=sharebar_twitter [Accessed 20 December 2015].

O'Toole, T., Meer, N., DeHanas, D. N., Jones, S. H., & Modood, T. (2016). Governing through prevent? Regulation and contested practice in State–Muslim engagement. *Sociology, 50*(1), 160–177.

Shah, S. (2008). Leading multi-ethnic schools: Adjustments in concepts and practices for engaging with diversity. *British Journal of Sociology of Education, 29*(5), 523–536.

Stevens, P. A. J., & Görgöz, R. (2010). Exploring the importance of institutional contexts for the development of ethnic stereotypes: A comparison of schools in Belgium and England. *Ethnic and Racial Studies, 33*(8), 1350–1371.

TellMAMA. (2015). Teacher in Rotherham under police investigation for alleged Anti-Muslim Bigotry, *TellMAMA*, http://tellmamauk.org/teacher-in-rotherham-under-police-investigation-for-alleged-anti-muslim-bigotry/ [Accessed 20 December 2015].

Thornton, R. (2011). Counterterrorism and the neo-liberal university: Providing a check and balance? *Critical Studies on Terrorism, 4*(3), 421–429.

Tindongan, C. W. (2011). Negotiating Muslim youth identity in a post-9/11 world. *The High School Journal, 95*(1), 72–87.

Verkuyten, M., & Slooter, L. (2008). Muslim and non-Muslim adolescents' reasoning about freedom of speech and minority rights. *Child Development, 79*(3), 514–528.

Verkuyten, M., & Thijs, J. (2002). Racist victimization among children in The Netherlands: The effect of ethnic group and school. *Ethnic and Racial Studies, 25*(2), 310–331.

Tania Saeed is an assistant professor at the Lahore University of Management Sciences, Pakistan. She is the author of *Islamophobia and Securitization. Religion, Ethnicity and the Female Voice*. Saeed's area of specialization is democratization and social exclusion with a focus on religious minorities, gender and security in the context of the UK and Pakistan.

INDEX

© The Author(s) 2017
M. Mac an Ghaill, C. Haywood (eds.), *Muslim Students, Education
and Neoliberalism*, DOI 10.1057/978-1-137-56921-9

Radicalization, 100–101, 108, 109,
    118, 119, 131, 218–222,
    226–228
(re) ethnicization, 193
Reflexive identity, 36–38
Reflexivity, 7, 12, 37–38, 44, 46,
    148, 202
Refugee, 87, 100
Religion/religious education/
    religious identity, 2, 3, 6, 7, 22,
    27, 38, 57, 58, 67, 103, 105,
    118, 147, 153, 164, 168,
    170–172, 174, 189, 200,
    206–210, 212, 217, 218, 226
Religious symbol, 162
Representation, 2, 3, 6, 7, 11, 12, 101,
    122, 149, 152, 162–164, 169,
    172, 174, 205, 210, 211–212
Repression, 9, 101, 107, 108–111
Re-racialization, 194, 202
Research/researcher, 2, 6, 7, 9, 11,
    12, 69, 72, 74, 75, 80, 99, 100,
    121, 122, 148, 149, 163,
    167–169, 172, 179–185, 187,
    189, 199–202, 206, 210–212
Risk, 8, 36, 41, 43–45, 57, 131, 218,
    220–222, 227, 228
Rural, 162, 183

S
Sample, 73, 74, 76, 78–80, 94, 201
Schooling biography, 203
Schooling self, 204
School management, 71
School performance, 152, 206
School/schooling, 7, 10, 12, 58,
    62–63, 70, 71, 73, 74, 76–80,
    89–96, 103, 107, 131, 133, 137,
    146, 149–155, 166, 168, 171,
    183, 187, 194, 199–213, 218,
    221–228

Secondary school, 10–11, 73, 90, 95,
    145–157, 194, 201, 224
Second generation, 87, 93
Secular education, 2
Securitization, 112
Securitize, 221, 226
Security, 3, 12, 17, 20, 23, 24, 28, 36,
    39, 40, 42, 46, 51, 99, 109, 118,
    121, 134, 135, 140, 161, 166,
    217–220, 222, 227, 228
Segregation/self segregation/spatial
    segregation/self- segregation, 17,
    117, 118, 134, 135, 205, 226
Self, 55, 60, 75, 146–147, 204,
    207, 213
7/7, 12, 28, 52, 53, 115, 218,
    223, 225
Sexuality/homosexuality, 4, 138–139,
    209
Shanghai, 181, 183, 187–190
Silicon Valley, 9, 100, 102, 103,
    109, 110
Sixth-form college, 201
Skill, 5, 25, 27, 68, 74, 179, 182, 192,
    202, 205, 206
Social contract, 2, 205
Social economic, 68, 70, 149, 179,
    182, 188–190, 193
Social field, 173, 174, 183
Social sciences, 168
Sociology, 9, 67, 68, 132
South Asian, 7, 9, 57, 99–112, 153,
    224, 225
Spiritual, 54–56, 68, 69, 72, 74
Sport activity, 40
State school, 6, 53, 54, 58–60, 132,
    205, 224
State system, 58, 59
Statistics, 59, 180, 206
Stereotype, 60, 77, 151, 154, 156,
    194, 221
Stop and search, 26, 52